P9-CLK-219
A12900 237168

The Inclusive Flame

The pure possession, the inclusive cloud
Whose heart is fire shall come . . .

Hart Crane

Glauco Cambon

The Inclusive Flame

Studies in Modern American Poetry

Indiana University Press
Bloomington

For Marlis

First Midland Book Edition 1965

This book was originally published in Italy by Edizioni di Storia e Letteratura under the title *Tematica e sviluppo della poesia americana.* Chapter Six, in a slightly different form, appeared as an article in *Papers of the Michigan Academy of Science, Arts, and Letters,* Vol. XLVII, 1962.

Manufactured in the United States of America

Library of Congress catalog card number: 63-16612

Foreword

PARTS OF THIS book first appeared in Italian magazines during 1955, and the book itself was published in Italy in 1956. In translating it for an American audience, I have made only minor changes, such as omitting what would have sounded superfluous in the changed context or tempering the exuberance of certain statements and turns of phrase. In so doing, however, I have not tried to conform to the academic dogma of impersonality, for the simple reason that the book, with whatever faults it may have, arose from my own response to American poetry and American life, and I hope it will indeed sound like the personal statement it was meant to be. The only addition to the work as published in 1956 is the chapter on Robert Lowell; but for this, and for some new notes that seemed advisable, the book is more or less as it stood then. This explains my failure to take into account later contributions like Mr. Pack's on Wallace Stevens, Mr. Miller's on Walt Whitman, Mr. Dembo's on Hart Crane, and Mr. Pearce's on "the continuity of American poetry." While making no claim to completeness, my work does attempt to probe into the recurrent American endeavor to grasp a totality of experience through poetry—hence its present title. References to Italian or generally European writers will, I hope, be taken as a tribute to the vitality of this American endeavor. The sounding board of a culture is always larger than the culture itself.

GLAUCO CAMBON

April, 1963
New Brunswick, New Jersey

Acknowledgments

MY GRATITUDE GOES to Professor Austin Warren of the University of Michigan and to Professor Newton P. Stallknecht of the Indiana School of Letters for encouraging me to give a fresh chance of life to the volume. I am also indebted to my Columbia classmate, Mrs. Ernst Rothkopf of Berkeley Heights, N. J., for editorial assistance, and to the Research Council of Rutgers University for generous financial help. Before my self-translation work began, a grant of the Horace Rackham School of the University of Michigan enabled me to consult valuable manuscripts, notably those by Edgar Allan Poe, Edwin Arlington Robinson, Herman Melville, and Emily Dickinson, at the Houghton Library of Harvard University.

The quotations from T. S. Eliot's *Four Quartets* (copyright, 1943, by T. S. Eliot) are reprinted by permission of Harcourt, Brace & World, Inc. Quotations from Robert Lowell's *Lord Weary's Castle* (copyright, 1944, 1946, by Robert Lowell) are reprinted by permission of Harcourt, Brace & World, Inc. Quotations from *The Poems of Emily Dickinson* (copyright 1914, 1929, 1935, 1942 by Martha Dickinson Bianchi and copyright 1957 by Mary L. Hampson) are reprinted by permission of Little, Brown & Co. Quotations from *The Poems of Emily Dickinson* (Thomas H. Johnson, editor, published by The Belknap Press of Harvard University Press, Cambridge, Mass., copyright, 1951, 1955, by the President and Fellows of Harvard College) are reprinted by permission of the publishers and the Trustees of Amherst College. Quotations from Edwin Arlington Robinson's *Collected Poems* (copyright 1896, 1897, 1902, 1910, 1915, 1916, 1917, 1920, 1921 1923, 1924, 1925, 1927, 1928, 1929, 1930, 1931, 1932, 1933, 1934, by Edwin Arlington Robinson; copyright 1935 and 1937 by The Macmillan Company) are reprinted by permission of The Macmillan Company. Quotations from *The Collected Poems* of Wallace Stevens (copyright, 1923, 1931, 1935, 1936, 1937, 1942, 1944, 1945, 1946, 1947, 1948, 1949, 1950, 1951, 1952, 1954, by Wallace Stevens) are reprinted by permission of Alfred A. Knopf, Inc., and of Faber and Faber, Ltd. Quotations from *The Collected Poems of Hart Crane* are reprinted by permission of Liveright, Publishers, N.Y., copyright © R-1961 by Liveright Publishing Corp. The selection from *The Letters of Hart Crane, 1916-1932,* ed. Brom Weber (copyright 1952 by Brom Weber), is reprinted with Mr. Brom Weber's permission. Quotation from Allen Tate's *Poems* (1960) is reprinted by permission of Charles Scribner's Sons. Quotations from *The Collected Earlier Poems of William Carlos Williams* (copyright 1938, 1951 by William Carlos Williams), from *The Collected Later Poems of William Carlos Williams* (copyright 1944, 1948, 1950 by William Carlos Williams), and from *Paterson 1, 2, 3, 4* (copyright 1946, 1948 by William Carlos Williams) are reprinted by permission of New Directions, Publishers.

Contents

	Foreword	v
	Acknowledgments	vii
One /	*Space, Experiment, and Prophecy*	3
Two /	*Edwin Arlington Robinson: Knight of the Grail*	53
Three /	*Wallace Stevens: "Notes toward a Supreme Fiction"*	79
Four /	*Hart Crane's "The Bridge"*	120
Five /	*William Carlos Williams' "Paterson"*	183
Six /	*Robert Lowell: History as Eschatology*	219
	Notes	229
	Index	246

One / *Space, Experiment, and Prophecy*

THE CONTEMPORARY luxuriance of American verse, especially in the United States, cannot be fully understood without taking into account the isolated efforts of nineteenth-century pioneers, who paralleled in literature the behavior of countless frontiersmen by obeying the urge to begin anew, in virgin space and virgin time. Hence the experimental approach to language, which goes hand in hand with a variously prophetic, or even "secessionist," attitude. These writers were exhilarated by so much geographic and cultural space to conquer, and maybe on the verge of losing themselves in it. The Founding Fathers of American literature are embodiments of Faust, the prototype of Western man, who, having rejected the burden of his cultural past, finds himself confronted by a horizon of unknown possibilities. Experience is his only guide, and the demonic drive, the quest for a new formula beyond the shattered old ones ("in the beginning was the deed"), can also be said to characterize the spirit of these iconoclastic prophets to whose homeland old Goethe yearningly looked when, in one of his "Xenien" poems, he praised America for being free from the fetters of European history.

On the other hand, in our century poetry in the United States has proved susceptible to the sophisticated examples of European achievement, mostly French, in a way that makes it impossible to speak of a parochial Yankee Muse. By the same token, modern

American poets have been able to sustain such challenging exchanges only because they had become aware of some cultural identity of their own; there was finally a measure of national self-reliance, however variable, to forestall literary frustration. The American identity, paradoxically, consists of a perpetual quest for itself between two diverse worlds. That makes it something to be found rather than something given, and in every significant writer, from Whitman to James, from Robinson to Eliot, it takes different forms, even that of self-negation. In this century, as a consequence, much of the liveliest work in English verse has come from America. And the essential traits of such modern achievement can be recognized in isolated forerunners like Poe, Melville, Whitman, and Emily Dickinson. To choose these writers for the purpose of a focused survey is to exemplify American poetical endeavor at its most poignantly typical in its formative age, even though the occasionally comparable verse contributions of Emerson and Thoreau, and of Freneau before them, should not be overlooked in a more systematic treatment.

Poe: space as nightmare and abstraction—absolute otherness

The seminal American poets of the nineteenth century resembled each other only in the uncompromising courage with which each faced his literary situation and went ahead on his own without bothering about the direction followed by official culture. In this individualist posture their American spirit expresses itself most clearly, whatever their respective philosophies or styles. Despite the reservations lately advanced against him, it would seem that this much at least applies to the controversial figure of Edgar Allan Poe. Yvor Winters and Aldous Huxley resent his "vulgarity," yet Gabriele Baldini[1], by no means an unexacting critic, senses in his strange genius an American quality to be recognized in the best part of his uneven prose and verse. Philip Van Doren Stern[2] ascribes to the frontier heritage his obsessive affinity for terror, and Elio Vittorini[3] sees in his "vampirism" a native growth of puritanical origin—a thesis that may remind us of D. H. Lawrence's vindication of Poe's work[4] as a necessary negative phase in America's quest for her own consciousness.

Edgar Allan Poe looked back, no doubt, to the romantic Europe of Coleridge, Byron, and E. T. W. Hoffmann—a fascination that he shared with many fellow American artists, and that often resulted in a Gothicized image of Europe. But this should not obscure the fact that in his very theatricality, mannerisms, and grotesquerie one can feel the savage violence of a pioneer American soul. His affinity for the grotesque and the abstract goes hand in hand with his experimental handling of verse and verse theory to proclaim that ultimate identity, even if all too often he indulged in the clichés of conventional Romanticism.

Perhaps the surest sign of Poe's basic allegiance to his own native culture in the making can be seen in his predilection for extreme adventures. Arthur Gordon Pym launched into an orgy of polar whiteness is the hyperbole of restless, exploring America, which clearly foreshadows Melville's Ahab. The Raven sitting in the poet's soul evokes the figure of a grim Prometheus, an overtone to be heard later on in much of Melville's American mythmaking. The incredible blending of apocalyptic hallucination and imperious mathematical logic that went into "science fiction" like "The Colloquy of Monos and Una" or "The Conversation of Eiros and Charmion," as well as into the Dupin detective stories, can be seen at work also in that amazing cosmological fantasy, *Eureka,* and in the self-dissecting cruelty of "The Philosophy of Composition." This very American work was the first case of poetry conceived as an experiment in verbal construction, to the distress of candid

Romantic souls who could not see that this was Poe's way to exorcise his own Romanticism. These are all weird adventures of a mind investigating its own frontiers, at the risk of sanity.

Much of Poe's verse hardly bears a second reading: it sounds too stiff, or coarse and padded. Yet his experiments in incantatory iteration, as in "The Raven" and "The Bells," seem to prelude luckier ventures of a comparable intent. Whitman, with his delight in repeated liquid sonorities, as in "Sea-Drift" ("Out of the Cradle Endlessly Rocking"), Eliot with the well-calculated iterative music of "Ash Wednesday" and "The Hollow Men," Gertrude Stein furiously wrenching sound from meaning through obsessive repetition, as if words were some kind of fissionable material to be bombarded in a cyclotron—they all have Poe as an ancestor, and his radical questioning of traditional prosody can be considered as the rough draft of a Declaration of Independence of modern poetry.

The author of *The Waste Land* owes an undeniable debt to the American "Founding Father" of *symbolisme,* who bequeathed a legacy to him through Baudelaire and Laforgue, and certainly the "familiar compound ghost" that the contemporary poet meets in Section II of "Little Gidding" exhibits in his ambiguous physiognomy many a trait of the visionary writer killed by alcohol in Baltimore:

> Since our concern was speech, and speech impelled us
> To purify the dialect of the tribe
> And urge the mind to aftersight and foresight,
> Let me disclose the gifts reserved for age
> To set a crown upon your lifetime's effort.
> First, the cold friction of expiring sense
> Without enchantment, offering no promise
> But bitter tastelessness of shadow fruit
> As body and soul begin to fall asunder. . . .

Sorrow, alienation, and death's shadow are the poet's lot; shortly before, he had

> . . . assumed a double part, and cried
> And heard another's voice cry: "What! are *you* here?"

with an act of self-duplication not unlike that of Poe's William Wilson. A few tercets further, the "compound ghost" explains:

> But, as the passage now presents no hindrance
> To the spirit unappeased and peregrine
> Between two worlds become much like each other,
> So I find words I never thought to speak
> In streets I never thought I should revisit
> When I left my body on a distant shore.

The "two worlds become much like each other" seem to be, at least in one sense, America and Europe, and the irony of the ambiguous situation involves Eliot himself with his Jamesian choice of England for a country; the body left on a distant shore could also be that of Poe, for obvious reasons. But the specific clue comes from the line, quoted above, that is a direct quotation from Mallarmé's "Tombeau d'Edgar Poe": "to purify the dialect of the tribe" ("donner un sens plus pur aux mots de la tribu"). Thus the shade of the "dead master" confronting Eliot in a twilit London street is compounded of Poe and his French *symboliste* disciples (among others), who played such a decisive part in the aesthetic education of the St. Louis-born poet.

Poe's relation to an indigenous American symbolism is well explored by Charles Feidelson in a book[5] that puts Poe in the company of Hawthorne, Melville, Whitman, Emerson, and Thoreau. Symbolism as the will to construct an abstract world, and a conscious reliance on the "poetic principle" of rhythm as the dynamic source of poetry, in a climate of experimental restlessness, make Poe a prototype of the American writer who must operate in a relative cultural void that arouses the joy of unhampered creative freedom and, at the same time, the fear of unsustaining emptiness. The imaginative embodiment of this American situation, in which language tests its precarious power against the inevitable dearth resulting from the loss or rejection of a time-honored tradition, can be viewed in Poe's recurrent sense of space as terror and, conversely, in his complementary claustrophobia. When he sets space in motion, the consequence is the whirlpool of "Ms. Found in a Bottle" or "A Descent into the Maelstrom," which may be taken to symbolize a renewing plunge into the unconscious, a return to the mother, to the principle that shelters existence from the merciless exposure of free space.

The sheltering mother may be death itself, for death dominates Poe's imagination to the extent of making it in many respects an alienated expression of decadent sensibility; if so, the fury with which he pushes that spiritual situation to the limit in the domain of poetry is the mark of an American adventurer. Allen Tate[6] sees in him an example of "angelic imagination." By angelic he means abstract, disembodied, Lucifer-like (we might add, "uprooted"). Isn't this, too, characteristic of a citizen of the New World who is still mentally grappling with the experience of virgin space without quite mastering it? The angelic curse finds in the rhythmical prose of "Silence" and "The Shadow," so sensitively focused by Philip Van Doren Stern, a memorable utterance to be recognized as one decisive episode in America's struggle to find her own voice. Between the formidable excess of spatial-expressive possibility and the impoverishment of "unmoored" language, Poe gropes toward the freedom of later poets; and it will be advisable to take into account this double facet of his in judging his macabre romanticism. The prevalent tendency nowadays, after some overrating in the wake of the French-born Poe myth, seems to be hostile to Poe, regarding him as a literary freak. Yet we might do well to consider the achievement of "To Helen," "The City in the Sea," and "Fairyland," and of some stanzas from "The Raven" or "Annabel Lee," before accepting a wholesale devaluation of Poe the literary artist, who was paving the way for the unrestricted liberties of Whitman as well as for the strict formal purity of Emily Dickinson.

Melville: *otherness as the threshold experience of the self; space as arena*

Melville as a poet in verse is a belated discovery,[7] and even if his uneven accomplishment in this area is overshadowed by the far more consistently impressive success of his prose, one can hardly turn a deaf ear to the music of poems like "Pebbles," "Misgivings," "The Portent," "The Apparition," "The Maldive Shark," "In a Bye-Canal," "Southern Cross," 'Shiloh," "Commemorative of a Naval Victory," "Art," "The Berg," and particularly "A Requiem for Soldiers Lost in Ocean Transports":

> When laughing light of hoyden morning breaks,
>   Every finny hider wakes—
> From vaults profound swims up with glittering scales;
>   Through the delightsome sea he sails,
> With shoals of shining tiny things
> Frolic on every wave that flings
>   Against the prow its showers spray;
> All creatures joying in the morn,
> Save them forever from joyance torn,
>   Whose bark was lost where now the dolphins play;
> Save them that by the fabled shore,
> Down the pale stream are washed away,

> Far to the reef of bones are borne;
> And never revisits them the light,
> Nor sight of long-sought land and pilot more;
> Nor heed they now the lone bird's flight
> Round the lone spar where mid-sea surges pour.

The sustained tone of these lines reminds one of "Animula" 's conclusion with its vibratory dryness, and of the prayer that constitutes the fourth section of "Dry Salvages":

> Pray for all those who are in ships, those
> Whose business has to do with fish, and
> Those concerned with every lawful traffic. . . .
>
> Also pray for those who were in ships, and
> Ended their voyage on the sand, in the sea's lips
> Or in the dark throat which will not reject them
> Or wherever cannot reach them the sound of the sea bell's
> Perpetual angelus.

Melville's "Requiem," one of the most remarkable poems to come from nineteenth-century America, foreshadows Eliot, while "Pebbles" recalls Baudelaire's "La Mer":

> Healed of my hurt, I laud the inhuman Sea—
>
> Yea, bless the Angels Four that there convene;
> For healed I am even by their pitiless breath
> Distilled in wholesome dew named rosmarine.

Within the framework of a conventional approach to prosody, which so often weights it down, Melville's verse attains certain felicities that make one wonder how his poetry books—*Battle Pieces, Timoleon, John Marr,* not to speak of the ponderous philosophical poem *Clarel*[8] could have been ignored when Longfellow's more superficial song exerted such a widespread appeal. The supporting quotations could be multiplied; one thinks of the lines that ironize the *Monitor*'s fight against the Confederate ironclad *Merrimac* as a triumph of mechanical industry over old-time heroism, now superseded by "calculations of caloric," while the resulting gunshots, heard round the world, drum a very different message from that of the Emersonian farmers embattled at Concord. One also thinks of the nightmarish vision embodied in "The Berg," "adrift dissolving, bound for death," even though at one point the alliteration sounds overplayed; one remembers forever the "basilisk" eyes of a secretive Venetian beauty, glimpsed through the slats of a Venetian blind on the canal; one sees the beard of John Brown metamorphosed into ominous fire, "the meteor of the war."

In these and other pieces, at which Melville worked carefully (as the revisions in the Houghton Library manuscripts show), his imagination has found an adequate outlet in verbal sensibility. Alliterative music combines with refreshingly unexpected word usage to animate the rhythm; objects are rendered in sharp outline, without embellishing fringes; and perception rises to a metaphysical awesomeness not unworthy of those climactic pages in *Moby Dick* where prose naturally heightens itself into visionary song. In its felicitous moments (and they were not so few) Melville's versification was almost as far from Victorian conventionality as the innovating achievement of Hopkins and of Whitman himself.

Readers desiring to obtain a closer knowledge of Melville's craftsmanship as a poet can peruse the three versions of "The Gannets" (originally entitled "The Admiral of the White") in the manuscript collection of the Houghton Library at Harvard, or they can study the delicate color patterns of "Sheridan at Cedar

Creek," or probe the kinesthetic effects of "The House-Top," where imitative sound powerfully evokes the roaring guns in the sultry atmosphere of a sinister summer night:

> Hail to the low dull rumble, dull and dead,
> And ponderous drag that jars the wall.
> Wise Draco comes, deep in the midnight roll
> Of black artillery. . . .

The sarcastic ambiguity of that "wise Draco" springs convincingly from the terrifying scene sketched by the previous lines and prepares us for the bitter gnomic conclusion. Melville's American fury manifested itself in a symbolic challenge to the cosmos, in the intoxication of space, in the breakthrough across ideal frontiers, but also as human and social self-criticism; and this is what sets him above his close literary kinsman, Edgar Allan Poe. In Poe the vortex of defeat is a terror having its end in itself, while in Melville the same archetype arouses ethical reverberations and might be defined as a graphic expression of what the existential philosopher Karl Jaspers, in our time, has called "metaphysical shipwreck." Poe's imagination verges on the inhuman; Melville's "lauds the inhuman" and is "healed" by the "pitiless breath" of the devouring sea, but only because the elements' inhumanness, at the weird zenith of their power, throws into sharper relief the precarious value of the human being who confronts them. Poe's terror, being an abstract hallucination, has no limits, but Melville's is to be defined in relation to man, who withstands it in the very act of being overwhelmed.

Poe's characters are more or less shadowy or ghostlike; Melville's characters, steeped though they may be in a symbolic ambience, are much closer to flesh and blood. Poe's terror could be called a preordained absolute, while Melville's has a human dialectic, therefore a dramatic movement. Death vampirizes life in Poe, but not in Melville, who can come to terms with death because he fights it; the predicament of Jacob struggling with the angel, as outlined by Melville in the late poem "Art" to symbolize the essence of creative work, lies at the root of his writing. Melville's tragic sense is absent from Poe's world, for the latter's one-sided hallucination can know only a progressive heightening of fear, not a qualitative transition. The ethical, or we might say human, dimension is what transforms *The Narrative of Arthur Gordon Pym* into *Moby Dick,* and as for *Billy Budd,* it is easy to see how inconceivable that work would be in the Poe canon. A comparison of Poe's and Melville's achievement beyond the technical province of verse, such as has been here essayed, might seem to exceed the limits of our treatment only if we were to overlook the vital nexus of each author's prose to his poetry, and the salient traits their imagination shares.

Melville's richer human sensibility accounts for lively verbal compounds like "laughing light of hoyden morning" or "delightsome sea" (where the syllable "light" mirrors in its echo-like effect the actual "light" of morning from the previous line), or again (to continue with his "Requiem") "shoals of shining tiny things," with the subsequent transition from the joy of marine creatures, rising to the sunlit surface, to the descent of shipwrecked sailors into the dark depths. Here it is unimprovably said of light that it "revisits them" no longer, while the stress placed on the preposition "save" (twice used at the beginning of a line) seems to revive its etymological link with the verb "to save" and thus arouse an overtone of prayer beyond the syntactical meaning of the context.

Furthermore, after the electrifying transition to "Save them forever from joyance torn" we are exposed to the solemn slowness of "Far to the reef of bones are borne," which is emphasized by a labial alliteration as well as by the chromatic insistence on the "o" sounds in "bones" and "borne," while the metaphor makes an ossuary of the coral-overgrown sea bottom. Internal echoes, whether vocalic or consonantal, count for much in the over-all impact of this poem; we have only to remember the "sight of long-sought land" in the last line but two, and again the rich play of sibilants in the last line, with the "lone spar where mid-sea surges pour" that, bird-haunted, recalls the catastrophe of the *Pequod.* Another striking example of expressive alliteration in Melville's poetry could be gleaned from "Pebbles" as above quoted, where the repeated spirants ("*H*ealed of my *h*urt, I laud the in*h*uman Sea") kinetically create the "pitiless breath" of the Four Angels in the following line, with a resultant sense of majesty and release in the very action of the voice. To sum up our analysis of "Requiem," we may observe how the whole poem pivots on a structural inversion of theme and tone (from morning light to dark abysses, from surfacing fishes to sinking corpses, from animal joy to the solemnity of human death, from lively description to a perceptible overtone of prayer) that evokes in its overturning movement an image of shipwreck. The joyful light of the first part interplays with the funereal darkness of the second, not as a mechanical contrast, but in a reciprocal heightening of mystery.

The typical American myth, from the frontier tall tales to the legendary pattern of an Andrew Jackson or an Abraham Lincoln who rose from the log cabin to the White House, not to speak of cruder "self-made men" of a later generation, has always been, ever since the political emancipation of the thirteen states, the myth of success—a sort of dialectical inversion of the original gloomy Calvinism. But writers like Melville (and there were many after him) based their work on a critique of this myth, at the levels and in the forms allowed by the different talent of each. Melville is among those who brought this critique to its deepest range, by developing its social basis (as evidenced in *Typee* and *Omoo*) into a far-reaching ethical and metaphysical inquiry. It is in failure or "shipwreck" and not in success that Melvillian man finds his own significance. With such an approach, Melville could not help remaining isolated, and all but totally obscure, in nineteenth-century America, as his posthumous critical discovery in the postwar period seems to confirm.

America as a whole did not believe in the value of suffering and defeat. But America needed and will always need her Socratic gadflies to save her from the shallowness that can all too easily result from the philosophy of official optimism. Thus Melville can be viewed as an individualist exploring the frontiers of his culture, where he ideally met a Dostoevski and a Kierkegaard, even though, or rather because, the respective departures were so different. The Promised Land of democracy, immune from anguish of the Russian or Danish variety, believed pragmatically in the best of futures. But the scandal of American democracy, slavery bred in the midst of affluence, was soon to explode in the Civil War. This "moment of truth" was what gave a historical focus to Melville's imagination, so that he could share with his unknown transatlantic brethren their ultimate existential concern, the belief in crisis as the basic experience in the human condition. For Melville, this was a natural result of his "frontier" situation—if by frontier we mean the divide between man and nature, between civilization and barbarism, between innocence and corruption, West and East, life and death.

Whitman: space as the expanding self—the prophecy of total identity

Walt Whitman was luckier, for he was able to endow the growing American nation with a congenial, if unwonted, voice. He shares with Melville the titanic attitude, but his is a different tone;

Pierre-Enceladus defeated by the white mountain, Ahab-Prometheus destroyed by the white whale, are giants of sorrow; while Walt, who "contains multitudes," who can effortlessly identify himself with seething America, who says "Yes" to everything, is the giant of joy.

"I celebrate myself, I sing myself": here is the individualist encamping in the virgin space of the North American continent to found there a world that begins from him. With Whitman, the American imagination takes possession of its land—the land of possibility, or better, the land *as possibility*. This barbaric courage to place the individual self at the originating center of a social world, without any fear of anarchy, this faith in the coincidence of individual and community, proclaimed in loud song, this measureless gesture makes Whitman a Don Quixote of letters, to whom it is hard to play Sancho Panza, even if Henry James[9] tried it early in his career. Henry David Thoreau,[10] who believed that anything good was wild and free, had no such trouble with the explosive poet he had practically prophesied in a climactic passage of his essay "Walking;" and this despite the utter difference in personality between Thoreau the secularized Puritan and Whitman the shocking faun.

The Concord writer, who had something of John the Baptist in him, had withdrawn to the lovely wilderness of his native New England countryside in order to start anew the experience of civilization as individual creation, to shake off the dead weight of drawing-room artificiality, to become himself; and that meant to find one's American identity in language, themes, way of life, and civil intransigence. In terms of A. J. Toynbee's philosophy, Thoreau represents the phase of "withdrawal" that was to culminate in Whitman's social "return."

If for Poe (and later for his close literary kinsman, Lanier) space was terror, and for Melville an ambiguous indifference charged with every seduction and every danger, for Whitman space was pure laughter. The sense of limit always supervenes, in Melville, to determine the experience of infinity, on the frontier between civilization and primitiveness, man and nature, life and death; behind him there is the dramatic Calvinism of Jonathan Edwards. In Whitman the Dionysian effusion obliterates all boundaries, it is an infinite in the making. In Melville the limit is always dynamic and qualitative, rather than statically spatial; it does not abolish, in the emergent crisis, the experience of infinity, which it may be said to elicit instead. Whitman's limit is always provisional, internal to his germinating world. Emerson's limitless optimism has found in him an adequate expression—the antiphon to that infinite sense of tragedy which characterizes Melville's confrontation of the "inhuman Sea." In Melville, the Puritan conception of Nature as an inimical Otherness rises to mythical proportions with the "mask" of Moby Dick, the ocean's "tiger heart," the white mountain of Pierre's dream, the iceberg of "The Berg," the wasteland of *Clarel,* the "reef of bones" of "Requiem," and it compels man to assert himself in a clash with the enormous inhuman; in Whitman rejection of puritanism goes so far as to deny any "otherness" in living or inanimate Nature.

That rejection enhances in Whitman a sensuality reaching toward any other human being, no matter how low, and toward the whole cosmos; Whitman enjoys touching everything, he wants interpenetration, his eroticism has a symbolic value as an anti-Puritan gesture, liberation from limits, from original sin, from the burden of history. That is why his love instinct lives homosexually; what matters to him is the experience of identity, of affinity and touch, hence sex stimulates him as identity, not as opposition. Melville too can deal with homosexual attraction, yet he portrays Claggart and Billy Budd as so radically opposite that otherness becomes mutually incommensurable.

The violence of Melville's yearning for the wholly other equals the violence of Whitman's love for the world, felt as an infinite expansion of the self. Whitman's ability and will to embrace the cosmos is no less heroic than Melville's determination to break through the extreme boundary of existence; they are both romantics whose basic attitude has to do with the expanding self, whether it crashes into ultimate cliffs or submerges all in its pantheistic joy. There is a theatrical impetus of Elizabethan flavor (as Matthiessen has observed)[11] in the surging monologue of *Leaves of Grass* as well as in the narratives, dialogues, and asides of *Moby Dick;* it verges in both cases on the melodramatic, though an authentic tragic theme inspires Melville, while Whitman's endless declamations to an endless audience seem attuned to something we should like to call cosmic comedy—the laughter of vital assurance.

Melville's tragic concern with otherness has also a comic counterpart, if we keep in mind the scene between Queequeg and Ishmael at the beginning of *Moby Dick,* or the later episode of the Negro cook's address to the sharks, or the picturesque ships the *Pequod* meets toward the end. Likewise, his basic sense of alienation or Otherness can be counterpointed by occult identity: Ahab somehow identifies with the hated cetacean, as his ivory leg suggests, and Ahab again, as the demonic embodiment of Western Faustianism, is bound by a weird sameness to Fedallah, the demoniac incarnation of Eastern fatalism. Pierre shades into Isabel and vice versa, and life and death rise in Moby Dick to the symbolic pitch that makes the whale a simultaneous manifestation of God and Devil, Nature and the Invisible, or they invert into each other, as when Queequeg's coffin becomes a "lifebuoy." Needless to say, this identity-through-opposition results in a heightening of the tragic paradox rather than in a comic view of existence, unless we taken into account the *Confidence Man* with his ironic welter of transformations.

Irony is not the keynote of Whitman's metamorphoses, which all spring from the basic assumption of universal identity, like a Vedantic "Tat twam asi" underlying every gesture of our restless poet's imagination. Since, however, an absolute metaphysical identity would leave no room for life or thought itself, we find Whitman's "Song of Myself" developing through internal oppositions ("Do I contradict myself? Very well, then I contradict myself") in a sensuous dynamism far removed from self-contained quietude. Whether it be Nature, Death, or the Godlike-demoniac Invisible, Otherness is an outside barrier looming against Melvillian man's explosive energy, while Whitman, having confidently appropriated the whole universe, eventually has to rediscover it as somehow "other" in order to keep moving. He has, in other words, to project or shed reality from the bosom of his own cosmic Self, initially posited as the creative principle ("Song of Myself," stanza 1) to encompass all, and finally to be found in "eddies of the sun" or "under your bootsoles" (stanza 52). Thus from within his all-absorbing Identity there rises a qualified Otherness as the dialectical term of an ever-renewed inner tension; it will be Death,[12] India and more than India, the mask of elusive Nature:

> A mask, a perpetual natural disguiser of herself,
> Concealing her face, concealing her form,
> Changes and transformations every hour, every moment,
> Falling upon her even when she sleeps.
>
> ("Visor'd")

Through this mask Melville's Ahab, of course, would strike frantically in the attempt to seize the hidden deity, but Whitman simply marries it. "Changes and transformations" are the stations of the cosmic Self's pilgrimage away from and back to itself; one only has to remember the strongly focused use of the verbs "to be" and "to become" in the "Song of Myself." ("I myself become the wounded man. . . ." "I am the man, I suffer'd, I was there. . . ." "I am Walt Whitman, a kosmos. . . .") to realize how the disguises here are not a matter of estranging deception as they are in *Confidence Man,* but Eros-charged metamorphoses having death itself for a catalytic force or phase: "Agonies are one of my changes of garments." Apropos of his own changes of garments, the Confidence Man would substitute "ironies" for "agonies."

Whitman the yea-sayer can sing "death, many deaths—not life alone," plying "as a ship on the waters advancing" the seas of existence in the archetypal "voyage of the soul" ("Gliding o'er All"). In this extreme venture, joy is his "shipmate" ("Joy, Shipmate, Joy") and he proclaims in his way that in his end is his beginning:

> Our life is closed, our life begins,
> The long, long anchorage we leave. . . .

Death, then, is to the joyous voyager the other face of the moon, the further and integrating dimension of life:

> The untold want by life and land ne'er granted,
> Now voyager sail thou forth to seek and find.
> ("The Untold Want")

The death wish becomes a projection of the life force, Otherness an inner discovery of the world-encompassing self, the final invitation to self-transcendence:

> Sail forth—steer for the deep waters only,
> Reckless O soul, exploring, I with thee, and thou with me,
> For we are bound where mariner has not yet dared to go,
> And we will risk the ship, ourselves and all.
> ("Passage to India")

These lines from one of the best-known poems in *Leaves of Grass* could have been written by the author of *Moby Dick,* and the convergence of the two otherwise so different writers will be even better documented when we read the following passage from Chapter CLXIX of *Mardi*:

So, if after all these fearful, fainting trances, the golden haven was not gained—yet, in bold quest thereof, better to sink in boundless deeps than float on vulgar shoals; and give me, ye gods, an utter wreck, if wreck I do.

Melville liked those who "dive deep," as he once defined Emerson; and Whitman was of his own kind, even if they started from opposite points. They both loved the sea as an image of life and death. The chapter titled "Pacific" in *Moby Dick* finds a counterpart in "Out of the Cradle Endlessly Rocking," where "Death, death, death, death, death" becomes the ecstatic syllable of the sea. When in *Moby Dick,* Chapter LXI, we read:

Death seems the only desirable sequel for a career like this; but Death is only a launching into the region of the strange Untried; it is but the first salutation to the possibilities of the immense Remote, the Wild, the Watery, the Unshored. . . .

our thought goes to Whitman's "Sea-Drift" ("As I Ebb'd with the Ocean of Life"):

As I wend to the shores I know not,
As I list to the dirge, the voices of men and women wreck'd,
As I inhale the impalpable breezes that set in upon me,
As the ocean so mysterious rolls toward me closer and closer,
I too but signify at the utmost a little wash'd up drift,
A few sands and dead leaves to gather,
Gather, and merge myself as part of the sands and drift.

O baffled, balk'd, bent to the very earth,
Oppress'd with myself that I have dared to open my mouth,
Aware now that amid all that blab whose echoes recoil upon me I have
  not once had the least idea who or what I am,
But that before all my arrogant poems the real Me stands yet untouch'd,
  untold, altogether unreach'd,
Withdrawn far, mocking me with mock-congratulatory signs and
  bows,
With peals of distant ironical laughter at every word I have written,
Pointing in silence to these songs, and then to the sand beneath.
I perceive I have not really understood any thing, not a single object,
  and that no man ever can,
Nature here in sight of the sea taking advantage of me to dart upon
  me and sting me,
Because I have dared to open my mouth to sing at all.

Here the experience of inner otherness attains in Whitman a crucial high point, for it springs from his sense of cosmic identity, of mystical possession of the All, of verbal effusion that negates itself in the humility of the powerless word; and the recognition of sought-for otherness brings him from the "old thought of likenesses" to the creation of a genuine myth:

Ebb, ocean of life, (the flow will return,)
Cease not your moaning you fierce old mother,
Endlessly cry for your castaways, but fear not, deny not me,
Rustle not up so hoarse and angry against my feet as I touch you or
  gather from you.

I mean tenderly by you and all,
I gather for myself and for this phantom looking down where we lead,
  and following me and mine.

Me and mine, loose windrows, little corpses,
Froth, snowy white, and bubbles,

(See, from my dead lips the ooze exuding at last,
See, the prismatic colors glistening and rolling,)
Tufts of straw, sands, fragments,
Buoy'd hither from many moods, one contradicting another,
From the storm, the long calm, the darkness, the swell,
Musing, pondering, a breath, a briny tear, a dab of liquid or soil,
Up just as much out of fathomless workings fermented and thrown
A limp blossom or two, torn, just as much over waves floating, drifted
at random,
Just as much for us that sobbing dirge of Nature,
Just as much whence we come that blare of the cloud-trumpets.
We, capricious, brought hither we know not whence, spread out before you,
You up there walking or sitting,
Whoever you are, we too lie in drifts at your feet.

After identifying with the ocean (which is also a definition of his poetics) Whitman experiences a sudden estrangement in the sense of the unknown and of death, and the latter progressively focuses in a phantom "other self" that in the end dominates like a sea-born god the sacrificially surrendered poet, now speaking in the plural as the chorus of all mankind. Whitman has grasped here the projection of his own double into myth, for the sea god of the end is none other than the "real Me . . . untouch'd, untold, altogether unreach'd" of stanza 2. Death and rebirth, identity and otherness, world ocean and ocean of the self; we have here an archetypal movement of being.

Thus the romantic yearning for the unknown finds in America its proper locus, possibly with accents of greater assurance than in the poetry of Old-World romanticists, for there the systole of the ego that acknowledges itself as a minimal particle of the cosmos takes place without fear and modulates into the diastole of total identification with the sea, with a resultant deepening of perception into mythical vision. Here the imagination seems to be at home in the vastness, while John Keats, though ideally ranging with his mind's eye over the wide Pacific from a peak in Darien, shuddered with fear at the actual experience of the dwarfing unknown. The thematic affinity of his sonnet "written on Ben Nevis" with Whitman's poem just discussed underscores a difference in attitudes between the Old-World dreamer who recoils from the challenge of unplied reality and the transatlantic pioneer who is not afraid to lose his identity if he sheds its earlier form. The refinement of Keats' art may put to shame Whitman's rawness, yet it remains true that the "barbaric" singer evinces an original mythopoetic impulse of which Keats himself was not capable, great though he was at poetically reinterpreting the old Greek myths.

For, unlike the pensive British poet, whose attitude to the universe was one of dreamy and sorrowful questioning, the uncontainable "I" of Whitman's poetry is America itself in its growing buoyancy, one and manifold, and ultimately coincides with the very space of total reality; or, better, it creates a wider and wider space:

> Swiftly I shrivel at the thought of God,
> At Nature and its wonders, Time and Space and Death,
> But that I, turning, call to thee O soul, thou actual Me,
> And lo, thou gently masterest the orbs,
> Thou matest Time, smilest content at Death,
> And fillest, swellest full the vastnesses of Space.
>
> ("Passage to India")

In its self-transcendence, the Whitmanian "soul" pours itself out into the whole universe, not being satisfied with social expansion alone; it behaves like the Atman of that mystical Indian philosophy which was so dear to Whitman's Transcendentalist inspirers, Emerson and Thoreau.

But see if the same ecstasy of effusion does not sing out loud in Melville's "Song of Myself." namely, Chapter CXIX of *Mardi,* where an individual speaker, America, and the world are identified in waves of rapturous utterance:

> Dreams! dreams! golden dreams: endless, and golden, as the flowery prairies, that stretch away from the Rio Sacramento, in whose waters Danae's shower was woven;—prairies like rounded eternities; jonquil leaves beaten out; and my dreams herd like buffaloes, browsing on to the horizon, and browsing on through the world; and among them I dash with my lance, to spear one, ere they all flee.
>
> Dreams! dreams! passing and repassing, like Oriental empires in history; and scepters wave thick as Bruce's pikes at Bannockburn; and crowns are plenty as marigolds in June. And far in the background, hazy and blue, their steeps let down from the sky, loom Andes on Andes, rooted on Alps; and all round me, long rushing oceans, roll Amazons and Orinocos; waves, mounted Parthians; and, to and fro, toss the wide woodlands; all the world an elk, and the forest its antlers.
>
> But far to the South, past my Sicily suns and my vineyards, stretches the Antarctic barrier of ice. . . . Deathful, desolate dominions those; bleak and wild the ocean, beating at the barrier's base, hovering 'twixt freezing and foaming, and freighted with navies of icebergs. . . . But beneath me, at the equator, the earth pulses and beats like a warrior's heart; till I know not, whether it be not myself. And my soul sinks down to the depths, and soars to the skies; and cometlike reels on through such boundless expanses, that methinks all the worlds are my kin, and I invoke them to stay in their course. . . . And like a frigate, I am full with a thousand souls. . . .

For a moment the hero of darksome Otherness enters the paradise of all-inclusive Identity, and Melville becomes Whitman, to the point of speaking almost in the same voice. Adolescent America expresses herself in these blood brothers, the irrepressible America of frontiersmen who learned to look beyond all boundaries. Whitman in his turn comes close to the somber tone of Melville when, in *Democratic Vistas* (1871), he issues on the scanty spiritual accomplishment of his beloved democratic fatherland a verdict comparable in severity to that which Melville had passed in *Mardi* a dozen years before the outbreak of the Civil War. The ideal dialogue between the aristocratically minded poet of Otherness and the democratic enthusiast of Identity has several beats, and seems to point in its dramatic development to the sequence of alternating successes and crises, broken barriers and formidable new problems that may be said to constitute the essential rhythm of American history.

Whitman's recurrent rhetoric, his painfully official postures, are too obvious to be emphasized in this context, were it not that the devotees of formal refinement and literary "good manners" have taken advantage of this weakness, as well as of his loose form,[13] to discredit his real achievement. Dilution, static repetitiousness, enumerative catalogues to exhaustion, yes; these flaws cannot be denied, but see what Matthiessen and his Italian friend, Pavese,[14] have to say on the Biblical structure of Whitman's free verse bordering on prose. The open form in which his utterance unfolds has finally been of some use, not just to the avowed Whitmanians like Williams, Jeffers, and Sandburg, but to Ezra Pound, who had some trouble admitting this literary kinship yet couldn't help signing a "Pact" with his all-too-crude forebear that "broke the new wood." Whitman's "formlessness," variously resented by genteel formalists like Yvor Winters, was something that had to be risked, a gesture that helped to rejuvenate Western poetry, as the testimonials[15] of Paul Claudel and St.-John Perse, of Italian and Russian Futurists and German Expressionists may confirm. It was chiefly to Whitman that they all looked for an example of liberating courage in their several experiments. The looser type of rhythmical form his verse attains in its unrestrained modulations makes for a wave-like effect to which prose writers like Wolfe and Faulkner have been heavily indebted; and in the "chaotic" enumerations of *Leaves of Grass* we can already see, as if in solution, the elements of coming American realism.

Dickinson: confrontation of the self with otherness in the inner space

From Whitman to Emily Dickinson the transition is so abrupt as to make any attempt to include them in a common perspective seem hopeless. What relation could ever subsist between the solitary introvert of Amherst, Massachusetts, and the vehement singer of democracy? In Whitman everything is gigantic, he multiplies his own ego by identifying with all human beings, from the victim to the murderer, and when he mythifies himself, he walks in cosmic space as an unquenchable god, a compound of Davy Crockett, Prometheus, Dionysus, and Jesus:

Solitary at midnight in my back yard, my thoughts gone from me a long while,
Walking the old hills of Judaea with the beautiful gentle God by my side,
Speeding through space, speeding through heaven and the stars,
Speeding amid the seven satellites and the broad ring, and the diameter of eighty thousand miles,
Speeding with tail'd meteors, throwing fire-balls like the rest,
Carrying the crescent child that carries its own full mother in its belly,
Storming, enjoying, planning, loving, cautioning,
Backing and filling, appearing and disappearing,
I tread day and night such roads.

("Song of Myself")

Whitman appropriates reality with a loving assault, and he inhabits an imaginative space well proportioned to the range and intensity of his effusion. His words, sometimes unsyntactically aligned, strike the ear as a marching mass, and often their effect is one of spatial addition rather than progressive integration. Emily Dickinson, the daughter of a declining New England, withdraws into herself and in so doing internalizes space. Whitman's basic note, even if death has a conspicuous place in his best poetry, is affirmation; Emily Dickinson's keynote is negation, a dialectical negation of religious origin that waives possession in order to recover reality on a spiritual level. Whitman's effusive poetry ranges camera-like throughout the external world; his heart reaches out from the great city toward the advancing frontier. Emily's poetics germinate from a sedentary soul and culture, firmly rooted in a local soil, for New England is the most "European" part of an America that has remained so nomadic elsewhere:

> I see—New Englandly—
> The Queen discerns like me—
> Provincially—[16]

Doubtless Emily Dickinson's verse is the most exquisite fruit of that particular world which is the American, and more specifically the New England, small town. If Whitman is at home in the vast spaces of the prairie, of expanding cities and of the whole world, Emily lives with little things, she converses with diminutive creatures and sings a thin birdlike solo; hers is chamber music, not Whitman's full orchestra:

> The Robin's my Criterion for Tune—
> Because I grow—where Robins do—

If the New York rhapsodist tends to populate the blank spaces of silence with the luxuriant aggressiveness of his lines, as though they were symbolic equivalents of the towns that mushroomed all over the American continent in the wake of the westering settlers, the genteel spinster contracts her vibrant words in a space where silence impinges relentlessly. The difference between her and Whitman is comparable to that between Ungaretti and d'Annunzio in Italian poetry, or between Mallarmé and Verhaeren in French. Both know ecstasy, but compared to his Dionysian kind, hers may call to mind the convent variety. Her aristocratic introversion is the opposite of his democratic faith, for he—as D. H. Lawrence[17] well saw—accepts the gospel of "sympathy" or dynamic Identity, while she, according to Allen Tate,[18] has built her house on the rock of otherness. And with otherness she endeavors to live, unlike Melville: we cannot imagine her brandishing Ahab's harpoon against it. Nature, says Tate, is the Number One enemy of New England puritanism, and Emily has faced it by placing on it the mask of Death. Intimacy with death is indeed a constant dimension of her poetry:

> Because I could not stop for Death
> He kindly stopped for me,

but perhaps it isn't the only one, nor does Nature appear to our poetess necessarily in that guise; she often feels it as a domestic entity:

> She sweeps with many-colored Brooms—
> And leaves the Shreds behind—
> Oh Housewife in the Evening West—
> Come back, and dust the Pond!
>
> You dropped a Purple Ravelling in,
> You dropped an amber thread;

And now you've littered all the East
With duds of emerald!
(No. 219)

Hence Henry Wells' claim [19] that Dickinson's verse is, in a way, "domestic comedy"—a claim supported by Constance Rourke's general thesis [20] on American literature, which she sees as an expression of frontier humor, and by George Whicher's monograph.[21] Of course Emily's comic spirit is far more refined than that of the tall tale, if we think of the cosmic gossip she establishes between birds, bees, flowers, and winds, "practising Titanic Opera." Nature is for her, in one of its aspects, a great theater, the projection of garden and drawing room, the magnified counterpart of the inner theater of the soul; Nature is "the gentlest Mother" (No. 790) and an impresario figure:

We spy the Forests and the Hills
The Tents to Nature's Show
Mistake the Outside for the in
And mention what we saw.

Could Commentators on the Sign
Of Nature's Caravan
Obtain "Admission" as a Child
Some Wednesday afternoon.
(No. 1097)

Thus the range of Emily's poetry will escape us if we only look, with Tate, at the pole of otherness and religious crisis and ignore the pole of "domestic" identity or comedy. By virtue of such a paradoxical inclusiveness she attains her magic effects, evoking for us a vividly familiar and quotidian reality which at the same time strikes us as enigmatic in its poignant ephemeralness:

I've known a Heaven, like a Tent
To wrap it's shining Yards—
Pluck up it's stakes, and disappear—
Without the sound of Boards
Or Rip of Nail—Or Carpenters—
But just the miles of Stare—
That signalize a Show's Retreat—
In North America—
No Trace—no Figment of the Thing
That dazzled, Yesterday, . . .
(No. 243)

Intensely perceived reality becomes a theater of spirits. Because Emily's strong religious conscience daily converses with eternity, she can so keenly feel the value of the transitory, of what can be there only once and then irrevocably disappear. Time and eternity for her are not two rigidly opposed concepts, as they would have been in a more orthodox Calvinist, but two dialectical poles of existence.

Allen Tate says that Emily's religion is wholly personal, a phenomenon of individual revelation tinged with heresy, and that in Cotton Mather's time they would have burned her for a witch; hence he links her poetical performance with the crisis of her regional culture as the "ideal literary situation." That indeed helps our poet to feel the transcendent in terms of the domestic, to play or to quarrel with God the Father, to see nature in terms of spirituality, sensation in terms of thought, thought itself as image. Thus in her metaphysical comedy confidence and dismay, smile and shudder, identity and otherness, quotidian and eternal intertwine to deepen the paradox of a reality virginally experienced:

Experience is the Angled Road
Preferred against the Mind

By—Paradox—the Mind itself—
Presuming it to lead

Quite Opposite . . .
(No. 910)

And Emily can, as a consequence, "dwell in Possibility" (No. 657) and practice sorcery:

This was a Poet—It is That
Distills amazing sense
From ordinary meanings
And Attar so immense

From the familiar species
That perished by the Door—
(No. 448)

Hers is a poetics of paradox and poverty:

Of Pictures, the Discloser—
The Poet—it is he—
Entitles Us—by Contrast—
To ceaseless Poverty—
(No. 448)

This is the reverse of Whitman's orgiastic sensuality; it would be hard to find in modern literature a more genuine example of spiritual awareness. Emily Dickinson's Franciscan aesthetics has purified life into image without leaving any dross; starting from the experience of a familiar private world, she has been able to rediscover the world at large in the inner space of her spirit, and vivify everything there with an ethereal touch. On the other hand, she shares with Whitman, different as he may be in every other regard, a resolute individualism that gives her the courage to make the world anew in the word, by herself in utter loneliness uttered; it is clear why both poets come to portray their existential plight in the image of the tireless spider.

The pure self becomes its own theater, "full as Opera," where she is "out of sight, in sound." The latter metaphor from poem No. 326 supplies us with a precious clue to Emily's poetics: the transition of the visible into the invisible, which then affords a purified return to the visible, to be performed only by a celestial eye. Imagism and symbolism, the image perfectly realized in itself as pure apparition and its fading into the encompassing symbol, are two coeval or alternating phases of Dickinson's poetry, for, as she has it, "to disappear enhances"—a statement Rilke would have subscribed to. To express the inexpressible is her divinely obscure task:

> To tell the Beauty would decrease
> To state the Spell demean
> There is a syllableless Sea
> Of which it is the sign.
> My will endeavors for it's word
> And fails; but entertains
> A Rapture as of Legacies—
> Of introspective—Mines—
>
> (No. 1700)

The poet's struggle with the word and his defeat by the august silence of the Inexpressible, which make up the essence of symbolism, have never been more vividly stated, perhaps not even by Mallarmé or Rilke, who were Dickinson's kindred souls in Europe.[22] At the same time, the dynamics of paradox prevented Emily from drowning in the "syllableless sea," for from her uneven struggle with that seething indefiniteness she derived the sense of individualized power that concentrates in the word when everything has been staked on it:

> Could mortal lip divine
> The undeveloped Freight
> Of a delivered syllable
> 'Twould crumble with the weight.
> (No. 1409)

On the verge of mystical ecstasy, Emily always recovers the sense of the finite, of the uniquely real, for she is an offspring of those hardy people who had known how to make New England a garden:

> On the Bleakness of my Lot
> Bloom I strove to raise—
> Late—my Garden of a Rock
> Yielded Grape—and Maise—
>
> Soil of Flint, if steady tilled—
> Will refund the Hand—
> Seed of Palm, by Lybian Sun
> Fructified in Sand—
> (semifinal version of No. 681)

Here Emily Dickinson's spiritual autobiography coincides with the history of New England, a history of long struggles with an alien environment and with oneself, of spiritual blossoming dearly paid for. But in another aspect, hers is the predicament of many a representative modern poet who, thrown back upon herself, has to make the best of his "estranged" situation by conquering sterility; whether we think of Mallarmé's spiritual wanderings "à travers un Désert stérile de Douleurs," of his proud Hérodiade, or of Paul Valéry's "Narcisse" (and "Palme"), the relevance will be clear. The strong existential motivation accounts in any case for the absence of idle aestheticism in Emily's frequent abandon to the sheer pleasure of imagery, where we find only the purity of an eye and of an ear utterly absorbed in their fairy world:

> How still the Bells in Steeples stand
> Till swollen with the Sky
> They leap upon their silver Feet
> In frantic Melody!
>
> (No. 1008)

Sound and vision vibrate so keenly that when we afterward read the Wallace Stevens of *Harmonium* and the John Gould Fletcher of *Irradiations,* we sense in most of these Imagist performances a certain thinness not to be redeemed even by an exceptional gift for verbal capers. It is of course true that Emily Dickinson affords, among other things, the ideal introduction to twentieth-century Imagism and its affiliates like Marianne Moore, who has not turned a deaf ear to Emily's conversational tones. If Emily Dickinson can be claimed as ancestor by some of the outstanding contemporaries, it is because she was engaged, like Whitman, in the intransigent task of founding an American idiom in poetry. Miracle rewarded her assiduous experiment when she conferred expressive density on lace-thin lines, airy lightness on a dry, exact language, and the freshness of an ever-renewed surprise on the well-known world of drawing-room, garden, church, school, bank, law firm, village, and surrounding countryside.

Emily's microscope discovers unsuspected vastnesses:

> Immured in Heaven!
> What a Cell!

This excerpt from poem No. 1594, which can be seen in manuscript at the Dickinson home in Amherst, shows how the artist could translate an "occasional" composition like a poem on her nephew's death into a metaphysical epigram that reverses the closure of the coffin (and of the isolated self) into the liberating spaciousness of an inner sky (Rilke's idea of "openness"). Such reversal of the negative into the positive constitutes the paradox of poetry, the highest affirmation of a spirit that "dwells in Possibility" waiting for "the slow fuse of the Imagination" to set fire to her inner charge, and achieving victory in defeat.

In her critique of the Yankee myth of secular success Emily was brought by her religious background very close to Melville's stance:

> Success is counted sweetest
> By those who ne'er succeed.
> To comprehend a nectar
> Requires sorest need. . . .
> (No. 67)

That paradoxical definition of victory seems to anticipate poem No. 1249:

> The Stars are old, that stood for me—
> The West a little worn—
> Yet never glows the only Gold
> I ever cared to earn—
> Presuming on that lone result
> Her infinite disdain
> But vanquished her with my defeat,
> 'Twas Victory was slain.

America as dream and as the reality of struggle inspires poem No. 555, and existence in general must define itself in struggle to attain the realm of miracle:

. . . 'Tis when

A Value struggle—it exist—
A Power—will proclaim
Although Annihilation pile
Whole Chaoses on Him—

(No. 806)

This is the heritage of the Pilgrim Fathers, an American light dawning on Plymouth Rock after two centuries and a half; but it is also an insertion of quotidian experience into the sphere of universal problems.

Thanks to such a purity of approach, Emily was able to become the most universally valid American voice of her time in poetry, without leaving her beloved small-town world. The limited world of a provincial village, of a sheltered home, and finally of the self-questioning ego, was her frontier; by deepening the sense of finitude she discovered infinity, infinity as sorrow:[23]

Pain has an Element of Blank—
It cannot recollect
When it begun—or if there were
A time when it was not—

It has no future but itself,
Its infinite realm contain
Its past, enlightened to perceive
New periods of pain

(No. 650)

She could also discover infinity as joy:

Inebriate of Air—am I—
And Debauchee of Dew—

Reeling—thro endless summer days—
From inns of Molten Blue—
(No. 214)

or as Kierkegaardian despair:

No Man can compass a Despair—
As round a Goalless Road
No faster than a Mile at once
The Traveller proceed— . . .

His ignorance—the Angel
That pilot Him along
(No. 477)

a despair drunk to the dregs:

No Man can understand
But He that hath endured
The Dissolution—in Himself—
That Man—be qualified

To qualify Despair
To Those who failing new—
Mistake Defeat for Death—Each time—
Till acclimated—to—
(No. 539)

Beyond the ordeal of despair there was the reward of eternity, an eternity experienced as spatialized time:

Time feels so vast that were it not
For an Eternity—
I fear me this Circumference[24]
Engross my Finity—

To His exclusion, who prepare
By Processes of Size
For the stupendous vision
Of his Diameters—

(No. 802)

For inner space is an infinity to be sensed in its outer reflection as external space ("The Outer—from the Inner/Derives it's Magnitude—" No. 451), and eternity can be experienced as ecstatic space, in a multiplication of oceans of light:

As if a Sea should part
And show a further Sea—
And that—a further—and the Three
But a presumption be—

Of Periods of Seas
Unvisited of Shores—
Themselves the Verge of Seas to be—
Eternity—is Those—

(No. 695)

Ecstasy is reversed into terror when eternity becomes a Pascalian chasm:

There is a pain—so utter—
It swallows substance up—
Then covers the Abyss with Trance—
So Memory can step
Around—across—upon it—
As One within a Swoon—
Goes safely—where an open eye—
Would drop Him—Bone by Bone

(No. 599)

Having started from the infinitely small, Emily finds herself again in the vertigo of the infinitely vast, as her microscope's lens dilates the scrutinized self and pushes its boundaries farther and farther:

> Then Space—began to toll,
> As all the Heavens were a Bell,
> And Being, but an Ear,
> And I, and Silence, some strange Race
> Wrecked, solitary, here—[25]
>
> (No. 280)

Thus spatial imagination, with her, is an adventurous phenomenology of existence; her talk of death, eternity, and infinity would make little sense were it not for its relation to existential concreteness:

> To be alive—is Power—
> Existence—in itself—
> Without a further function—
> Omnipotence—Enough—
>
> To be alive—and Will!
> 'Tis able as a God—
> The Maker—of Ourselves—be what—
> Such being Finitude!
>
> (No. 677)

Time, anguish, and lostness are transcended in a strangely placating spatial vision:

> Great Streets of silence led away
> To Neighborhoods of Pause—
> Here was no Notice—no Dissent—
> No Universe—no Laws—

By Clocks, 'twas Morning, and for Night
The Bells at Distance called—
But Epoch had no basis here
For Period exhaled

(No. 1159)

The confusion of clocks is both dread and liberation, for it results from the intentional probing of all-transcending solitude:

There is a solitude of space
A solitude of sea
A solitude of death, but these
Society shall be,
Compared with that profounder site
That polar privacy
A Soul admitted to Itself—
Finite Infinity

(No. 1695)

This poem reminds us of the Nietzschean "fisher of seven solitudes," just as poem No. 139 ("Soul, wilt thou toss again?") brings to mind Pascal and the Mallarmé of *Un coup de dés*. "Domestic" as she may be, Emily pushes to the limit the adventures of solitude. Privacy becomes a thematic symbol in the form of the ever-recurrent "cocoon," which hides in itself the future of the "Butterfly." In poem after poem the release Emily attains by withdrawing from the outer world and communing with herself is conceived as the blossoming of a butterfly from the cocoon of inwardness.

This is a clear image of liberating transcendence, but even in her own solitude Emily cannot install herself without incurring further troubles. Privacy does shelter also the worm of "otherness," and from her culminating ecstasy the mystical contemplator is mercilessly evicted. Thus the absoluteness of an identity sought at the cost of utmost renunciation breaks under the inroad of otherness, which appears as love, or as grass-shivering wind, or a fire-hatching volcano near the doorstep, or as a snake focusing the fascination-repulsion of sex. The latter is to be unmistakably recognized in poem No. 986 and even better in No. 1670, where Emily-Eve flees from the phallic, Satan-like reptile, in a negative inversion of the Eden myth:

> I shrank—"How fair you are!"
> Propitiation's claw—
> "Afraid, he hissed,
> Of me?"
> "No cordiality"
> He fathomed me—
> Then to a Rhythm *Slim*[26]
> Secreted in his Form
> As Patterns swim
> Projected him.
> That time I flew
> Both eyes his way
> Lest he pursue—
>
> (No. 1670)

This ambivalence of attraction and fear keeps threatening Emily's solitary Eden, after the tension of unrequited love. Otherness is a sphinx that menacingly confronts the poet's identity, as a "mighty Face" whose "Figure was withdrawn" in "the charms/Of Winter and of Hell" (No. 1649); all nature then reveals its demoniac cruelty, the wind growling "like hungry dogs/Defeated of a bone" and the trees holding up "their mangled limbs/Like animals in pain" (No. 1649).

Sphinxlike or hellish Nature is but the counterpart of the inner threat to the self, which writhes in self-alienation:

> Me from Myself—to banish—
> Had I Art—

Invincible my Fortress
Unto all heart—
But since Myself—assault Me—
How have I peace
Except by subjugating
Consciousness?[27]
(No. 642)

The buried volcano of the Unconscious might erupt at any time:

It's Hour with itself
The Spirit never shows
What Terror would enthrall the Street
Could Countenance disclose

The Subterranean Freight
The Cellars of the Soul . . .
(No. 1225)

And the most dreadful battle is that which one wages against the formless forces of the psyche, in the secret battlefield:

The Battle fought between the Soul
And No Man—is the One
Of all the Battles prevalent—
By far the Greater One . . .
(No. 594)

The "legions of night" besiege the self; one thinks of Marlow's fight against death in Conrad's *Heart of Darkness.* Emily does not succumb to this dangerous ordeal; she girds herself like David and flings her stone at the phantom of Otherness, but like a newfangled William Wilson, she hits only herself:

'Twas not so much as David—had—
But I—was twice as bold—

I aimed my Pebble—but Myself
Was all the one that fell. . . .
(No. 540)

Otherness in identity, the splitting of the self, is the Damocles sword hanging over our solitary dreamer; she thus knows the obsession of Poe's Wilson and of Dostoevski's *Double*. It is an insidious specter, weirdly laughing (No. 274), and it can appear in the "Corridors" of the "Brain":

. . . Far safer, of a Midnight Meeting
External Ghost
Than it's interior Confronting
That cooler host.

Far safer, through an Abbey gallop,
The Stones a'chase,
Than unarmed, one's a'self encounter—
In lonesome Place
(No. 670)

In the face of that terror, death is salvation, "overtakelessness," or inaccessibility to disintegration, for, as Dylan Thomas has said in another age, after the first death there is no other; and to be "beyond the hope of touch" is the reward of those "who have accomplished Death" (No. 1691). Special attention should be given here to the verb of fruition, "to accomplish" which denotes the crowning of a process of endeavor. In her drama of identity versus otherness Emily knows the horror of the demoniac, the Devil appearing as an ambiguity enticingly close to the Divine (No. 1479), while God Himself, on the other hand, stands accused of "Duplicity" (No. 1462). Thus the personification both of the infinitely negative and of the infinitely positive is questioned by our gentle rebel, who takes toward both an attitude not very unlike Blake's or Melville's, if we overlook the ironic curtseying in the style—an elegance meant to heighten cunningly the radicalness of the gesture. Heresy springs from the obsessive Puritan conscience that haunts Emily's pillow and arouses a wish of annihilation in the "phosphorus of God" (No. 1598). Nor is this a mere fleeting mood; our poet had eventually denounced the rigor of Biblical literalism, by upholding Orpheus, the singer prophet who charmed and "did not condemn," against a dogmatized myth supported by arbitrary religious sanctions that divide mankind into elect and damned (No. 1545). When, in the same poem, she attacks the Church's notion of sin, she is formulating on an intellectual basis the imaginative revolt that had brought her to identify with the criminal in No. 1470:

> The sweets of Pillage can be known
> To no one but the Thief,
> Compassion for Integrity
> Is his divinest Grief.

If ever a poet was "of Hell's party," she was one. For in her boldness she accepted sin as an affirmation of existence, a possible way out of demoniac ambiguity. In this light we can perhaps read her early poem on that favorite subject of several modern writers, Melville among others: Jacob's struggle with the angel, which she interprets as the victory of one who "found he had worsted God!" (No. 59). The struggle with the divine-demoniac angel was renewed whenever Emily, by defining herself in verse, reasserted her identity against the chaos of formlessness, of ambiguous silence; the angel was the Sea trying to lure her into destruction (No. 520), or else the Wind of No. 436, who had "no Bone . . . to bind Him" and a "Countenance" like "a Billow." The Wind "visited" flurriedly, and she "became alone—." A poem like this documents Emily's sense of spiritual event—in the circumstances, a sterile Annunciation, betokening a final solitude. Revolt and transcendence, the will to affirm and the ability to renounce, bred an intimate acquaintance with sorrow, fear, and ecstasy, and the resultant deepening of consciousness enabled the poet to concentrate her language into pure vibrancy. Words are distilled, etherealized, and yet sharpened in their outline; they are juxtaposed by sorcery. In the poem under examination, one should notice a modifier like "impossible," a verb like "to visit" (loaded with Biblical overtones), a conclusion like "became alone," which recapitulates the whole composition. Intensity focuses those words into individual expressiveness, while others are paired so as to pass into each other: chair-air, speech-push, countenance-billow, flitting-Man, fingers-music. They dramatize the interplay of shape and shapelessness, a presence that almost becomes tangible and yet dissolves on the verge of total realization—after which the condition of loneliness is deeper.

Emily Dickinson is the poet of the inner theater that is the heart, the only one owners cannot close (No. 741). In such a theater the drama of her existence is played out over and over again under the watchful eyes of the stage manager, who is also actor and public—the "single hound" of her identity (No. 822). The action of the play may also feature an endless journey beyond three Rivers and a Hill, a Desert and a Sea (No. 1664) toward the beloved, toward God, toward the conquest of the challenging Other. The arrival at the goal takes place as a transfiguring metamorphosis of our traveler into the bodiless:

> We step like Plush
> We stand like snow
> The waters murmur new

Three rivers and the Hill are passed,
Two deserts and the sea!

She has shed the weight of matter, yet Death denies her the ultimate vision; so that in a way the trip never finishes, its goal being everywhere and nowhere. And the trip actually symbolizes the finite-infinite process of existence toward, through, and beyond consciousness; by the same token, it also alludes to the trajectory of poetry as a consummation of language (since this can only coincide with the gradual heightening of consciousness); finally, its meaning can be extended to adumbrate, prophetically, the posthumous adventure of Emily's verse into the awareness of modern readers the world over—an eclipse to be followed by apocalypse.

Pioneering critics like Mark Van Doren, Allen Tate, Conrad Aiken, and John Crowe Ransom[28] have contributed to the apocalyptic discovery, one that parallels that of Melville in the realm of prose, but its climax came in 1955 with the publication of Thomas H. Johnson's critical edition of the poems. Only with this text at our disposal could we begin to glimpse the full extent of Emily Dickinson's achievement, her art's "circumference," in her own pregnant idiom. It is a circumference that encompasses clear intimations of the very best Anglo-American poetry to come in the twentieth century: the conversational irony of Eliot, Pound, and Marianne Moore, the vivid elegance of Stevens, the intermittent illuminations of Hart Crane. Whatever is bold or vital—and that includes the best part of E. E. Cummings' verbal experiments—may be said to have some antecedent in the work of the Amherst poet, who can claim at the same time a primacy of refinement. Whitman was just as bold if not bolder, but none of the American poets of her century can compare with the unequaled sophistication of her style. Within the framework of very limited metric patterns, she attained an incredible resilience by making rhythm and diction in turn supple, brittle, or taut, rich or abstract, direct or oblique. Only in rare moments does Thoreau's or Melville's verse approach anything like this felicity of statement.

If her poetry's "circumference" is so vast, it is because she combines a sharp intellectual lucidity with a naïve sensuousness, harboring in her soul the *naiven Dichter* along with the *sentimentalischen Dichter,* which both conspire to give her diction is uniquely modern flavor. No wonder, then, that poems like No. 204, No. 552, and No. 632 sound like Stevens. They exhibit the same Transcendentalist concern with the mind, tempered by a comparable dryness or irony; and the result is an effect of weird lucidity that radiates dreaminess:

An ignorance a Sunset
Confer upon the Eye—
Of Territory—Color—
Circumference—Decay—

It's Amber Revelation
Exhilarate—Debase—

When, in the first of his *Notes toward a Supreme Fiction,* Wallace Stevens asks his aesthetic disciple to "become an ignorant man again" in order to see the sun in the purity of its "first idea," untainted by human intrusions, he is restating the theme Dickinson had touched upon in the above lines; with both poets, "ignorance" becomes something positive, a state of unknowing that prepares the mind for an unclouded revelation that has the power of radically transforming its beholder. At the same time, one cannot help noticing how differently they handle their theme of *docta ignorantia:* the more logical Stevens pleads for phenomenology, the more mystical Dickinson is seized by the rapture of mystery.

It could also be added that Stevens' more artfully intellectual verse sometimes moves on a more gratuitous level, verging on decadent word play, while Dickinson's experiments show an existential motivation that redeems their occasional naïveté. She is familiar with death and can interpret it either as the shudder of an inconceivable experience that totally transcends our world, or as the integrating dimension of existence. Formally, she seems to recapitulate in a subtler way the various fortunate attempts of her predecessors, from Freneau to Poe and Melville, from Thoreau and Emerson to Whitman; the sense of space reappears in her as a totally internalized spiritual vastness, the sense of identity manifests itself as a continuous adventure and a perpetual crisis. And since from that predicament can spring either a radical renewal or an insidious disintegration of the soul which, if complacently savored, engenders the literature of decadence, even the twentieth-century American decadentism of French derivation has a national antecedent in Emily Dickinson's obsessively refined sensibility. Hart Crane, who spent himself in "this cleaving and this burning," Conrad Aiken, who knows the literature (and the pleasure, along with the pain) of dissolution, John Peale Bishop, who felt death as a music, are all related somehow to the poet who "felt a cleaving" in her mind until she could no longer unravel the sequence of her thoughts.

Prophetic Heritage

Since, with Emily Dickinson, nineteenth-century American poetry seemed to have reached its deepest intensity and its widest "circumference," it was historically fitting that the cycle should close with her and reopen at the beginning of our century with the powerful injection of French symbolism[29] that started Ezra Pound, T. S. Eliot, Wallace Stevens, and Marianne Moore on their thriving careers. The American "Renaissance" officially blessed by Harriet Monroe in 1912 with the foundation of this country's veteran magazine of verse, *Poetry* (Chicago), had nothing to do with Dickinson and little with Whitman, though one of its most impressive exponents, Hart Crane, claimed both as direct ancestors in his effort to create an American epic. Nowadays we are in a position to revaluate *Leaves of Grass,* grossness and all, while reading the *Cantos* and the *Waste Land.*

The sense of space is expressed in vision, the sense of time in rhythm, and rhythmical experimentation has marked the achievement of several twentieth-century poets, some of whom, like Vachel Lindsay, Gertrude Stein, William Carlos Williams, and Hart Crane, have variously responded to the stimulus of jazz. Its languor and frenzy appeal to the sensibility of an age beset by experiential discontinuities, whether of mechanical, social, or psychological nature. There was nothing to compare with this in the nineteenth-century world of American poetry's Founding Fathers, yet even here one can say that their pioneering counted for much in the way of making new rhythms possible.

The French-inspired experimenters of our time have been able to extend the range of poetical language, but their inspiration was not completely "foreign," for their French models looked up to Edgar Allan Poe and made his exacting poetics their own. Thus the quest for "pure poetry," for the perfectly constructed and mysteriously revelatory poem, has been a joint Franco-American venture from the outset; and the same applies to the parallel, and antithetic, quest for the "open" poem, for the poem conceived as an unbounded act of the voice, as a prophetic statement: Rimbaud, Laforgue, Claudel, and St.-John Perse have all listened to the unevenly powerful song of Walt Whitman. Current appraisals that stress America's (and the whole West's) modern indebtedness to French nineteenth-century sources generally overlook the fact that Emily Dickinson was paralleling in her provincial isolation the great enterprise of Baudelaire, Mallarmé, and Rimbaud in developing Poe's initial cue. She, too, was "purifying the dialect of the tribe" in an imperishable way, though nobody knew it at the time; for the efforts of American literary explorers, unlike those of their French brethren, did not benefit by a tightly knit cultural milieu, and could not, as a consequence, thrive on a continuous rising tradition; the more astonishing their breakthroughs.

The Paris salon made for the gradual shaping of rigorous craftsmanship in the pursuit of *poésie pure,* though it could also take to heart a rebellious visionary like Rimbaud; the scattered, restless life of young America had to evolve an image of the poet as prophet as well as craftsman. The prophet often speaks up against his nation, to warn her of impending doom or corruption; the American writer, Bible-inspired even when he does not know it, has often taken the posture of the rebel within his own society to decry injustice or looming arrogance—the hybris attendant upon victory—and stagnation—the temptation of prosperity. In this function, prose and drama writers have claimed, of course, the larger share of the work, but poets like Eliot, Pound, MacLeish, Jeffers, a maverick like E. E. Cummings, Robert Lowell, William Carlos Williams, or Southern "rebels" like Allen Tate or Robert Penn Warren have vied in reminding their giant country of the dangers that beset its triumphant path after so many victories. Expressed in whatever symbols, the protest of the poet against a mechanical, thing-minded civilization that risks idolizing its own power at the cost of its soul and future life is always fundamentally a plea for the vital versus the stagnant, for the perennial in man versus the extrinsic, for quickening form versus deadening inertia or apoplectic fury. Whitman already knew, as did Thoreau, that the Promised Land was a possible Eden but also a possible Babel; subsequent history has not proved their fears totally unfounded. Here, too, the nineteenth-century pioneers of American poetry paved the way for their modern descendants, whose struggle for new, enduring forms has been inspired by a common dream of that fulfilled humanity without which all technological boasts are empty. This rage, and this love, are the fire from which even the rarest alchemies of the word draw their distilling energy; nor are they wanting in the dedicated endeavor of those devotees of tradition who, like Robinson and Frost, have preferred to stand quietly apart from the experimenters. It can be said that experiment and prophecy are the main fuel of the "inclusive" flame that is American poetry.

Two / *Edwin Arlington Robinson: Knight of the Grail*

THE GENTLEMAN from Gardiner, Maine, was an isolated conservative in a literary world that had seen the triumph of an aggressive Imagism. He refused to court public favor by joining the winners,[1] and kept on writing, mostly in a narrative vein which, in the changed climate of American letters, seemed to be obsolete. In the deafening labyrinths of Manhattan he would walk like a shadow of his own characters besieged by time and enlightened by defeat—Captain Craig, Fernando Nash, Merlin, Lancelot, Ferguson.

Yet today, when a generation of careful craftsmen has succeeded yesterday's iconoclasts, and the New England voices of Robert Frost and Robert Lowell have won enduring attention, it does not seem right to relegate Robinson to a prewar poetic interregnum, or to make him the mere gifted epigone of a discursive nineteenth-century romanticism.[2] Perhaps Robinson's best achievement is to be found not in the long Arthurian poems but in the short compositions sprung from native New England soil. Thus we shall peruse volumes like *Children of the Night* (1890-97), *The Town Down the River* (1910), *The Man Against the Sky* (1916), *The Three Taverns* (1920), and *Avon's Harvest* (1921) to map the "Tilbury Town" which, among the small towns of the imagination, claims a priority over Masters' Spoon River, Anderson's Winesburg, and Wilder's unnamed municipality. For here the dry comical vein so well identified by Horace Gregory fuses or intertwines with the tragic and elegiac introversion of the New Englander who feels he has come at the end of a cycle in his native culture.[3] On the other hand we should beware of wholesale condemnation of the long poems. "Captain Craig" is generally acknowledged as rather successful but the compositions dealing with Arthurian romance—particularly the remarkable *Tristram*—are not given their due. Apart from the *Tristram's* glittering final sequence, which wrests admiration from sensitive critics, the prevailing indifference to the Arthurian poems seems to rest on the assumption that they are cases of belated romantic sentimentalism in a derivative vein. I believe, on the contrary, that their genetic connection with the seminal part of Robinson's poetical canon can be demonstrated: his Camelot is an inverted image of Tilbury Town.

Tilbury Town is provincial America unable either to wrench itself loose from its Puritan roots or to draw nourishment from them; it is a world locked in a spellbound past, where individuals no longer communicate with one another. One need only remember what New England had been like at the time of its mid-century "flowering"[4] to realize the historical predicament that Robinson interprets symbolically in his clipped verse. Concord, the "shot heard round the world," the Transcendentalist circle, the zest for social and educational experiment, the courage of individualist defiance, Brook Farm and Walden, Emerson and Hawthorne, the fervor of an "American Renaissance" eventuating in pioneer literary achievement; and now the twilight of creativity, the loss of commercial primacy to the growing urban giants of New York, the Middle West, and California, the westward migration, the shadow of abandoned villages. When life subsides, then is a time for brooding.

The shadowy citizens of Tilbury Town, left behind by history's wave, passively await the consummation of time; the dead village is their focusing symbol:

> Here there is death. But even here, they say,
> Here where the dull sun shines this afternoon
> As desolate as ever the dead moon
> Did glimmer on dead Sardis, men were gay. . . .
> And over the forgotten place there clings
> The strange and unrememberable light
> That is in dreams. The music failed, and then
> God frowned, and shut the village from His sight.

In poem after poem we hear their voice as a gossipy chorus that establishes their collective presence as a limiting horizon while concentrating in turn on each of the town characters, the eccentric as well as the drab. Thus we get to know Tilbury Town as a perspective, as a state of mind reflecting a close community, and at the same time as a collection of failures. There is Bewick Finzer, the ruined millionaire, "familiar as an old mistake,/ And futile as regret;" there is Bokardo, resignedly "battered by the past" though "not yet/ Consumed or mourned;" there are John Gorham and Jane Wayland, who, through the years, keep up their mutual estrangement through inability to understand each other; and the "poor relation," abandoned by everybody, feels useless as if it were "wholly wrong/ Of her to stay alive so long." Therefore she secludes herself in the pastures of memory, "foraging/For bits of childhood song," and time slowly closes down on her, scanning for her a death sentence on the rhythm of the unknowing metropolis where she has migrated for refuge:

> And like a giant harp that hums
> On always, and is always blending
> The coming of what never comes

Outside, and through a thousand sounds
The small intolerable drums
Of Time are like slow drops descending.

Bereft enough to shame a sage
And given little to long sighing,
With no illusion to assuage
The lonely changelessness of dying,—
Unsought, unthought-of, and unheard,
She sings and watches like a bird,
Safe in a comfortable cage
From which there will be no more flying.

Of course in this masterpiece it is Robinson's own voice we hear, his sustained style, instead of the villagers' chorus, and just as the lady described is an exile from Tilbury Town, the poem itself is marginal to the Tilbury Town series. But Robinson's felicitous diction can range from the conversational to the lyrical and the dramatic. There are few things in modern verse worth comparing with the "largo" effect of the finale above quoted, where verbal precision, rhythmical strength, rhyme melody, and functional onomatopoeia combine to make the "small intolerable drums/ of Time" an orchestral commentary on the situation. If the rhythm of time and doom is expressed by the phonetic mimesis of those drums, that of the City comes through like the panting of a monster in heavily stressed spirant alliterations:

The City trembles, throbs and pounds
Outside, and through a thousand sounds. . . .

This driving pulsation in turn is echoed toward the end by a similar rhythmical phenomenon that embodies the very throb of our lady's heart; and since that heart is not named, the elusive tactics heighten our imaginative apprehension of the whole, by making us respond preeminently to the rhythmical component of expression:

> Unsought, unthought-of, and unheard. . . .

Similarly, in *Merlin,* Merlin and Vivian are overtaken by Time's assault, "cold angel of Change."

The roster of Tilbury Town's citizens includes loveless mates ("The Clinging Vine"), village sages who bear with good humor the curse of a degenerate offspring ("Old King Cole"), ghosts of vanished people and homes ("Stafford's Cabin"), posthumous accusers forever bound by mutual jealousy ("Lisette and Eileen"), jolly adventurers of love ("John Evereldown"), tight-lipped hypochondriacs ("Charles Carville's Eyes"), elemental types who crumble suddenly under the impact of grief ("Reuben Bright"), the rich man whose life is so empty that he astonishes his enviers by suddenly killing himself ("Richard Cory"), the gambler beaten by life ("Leffingwell"), the spiritualist questioning shades ("Lingard"), the old "Uncle Ananias" who, as the nicest of liars, kept telling fairy tales to the village children, the unforgettable Mr. Flood ("Mr. Flood's Party") who ironizes his irremediable loneliness by toasting himself as if there were two of them there on the hilltop overlooking the estranged town.

Robinson's art is discreet, aristocratic, and wiry. It muffles its effects in understatement without stifling them, for it partakes of certain qualities of American speech: precise diction, dry wit, colloquial directness. Who can forget the etching of "Aaron Stark," where the miser is caught in his devilish predicament, with merciless insight? In those eyes of his "like little dollars in to dark" we find a Dantean critique of character and culture, telescoped into the flash of one image. "Richard Cory," deservedly loved by anthologists, uses the traditional metric pattern of the sonnet for a very modern effect of dramatic transition that makes its point by sheer shock. Robinson has few rivals in the treatment of the sonnet, as his poems to Zola, Verlaine, and Crabbe, among others, show; of course the ideal specimen would have to come from the Tilbury Town series, and of these "New England" would not be an implausible candidate for primacy. The mockery here comes through in a terse satirical vein that is, itself, an understatement of love; there is a measured energy in the utterance, which modulates the rhythm and the syntax, besides concentrating diction into graphic imagery, and the total result is a sense of artistic finality. Nor should one forget the formal sharpness—and the compassionate insight—of another sonnet, "The Pity of the Leaves," where the dry leaves become the encompassing symbol that focuses a human condition:

> Words of the past that shook the old man's cheek
> Like dead, remembered footsteps on old floors.
>
> . . . Now and then
> They stopped, and stayed there—just to let him know
> How dead they were, but if the old man cried,
> They fluttered off like withered souls of men.

Louise Bogan has rightly said that Robinson's language, when free from Tennysonian influence, germinates from New England speech with its reticence, its incisiveness, its angular rhythm. This appears to be particularly true of "Isaac and Archibald," a narrative poem of intermediate length that meanders effortlessly through dialogue and monologue. The story is about two friends, old patriarchs, who are transfigured by a boy's nightly dream into time-conquering angels and in this imaginary guise enable him to converse with all ages and all heroes. Since they have faced time without cheating, they do ideally conquer it and thereby allow the poet himself to breathe a mythical aura of timelessness where the past is recoverable. The same motif can be found in *Tristram,* which thus "hinges" on Tilbury Town—the hinge being provided by "Isaac and Archibald." The latter poem also connects Robinson with Robert Frost; for here the use of speech in its conversationally subtler tones to effect a natural transition from reality to imagination and back clearly foreshadows Frost's analogous ventures. On the other hand, Robinson's New England roots show (less pleasantly) when he moralizes, whether allegorically or not, in a way that reminds us of Whittier, Longfellow, and Hawthorne.

And here a definite statement on our poet's situation in the "main currents" of American poetry may be in order. There are critics who deny his relevancy to contemporary poetry. But the art of Robert Frost and Robert Lowell, and, utterly different though it may be, of Wallace Stevens, has come to show the vitality of Robinson's heritage, at least in some important respects. The Italian critic Rolando Anzilotti[5] has said that Robert Lowell focuses in his use of the dramatic monologue a central strain of modern American poetry; monologues like "Falling Asleep over the Aeneid," "David and Bathsheba in the Public Garden," "Thanksgiving's Over," and "Mother Marie Thérèse" can be placed in an ideal continuity with "Captain Craig," "Ben Jonson," "Isaac and Archibald," "Lazarus," and "The Man Who Died Twice," provided we take into account the intervening influence of T. S. Eliot, Hart Crane, and Dylan Thomas, which makes for lightning-like metaphors and contractions in the texture of Lowell's discourse. Yet Robinson can approach that incandescent tenseness, for poems like "New England" and "Anchors" clearly anticipate the Lowell of "Where the Rainbow Ends" and "Children of Light." On the whole, however, Robinson's tone is brooding rather than explosive, meditative rather than apocalyptic; in this dimension, his Arthurian poems foreshadow Stevens' "The Comedian as the Letter C" or *Ideas of Order,* with which they share a sustained interest in certain existential problems. Finally, one might note in passing how, even in its conservative metric draping, Robinson's sensitive use of conversational irony partly points to T. S. Eliot's experiments. Unless we thus situate Robinson in the perspective of living, rather than past, history, we cannot understand why an exuberant avant-gardist like Amy Lowell insistently urged the shy New Englander to join her revolutionary ranks.

But he was a citizen of "Tilbury Town," and Tilbury Towners do not easily make revolutionary gestures; they are prisoners of dream. One thinks of "Shadrack O'Leary," of "Atherton," of "Miniver Cheevy," of "Vickery," who forever gazes at the western mountain beyond whose summits gleams phantom gold. "Miniver Cheevy" is a two-edged satire that gently mocks on the one hand the provincial character wavering in his cups between naïvely unfulfillable dreams and regrets of unachieved wealth, and on the other, the poet himself, "born too late," sighing "for what was not," dreaming "of Thebes and Camelot, and Priam's neighbors." The terse diction and affectionate humor recommend this poem to the modern reader, who soon realizes how Robinson's unobtrusive style grows on him at every reading. "Miniver Cheevy" parallels "Isaac and Archibald" in showing the nexus between Robinson's personal experience and the Arthurian fables that occupied the latter part of his creative life. But "Isaac and Archibald" is dreamy, while "Miniver Cheevy" parodies the poet and his world; if we chorally amplify the parody, without forgetting the dream, we get to "Captain Craig," where the local elegy and local comedy of Tilbury Town are transcended into a general vision of human fate as an overcoming of material defeat through the cult of innocence (the Child, of Wordsworthian memory, whom we must never kill in our heart; the Nazareth carpenter; the sage who laughs and understands because he has retained his purity.)

Captain Craig, in dreary New York poverty, tells his listeners that "success" is not everything, that indeed the only important success is to be attained through material defeat. He thus states (and embodies in his own destiny) a central theme of Robinson's, which runs full tilt against a widespread American gospel, the businessman's faith in "aggrandizement." "Cassandra" is another prophetically minded poem, though slighter in scope, which seems to prelude analogous statements by later writers like Robert Lowell or Robinson Jeffers (who indited a piece of poetry by the same title). Of course much of the best American literature, whether in verse or prose, revolves around a thorough critique of naïve optimism; here if anywhere the responsible writer has typically been some kind of social prophet periodically reappraising the "democratic vistas" of his materially privileged country—which also goes to explain the frequent estrangement of the American writer from his community, an estrangement generally dictated by a deeper commitment to that community's original values than the community's official sponsors seem ready to recognize. It might even be said that if God sent Gogol, Dostoevski, Tolstoi, and Gorki to Russia because she suffered too much, he sent to America Melville, Robinson, Eliot, Lewis, and Faulkner because she did not suffer enough. A nation that loses the tragic sense of existence risks drying up its culture's very sources, while a people steeped in tragedy risks foundering in fatalism. These, perhaps, are in the last resort the great alternatives of American destiny and of Russian destiny: uncritical faith in material success produces a Babbitt, a Prufrock, a Bewick Finzer, some kind of "hollow man," while the orgy of unhappiness without hope results in a Stavrogin—to be sure, these are prophetic images, projections of the possible, rather than accomplished verdicts.

If Tilbury Town is a closed world, a jail of ghosts, Robinson does not fail to show a way out. There is the way of death, the "western gate" through which Luke Havergal tries to join his beloved; but there is also the way of life, the temporary opening up of the whole community to the strange angel, Flammonde, who comes to renew that world with a breath of free air and then passes on, leaving the town in a state of uncomprehending amazement. But Flammonde is an exception; one never immigrates into Tilbury Town, one emigrates, like Captain Craig, like Robinson himself, who "went underground" into the New York subway to make a living—and a resurrection. From that daily faced Hades the poet emerged with a new wisdom; the provincial man from Gardiner lost in New York chaos found his Tilbury Town in a wider dimension, where anybody is a failure unless he has learned to master time in a pilgrimage to the Grail of love, for the whole world is, in a sense, Tilbury Town.

At this point fable supervenes in Robinson's writing, and for a very good reason. If the whole world is Tilbury Town, the whole world is fairyland. The perennial conflict of man with his dream, the perennial problem of quest and defeat, at times take on a metaphysical depth not unworthy of Melville.[6] And now the universal myths bud from Tilbury Town's reluctant clods: we meet Fernando Nash, the "man who died twice," the first time to be reborn in the spirit, the second to take leave of the world under the seal of wisdom, amid an intermittent throb of drums, life drums and death drums (reminiscent of Conrad's *Heart of Darkness*) that relentlessly scans the poem; for Fernando Nash beating the Salvation Army drum on Broadway is more than a wayside folklore type, he is a spiritual colleague of Marlow and Kurtz, a man going toward the farthest threshold where, by paying with one's life, one can glimpse the mystery of existence. We meet Lazarus, who rose from the dead only to realize that life is the more awesome riddle; we meet Nicodemus, well instructed by the words of Christ, who taught him how the only way to return to one's mother is to go straight on in time up to death, and death will conquer death; we overhear Shakespeare, who has learned to converse with nothingness because this is the tollway to a new hope; we renew our acquaintance with the Round Table knights and Merlin the wizard, who will never find the Grail because death is the quintessence of life.

The basic motifs luxuriating (often, unfortunately, to the extent of discursive prolixity) in that narrative cycle are neatly stated in a poem whose firm thirteen quatrains should put to shame the partiality of so many anthologists for the wordier "The Man against the Sky." For "Hillcrest" must count among the enduring examples of American poetry, and within the Robinson canon it easily takes its place beside gems like "Eros Turannos" and "For a Dead Lady." Here the experience of disappointment transcends itself into a sense of mystery; here Captain Craig, as a disciple of both Socrates and Christ, empties the cup of bitterness that will magically become a Grail for him, and vision rises from the chasm of thorough despondency to new quickening vistas—though not to a codified faith, for we can speak only of faith in man, vibrating in the atmosphere of the Unknown. The versification in "Hillcrest" is sustained and flexible, the diction untainted by padding, sagging softness, passive echoes, or rhetorical gestures; whereas "the Man against the Sky" ends on the note of "nothingness," here the game is subtler, outlining the paradox of an unknowing wisdom, of death that is "less than Change," of love that "builds of what Time takes away," of "triumphant" soul that recovers the "sight" of "a child who sees the whole/World radiant with its own delight."

The crystal phrasing here mirrors the purity of a world view which, instead of backing down before paradox, in paradox itself seeks and finds release. Both philosophically and stylistically, discretion keeps the poem from slipping into raw private ideology by insisting on the use of "if" and "may," those natural semantic messengers of Robinson's questing doubt. By comparison, the sonorous questions and answers of "The Man against the Sky," which likewise revolves on the problem of man's ultimate destiny and the meaning of existence, sound hollow, despite some brilliancies of diction. The comparison might be usefully extended to test Robinson's art against the passionately ideological assertiveness of his contemporary, Thomas Hardy, and perhaps also against the pure melody and bitter philosophy of Giacomo Leopardi, an earlier small-town gentleman who throughout his tormented life, like Robinson, kept up the inner debate between disillusioning Truth and delusive dream. To glean felicities from the imaginative whole of "Hillcrest" is to do less than justice to the harmonious poem, but one can at least point to the magic of the first two stanzas, to the modern elegance of diction in the fifth ("if here he venture to unroll/ his index of adagios . . ."), the seminal statement of the last but four, which condenses the themes of *Tristram, Merlin* and *Lancelot,* and the airy resolution of the last, which merges sound, image, and thought into effortless song.

Knowledge annulling itself in the child's vision, Jesus' *docta ignorantia,* makes the impossible possible; the return to the source, the reversal of time through poetry's magical metamorphosis that subdues the irreversible: the oaks will "return to acorns," Nicodemus' question will find a positive answer—not in simple regression, which equals involution, but in the authentic "return" of the imagination that frees reality from its limitations to bring it back to its moment of nativity:

He may by contemplation learn
A little more than what he knew,
And even see great oaks return
To acorns out of which they grew.

Isn't this the same as Kierkegaard's "resumption of the past," memory as the liberating act of consciousness? Indeed, the whole poem takes shape as such a resumption; we might say it is formally a creative reversal. It returns to its beginning, as one may verify by comparing the last stanza with the first; but the return is a discovery, made possible by the lightness of touch, since Robinson says great things here without seeming to, and the only word for that is grace.

If we keep in mind this poem, along with the self-parodying "Miniver Cheevy" and "Isaac and Archibald," which states the transition of Tilbury Town into pure fable, we shall understand why Arthurian myths should have seduced Robinson's imagination and what is their vital relation to the rest of his work. Tristram is man as the prisoner of ambiguity, caught between Isolt of Brittany and Isolt of Cornwall, between wife and mistress, love evenly flowing in a serene time and climactically violent love; caught, that is, between the experience of what is familiar and intimate and the yearning for the unknown. Perhaps, since the two geographic terms of the ambiguity are Europe and a western overseas land, we might even read into the situation a symbolic tension between Old and New World. Tristram eventually yields to the lure of Cornish Isolt's "new world" and thus chooses the consuming time that will burn him up, while Breton Isolt keeps waiting for him in the endless patience of her horizontal time. Meanwhile Tristram and Isolt of Cornwall have been killed by Andred, the trusted jackal of King Mark, but really by their own love, which, having burned all of life in its effusion, makes further time meaningless. Breton Isolt's love was an intimacy with horizontal time; Cornish Isolt's love is a refusal of time, a withdrawal from time and world, therefore an intrinsic death:

> You said once that whatever it is that fills
> Life up, and fills it full, it is not time.

Time as lived by, and shared with, Isolt of Cornwall is fire; time inhabited by Isolt of Brittany is water. Fire attains a climax of intensity, afterward to leave only the void of a "posthumous" time; water flows quietly on without failing. The two Isolts are at bottom two aspects of the same woman, the nocturnal and the diurnal, and together they form the sphinx of ambiguity that is existence as confronted by Tristram. Tristram is also Robinson spiritually moving between the two worlds of his heritage; he is another Hawthorne, another Henry James, and the New England legacy (or we should say the American) partakes of New and Old World alike. The resultant situation, as we know, posed for many a New World writer a problem not easily solved, the search for his own identity as definable within his homeland's tradition; and home was on both sides of the Atlantic!

Tristram is, then, the typical Robinsonian hero wrestling with time. For him and Isolt of the violet eyes time is a boundless availability that eventually loses meaning because daily life cannot fill it any more. After the fire of absolute love, after the violation of tranquil "marital" time, after surrender to the exceptional, only emptiness remains; the only open gate will be Luke Havergal's "western gate," death. Cornwall lies west of Brittany. A life founded on escape, on the supreme intensity of a beautiful moment, can hardly have another outcome. Tristram is the poet's escape from the quasi-Dostoevskian underground of New York's subway into pure fable; but fable here contains its own self-criticism. Tristram has chosen the lightning of an absolute instant, yet Isolt of Brittany loves him beyond desertion, since she embodies the continuity of domestic time, fidelity; and the poem closes with a sequence of high lyrical power that resumes the initial seascape's cue:

> . . . Yet there she gazed
> Across the water, over the white waves,
> Upon a castle that she had never seen,
> And would not see, save as a phantom shape
> Against a phantom sky. He had been there,
> She thought, but not with her. He had died there,
> But not for her. He had not thought of her,
> Perhaps, and that was strange. He had been all,
> And would be always all there was for her,
> And he had not come back to her alive,
> Not even to go again. It was like that
> For women, sometimes, and might be so too often
> For women like her. She hoped there were not many
> Of them, or many of them to be, not knowing
> More about that than about waves and foam,
> And white birds everywhere, flying, and flying;
> Alone, with her white face and her gray eyes,
> She watched them there till even her thoughts were white,
> And there was nothing alive but white birds flying,
> Flying, and always flying, and still flying,
> And the white sunlight flashing on the sea.

That contagion of whiteness engulfing all—seascape and "inscape" of the mind, things, animals, and thoughts—epitomizes in a concrete symbol the climate of the whole poem. It is a whiteness of death and liberation, the sign of a reached limit; it is Breton Isolt of the white hands, and it is Isolt of Cornwall; it is the soul migrating toward an infinite horizon.

Horace Gregory and Marya Zaturenska have noticed, in this poem, occasional slips into flatness—something hard to avoid in a long narrative composition. But one should also point out the several passages worthy of particular mention, like those vistas of a glittering iron ocean which might be the same that lashes the New England shores:

> Albeit the sun was high, the breath of morning
> Was in the trees where Tristram stood alone
> With happiness, watching a bright summer sea
> That like a field of heaving steel and silver
> Flashed there below him, and as harmlessly
> As if an ocean had no darker work
> To do than flash, and was to bear thereafter
> No other freight than light.

The next to last stanza of "Hillcrest" says:

> Peace, like a mask, hides everything
> That is and has been from his eyes;

and in *Tristram,* shortly after the quoted passage, we find:

> Security, the friendly mask of change
> At which we smile, not seeing what smiles behind it. . . .

Tristram is not merely a fable of romantic evasion, but an apologue of disenchantment that tells how Tristram and Isolt, by withdrawing from the world and disowning time in their ecstasy, have dissolved reality into a ghost fog:

> We are the last that are alive, Isolt,
> Where the world was. Somewhere surrounding us
> There are dim shapes of men with many names,
> And there are women that are made of mist,
> Who may have names and faces....

They have thus exiled themselves from the possibility of continuing to live, for their mode of existence has become an alienation, a loss of reality. Instead Isolt of Brittany,

> ... who sees enough in ... duress
> May go as far as dreams have gone.

The problems of dream versus reality, of man vis-à-vis the world, of the relation to what is other than self, underlie this retold romance.

Nor should we forget, if we want to do justice to the author, his delicately rendered women (they are portrayed as active presences, not as given objects):

> He felt her body throbbing
> As if it held a laugh buried alive,
> And suddenly felt all his eloquence
> Hushed with her lips. Like a wild wine her love
> Went singing through him and all over him;
> And like a warning her warm loveliness
> Told him how far away it would all be
> When it was warm no longer.

Time's steady trickling becomes the assault of a sea:

> Each with unyielding lips refused the other
> Language unasked; and their forgotten ears

> Knew only as a murmur not remembered
> A measured sea that always on the sand
> Unseen below them, where time's only word
> Was told in foam along a lonely shore,
> Poured slowly its unceasing sound of doom—
> Unceasing and unheard, and still unheard,
> As with an imperceptible surrender
> They moved and found each other's eyes again,
> Burning again the night between their faces.

The others, on the contrary, "were to fill life with time," accepting day-to-day existence.

Merlin (1917) and *Lancelot* (1920) are the same as Tristram's story but in reverse. Like him, the wizard and the Round Table knight savor for a moment the climactic joy of love outside time and outside the world—Merlin with Vivian and Lancelot with Queen Guinevere. But unlike Tristram, they re-enter time, they don't let it spew them back onto the sands of death. For they realize the impossibility of prolonging the ecstatic moment, and instead of being caught off guard by Change, the insidious Lucifer of their Eden, they face it and thus forestall it; so they leave each his beloved, to return to the real world. Only if one has the strength to renounce dream can one preserve it intact beyond its climax. Neither Merlin, nor Arthur, nor Lancelot will ever find the Grail; Galahad, who got a glimpse of it, was struck dead by its light, for the absolute does not forgive, it is the threshold situation of death. But this bitter wisdom saves the others from shipwreck.

Who willingly renounced the supreme happiness will not be robbed by Time; who clings to the privileged instant will lose everything, including himself. So Lancelot wandering into darkness until he meets a mysterious light, and Merlin leaving his Vivian to return with Dagonet to the world of men, are prototypes of the "pure fool" (Merlin indeed says of himself that he "shall die a fool"). Clearly this suffices to redeem Robinson's Arthurian fables from the imputation of soft romantic escapism; evasive fantasy is consummated and taken stock of by the poet within the fable itself. He never forgot the great adversary, Time, who offers existence his ambiguous factotum services in order to take a harsh revenge later on if it turns out that they have been wrongly used. The knights of the Grail are the heroes of time; they lose when they think they are conquering it, they conquer when they acknowledge its law.

The Grail is the ever-receding boundary of human experience, the furthermost term of any quest, Kant's "Highest Good;" it could also be taken to signify the American dream, the propelling vision of the Pilgrim Fathers, of the pioneers, of the later immigrants, the continuous challenge of a reality that refuses to be confined within a definitive horizon. Isn't this the very essence of the American adventure? And isn't it significant that medieval fables should conclude, with Robinson, on the note of a plea for reality? Merlin is Captain Craig, who went underground to rediscover his humanity, and Lancelot is Miniver Cheevy, who learned to come to terms with reality. They always took to the West—Tristram in the direction of Cornwall, Merlin

> . . . stared out into the West again,
> Where now no crimson cloud or phantom town
> Deceived his eyes.

They are brothers of the man against the sky who disappears beyond a hillcrest into sunset's blaze, of Vickery, who sees his mountain gleam blue in twilight, of Luke Havergal, who gazes spellbound into death's "western gate," or of the gold-seekers of "Klondike" who remain to waste and wane, victims of their mirage, on their march to a delusive goal.

We have here a basic ambivalence. The West is the American "call of the wild," the pioneers' lure, but it is also the sunset sky, the call of death. Robinsonian man looks west because he cannot invert the course of the sun, that is, of life; he knows that time is irreversible. But he does not give up the dream, since it is the dimension that gives scope and breath to reality. In dream one cannot install oneself permanently; from dream one proceeds toward death, the last issue of ecstasy, like Tristram and Havergal, or one returns to reality, like Merlin.

Here is Lancelot coming to grips with the angel of Time:

> "Yet here I am," he said,—"and here I am.
> Time, tide and twilight; and there is no twilight—
> And there is not much time. But there's enough
> To eat and drink in; and there may be time
> For me to frame a jest or two to prove
> How merry a man may be who sees the Light.
> And I must get me up and go along,
> Before the shadows blot out everything...."
>
> ... He rose and looked away into the south
> Where a gate was, by which he might go out,
> Now, if he would, while Time was yet there with him—
> Time that was tearing minutes out of life
> While he stood shivering in his loneliness,
> And while the silver lights of memory
> Shone faintly on a far-off eastern shore
> Where he had seen on earth for the last time
> The triumph and the sadness in the face
> Of Galahad, for whom the Light was waiting.
> Now he could see the face of him again,
> He fancied; and his flickering will adjured him
> To follow it and be free. He followed it
> Until it faded and there was no face,
> And there was no more light. Yet there was time

That had not come, though he could hear it now
Like ruining feet of marching conquerors
That would be coming soon and were not men.
Forlornly and unwillingly he came back
To find the two dim chairs. In one of them
Was Guinevere, and on her phantom face
There fell a golden light that might have been
The changing gleam of an unchanging gold
That was her golden hair. He sprang to touch
The wonder of it, but she too was gone . . .

Merlin abounds in subtly wrought passages that anticipate or parallel the best of Stevens; they develop the theme of Change as a law of life—life which, despite and through change itself, must somehow find a constancy, a fidelity. Merlin, like Craig and Nash, "knows beyond knowledge," and this makes him mysteriously inaccessible even in domestic intimacy. Vivian wants to keep him near herself, in an island outside time, for Merlin is a powerful king-maker and contriver of metamorphoses:

> You are the only thing there is alive
> Between me as I am and as I was
> When Merlin was a dream. You are to listen
> When I say now to you that I'm alone.
> Like you, I saw too much; and unlike you
> I made no kingdom out of what I saw—
> Or none save this one here that you must rule,
> Believing you are ruled. I see too far
> To rule myself. Time's way with you and me
> Is our way, in that we are out of Time
> And out of tune with Time. We have this place,
> And you must hold us in it or we die.

So she plays Calypso to Merlin's Ulysses, and at first she seems to succeed; he becomes a helpless prisoner—a prisoner of dream like many Tilbury Towners—and Vivian pities him:

> . . . and, pitying herself,
> She pitied the fond Merlin she had changed,
> And saw the Merlin who had changed the world.

If Merlin, who by his magic power changed the world, cannot come to terms with Change, he will be irremediably defeated. Vivian now becomes so necessary to him that "without her now there was no past or future;" without her, time loses its physiognomy to level out into a "desolation and a changelessness—defying reason." But then the angel of Change enters his paradise, and it is the revenge of excluded Time:

> For now to Merlin, in his paradise,
> Had come an unseen angel with a sword
> Unseen, the touch of which was a long fear
> For longer sorrow that had never come,
> Yet might if he compelled it. He discovered,
> One golden day in autumn as he wandered,
> That he had made the radiance of two years
> A misty twilight when he might as well
> Have had no mist between him and the sun,
> The sun being Vivian. On his coming then
> To find her all in green against a wall
> Of green and yellow leaves, and crumbling bread
> For birds around the fountain while she sang
> And the birds at the bread, he told himself
> That everything today was as it was
> At first, and for a minute he believed it.
> "I'd have you always all in green out here,"
> He said, "if I had much to say about it."

The interview that follows that (worthy of Henry James, as Babette Deutsch has aptly remarked) gives Merlin the revelation of inescapable truth: Time cannot be tricked, and it is better to accept its law than to stop life in a cocoon of delusion. Now Merlin finds his wisdom again and he can face the crucial moment of parting as if it didn't matter. By thus submitting to Time's inevitable victory, Merlin saves himself, for he affirms his integrity as man rooted in a world of other men to be helped:

> . . . The man who saw
> Too much must have an eye to see at last
> Where Fate has marked the clay; and he shall delve,
> Although his hand may slacken, and his knees
> May rock without a method as he toils;
> For there's a delving that is to be done—
> If not for God, for man. I see the light,
> But I shall fail before I come to it;
> For I am old. I was young yesterday.
> Time's hand that I have held away so long
> Grips hard now on my shoulder. Time has won
> . . . And in the end
> Are more beginnings, Dagonet, than men
> Shall name or know today. It was the end
> of Arthur's insubstantial majesty
> When to him and his knights the Grail foreshadowed
> The quest of life that was to be the death
> Of many. . . .

Here Merlin's Robinsonian voice forms a prelude to Eliot's *Four Quartets,* despite the different philosophy implied. Galahad, who has seen the Light, is dead but lives; Merlin has been buried at Broceliande but lives—he is the "man who died twice" to be reborn.

Instead of succumbing to his experience of love, knowledge, and power, he has mastered it with the courage of timely renunciation and the humility of the man who knows he will never be able to know everything because he does not want to dominate and accepts the human world. Merlin has transcended the world of restlessness, of lust for power and selfish love; he has found a different level of existence in a perspective of acceptance that is his Grail, the hemlock cup of Socrates-Craig emerged from underground to reassure his friends. On that world—which might even symbolize the feverish America of our century, so alien to Robinson's feelings—Merlin casts a detached glance, seeing

> . . . no more for me to do
> Than to leave her and Arthur and the world
> Behind me, and to pray that all be well
> With Vivian, whose unquiet heart is hungry
> For what is not, and what shall never be,
> Without her, in a world that men are making,
> Knowing not how, nor caring yet to know. . . .

Merlin has not only accepted time, but through his conscious renunciation he has risen above the level of his former existence; instead of a mere "return," his is a pilgrim's progress toward the further consummation. Touched by vision, he has known himself in truth, and this sets him apart from the common world. He is an ideal brother of Prospero:

> I saw; but I was neither Fate nor God.
> I saw too much; and this would be the end,
> Were there to be an end. I saw myself—
> A sight no other man has ever seen;
> And through the dark that lay beyond myself
> I saw two fires that are to light the world.

The two fires prophesied by Merlin are creative love, which does not consume or imprison the beloved in its laughter, and truth, the Grail men attain in Socrates' cup, revelation through suffering. It is the message of Captain Craig, addressed to Robinson's unheeding America.

The theme cluster of time, light, and darkness unfolds variously in Robinson's verse, often paralleling the twilight effects of Henry James' and Joseph Conrad's prose: witness the atmospheric beginning of *Cavender's House* (1929). That beginning shows how Tilbury Town's phantom air has touched all of Robinson's personae. But the result does not stop at the funereal presage of defeat. Captain Craig, who has "cursed the sun and the breezes and the leaves," thinking of human misery, believes in the mystery of the Child everybody can nurture within himself. The apparition of Christ is at first suffused with an unknown light, which then becomes the absolutely familiar, the always known light: Craig owns to being a "carpenter" and is invited to Nazareth for a chance to learn the trade anew. Craig, the hero of hemlock and laughter, has seen the Light, has attained his Grail; Merlin gets there by another way, having overcome the seduction of dream. Dream and sorrow are a viaticum, at this point, instead of snares; Robinson is not an ultimate pessimist, because with every fiber of his being he senses that intangible something which potentially dwells in every human being. Craig, Flammonde, Merlin, Rembrandt, Isaac and Archibald, Fernando Nash, all embody this mystery, they harbor this light no darkness will ever manage to stifle, for they have reconquered innocence through experience.

In view of all this, dare we still confine Robinson's poetry to a more or less remote past? In privileged moments he even anticipated the clear-cut diction of Yeats' last poems. In "The Man Against the Sky," wordy and prolix though it may be as compared to other Robinsonian works, we find these lines, which remind us of Yeats' "Byzantium":

> And with an aching strangeness viewed the last
> Abysmal conflagration of his dreams,—
> A flame where nothing seems
> To burn but flame itself, by nothing fed; . . .

"Byzantium" 's fourth stanza has:

> Flames that no faggot feeds, nor steel has lit,
> Nor storm disturbs, flames begotten of flame. . .

But "Byzantium" was written in 1930, fourteen years after "The Man Against the Sky." And one might call "pre-Yeatsian" Robinson's "Pity of the Leaves," or "Fragment," with its classically firm style so well climaxed by the final stanza; or 'For a Dead Lady," whose classicism is likewise anything but derivative; or "John Brown."

Now that the Imagist revolution has weaned us from whatever was stale, soft, or spurious in the romantic heritage of the nineteenth century, we can take a fresh look at Robinson's achievement and reappraise his solitary voice. He was a true knight of the Grail, born either too late or too soon, forever confronting in his quietly heroic isolation the perilous ordeal of a quest for the ultimate experience, the "inclusive flame" that would either destroy or remake the unappeased seeker. For him the way to this Grail started from Tilbury Town, while Hart Crane, who did not survive the quest, came from Garrettsville, Ohio, to find a gleam of the same holy cup in New York's ashcans, and Eliot, migrating from St. Louis, Missouri, to ancestral New England and England itself, kept looking for it through the waste land of modern civilization. Where was the roadblock on the way to fable?

Three / *Wallace Stevens: "Notes toward a Supreme Fiction"*

Gazing[1] at the sun of reality, Wallace Stevens refracts its "inclusive flame" into rainbows, which he then pursues to the boundaries of the invisible, and in this perilous game he uses for a prism only the word, which he handles with consummate rhetoric. If this is true of most of his work, from "The Man with the Blue Guitar" to "Esthétique du Mal," from "Peter Quince at the Clavier" to "Thirteen Ways of Looking at a Blackbird" and "Description Without Place," it finds a signal confirmation in *Notes toward a Supreme Fiction* of 1942. These thirty compositions, grouped in three dialectically related sections, rehearse the main themes of Stevens' poetry, and an analysis of them yields much that is of value for a better understanding of all of Stevens' work.

The word "rhetoric," as used above, refers to its Latin source, according to which a rhetorician was a master of language, a craftsman of speech. We might recall how Malcolm Brinnin,[2] in an essay on contemporary American poetry, classified Stevens as an "artifact" writer along with Marianne Moore, to separate their tradition from the "demoniac" one that runs from Poe to Crane as well as from the strain of "ironic conversation" that binds Laforgue to Pound and Eliot. We might also remember Richard Blackmur's[3] discussion of Stevens' "The Comedian as the Letter C," which he envisages as a "texture" of "rhetoric" retaining feelings and thoughts in such a way as to transform them through verbal chemistry, so that for this poet nature "becomes only words." If we compare these critical opinions with Malcolm Cowley's statement in "The Time of the Rhetoricians,"[4] that the poet or creator has been superseded in modern America by the "rhetorician," that is, by the refinedly competent critic, by the Alexandrian man of letters, we may realize with greater precision the significance of a poet like Stevens, especially in *Notes*.

For we shall see the historical value of his art of poetry as the American equivalent, and not merely derivation, of Mallarmé's and Valéry's self-mirroring aesthetic autonomy, which in its turn was the culmination of that tireless process of refinement that led European poetry, from Romanticism onward, to seek its own absolute essence in its very medium. We have here to do with a conscious maturity of American verse, where technical expertness, self-awareness, and extreme refinement go hand in hand. Both the advantages and the dangers of ripeness are conspicuous in Stevens.

At the same time, of course, his sophistication must be understood in the framework of America's genteel tradition, a New England phenomenon of recurrent vitality not to be underestimated when one is tempted to identify the native temper only with the "lowbrow" or "redskin" writers. Introverted Brahmins, spinsters, or dandies from the northeastern states have always vied with rugged muckrakers in intellectual courage, and in our century an effusive revolutionary poet like Hart Crane strove to unify in his art the two opposite strains of American culture by enshrining in his *The Bridge* the delicate memory of Emily Dickinson along with that of passionately invoked Walt Whitman. Crane was really a Dionysian type, unlike our quietly musing lawyer and adoptive New Englander, who contemplates reality with a detached curiosity and an intellectual urgency comparable to Ezra Pound's. The latter has been called by his friend Eliot *"il miglior fabbro,"* but when it comes to handling the chisel he has a strong rival in the author of *Notes toward a Supreme Fiction.*

Since Stevens has always proclaimed his allegiance to the cult of Mother Earth (witness "Sunday Morning" or "Credences of Summer"), it may be puzzling to find the first ten poems of *Notes* grouped under the postulate of abstraction ("It Must be Abstract"). Harold Watts[5] was one of several critics who used "Credences" as his basic text to prove Stevens a seeker of pure sensory perception, undisturbed by intellectual adulterations:

> Let's see the very thing and nothing else.
> Let's see it with the hottest fire of sight.
> Burn everything not part of it to ash.
>
> Trace the gold sun about the whitened sky
> Without evasion by a single metaphor.
> Look at it in its essential barrenness
> And say this, this is the centre that I seek.
> ("Credences of Summer," Stanza 2)

And indeed, later on, the same poem says:

> The rock cannot be broken. It is the truth. . . .
> It is the visible rock, the audible,
> The brilliant mercy of a sure repose,
> On this present ground, the vividest repose,
> Things certain sustaining us in certainty.
> (Stanza 6)

Yet even here we can see a different attitude emerge: though the poet relishes the immediate perception of reality, he cannot express it "directly," but must somehow detach himself from it and reach another plane from which to talk about it, or better, speak it:

Far in the woods they sang their unreal songs,
Secure. It was difficult to sing in face
Of the object. The singers had to avert themselves
Or else avert the object. . . .

(Stanza 7)

If so, Lloyd Frankenberg's reading[6] will have to be taken into account. Frankenberg interprets Stevens' poetry as a continuous variation on the theme of the ever-changing relation between appearance and being, and such a stance cannot ignore the intellect; on the contrary, it will necessarily take the intellect as a basis even if the final goal is its negation. Our poet's manifold and often contrasting attitudes have to do with this problem, as a careful reading of *Notes toward a Supreme Fiction* shows. William Van O'Connor's monograph[7] is another critical contribution to an understanding of the challengingly protean song. After a minute elucidation of Stevens' poetry in its symbolic leitmotiv, O'Connor concludes that he is preeminently an intellectual poet, for it is the intellect that enables him to introduce into his vision the element of relativity and irony. Intellect ultimately negates itself in this process to favor imagination—itself conceived as a relative faculty, unlike Coleridge's—and pure perception.

What, then, does Stevens mean by "abstraction"? Remember, he believes only in the concreteness of colors, of "summer," and in "Crude Foyer" he proclaims the innocence of the absolute to be a false happiness:

. . . since we know that we use
Only the eye as faculty, that the mind
Is the eye, and that this landscape of the mind
Is a landscape only of the eye; and that
We are ignorant men incapable

Of the least, minor, vital metaphor, content,
At last, there, when it turns out to be there.

He only seeks

... the dazzling, bulging, brightest core,
The furiously burning father-fire,

afterward to state:

Infant, it is enough in life
To speak of what you see. But wait
Until sight wakens the sleepy eye
And pierces the physical fix of things.
("The Red Fern")

And in "Description without Place" he affirms the identity of appearance and reality:

It is possible that to seem—it is to be,
As the sun is something seeming and it is. . . .
(Stanza 1)

Even if we were momentarily to forget the miraculous lightness of "The Man with the Blue Guitar," wholly played on the magical interaction of reality and appearance, fact and fantasy, nature and art, a first answer could come from "The Motive for Metaphor," where the poet desires

... The exhilaration of changes:
The motive for metaphor, shrinking from
The weight of primary noon,
The ABC of being,

> The ruddy temper, the hammer
> Of red and blue, the hard sound—
> Steel against intimation—the sharp flash,
> The vital, arrogant, fatal, dominant X.

Here we have the dramatic confrontation of two opposite terms: reality as a "thing in itself," a provocative sphinx, and the artifice of poetical metaphor, which here epitomizes all of human knowledge. Human fiction is incommensurate with reality, and reality is a never-to-be-exhausted challenge to human intelligence. But since the human mind is lodged in reality, it will have to find a way to overcome this paradox, at least provisionally.

If metaphor (and, by implication, all of poetry, all of knowledge) is a mere evasion, a "shrinking from" being, it has no value. If it merely duplicates being, it likewise has no value. The only way out seems to lie in discarding "metaphor" and confessing our impotence vis-à-vis the purity of being, which is ultimately inexpressible. Only thus, by such an act of humility in the renunciation of what we hold as our dearest power (language), will the grace of an illumination become possible, and if it does visit our eyes, our world, our words, it will regenerate us and bring to life in ourselves the "major man," him who communes with himself and with the very source of things. O'Connor says in this regard that Stevens' sun is a recurrent symbol of the "unthinking source" or irrational spring of existence.

Here, then, is the reason for abstraction: the "supreme fiction" must indeed "abstract" from any historical superstructure, from any anthropomorphic assumption; it must go back to the sun of the "first idea," to the integrity of Being that man has obscured with his religious myths and by the very act of giving arbitrary names to things. Stevens' abstraction is therefore not ultimately intellectual; it consists in a kind of Platonic contemplation that aims at seizing the fire of primeval reality by going back upstream over the course of human history—the latter being only a progressive removal from innocent origins and thus something like a degeneration, the loss of Eden, where, according to the Italian poet Montale, "even a name, a garment, were a vice."[8] This is, in summary, the theme that the ten poems of "It Must Be Abstract" develop with rich variations; the epic of the lost "first idea" which man, even though he cannot re-attain it, endeavors to adumbrate in the "supreme fiction" of poetry. The mobility of exploring intellect has brought Stevens from sensory imagination, through an immanent poetical phenomenology, to a Platonic stance where sense, word, and perception can exist only problematically in relation to the invisible magnet of pure idea; and human history is but a fall from that incorrupt principle, an invention of makeshift myths and names, an ineffective mimesis of the inimitable.

Plato (a Husserlian[9] Plato) really presides over this first section of the compositional series we are discussing—and Stevens has arrived here, obeying his dialectical urge, the way Bishop Berkeley once did, that is, on the spur of the senses. The "rock of summer," truth compacted of immediate certainty, has here dissolved into a supreme uncertainty, or better, it has receded into a far sky, refusing to be possessed by man or even defined; while the paradox of the human situation, which for Stevens is summarized in the tension of the poet confronted by his object, compels the craftsman to sing in his verse the impossibility of song. A drama is thus outlined, with the poet as the universal subject of poetry ("poetry is the subject of the poem"), not as a complacent idler brooding over himself, but as behaving in an ambivalent way toward reality, which he by turns seeks and eludes—

> It is never the thing but the version of the thing:
> The fragrance of the woman not her self,

Her self in her manner not the solid block,
The day in its color not perpending time,
Time in its weather, our most sovereign lord,
The weather in words and words in sounds of sound.
("The Pure Good of Theory," Part IV)

or affirms in its imperious irreducibility, as the "vital, fatal, dominant, arrogant X."

The Platonic antecedent of *Notes toward a Supreme Fiction* is to be found, of course, in the poem just quoted, and in a rather explicit form, as the utopia of a flight from the ruin of time; but also the third stanza of "Description without Place" contains something we would define as Platonic-Husserlian *Wesensschau:*

There might be, too, a change immenser than
A poet's metaphors in which being would
Come true, a point in the fire of music where
Dazzle yields to a clarity and we observe,
And observing is completing and we are content,
In a world that shrinks to an immediate whole,
That we do not need to understand, complete
Without secret arrangements of the mind.

The first idea is thus the "father-fire" of "Red Fern," it is the inexpressibly intact heart of the real. And in the first lyric of "It Must Be Abstract" it appears as "the inconceivable idea of the sun" which the "ephebe" must learn to perceive by "becoming an ignorant man again." This way he will

. . . see the sun again with an ignorant eye
And see it clearly in the idea of it.

He must

> Never suppose an inventing mind as source
> Of this idea nor for that mind compose
> A voluminous master folded in his fire.

In fact,

> How clean the sun when seen in its idea,
> Washed in the remotest cleanliness of a heaven
> That has expelled us and our images. . . .

And since

> The death of one god is the death of all,

the "ephebe" is advised to let mythology and theology go:

> Phoebus is dead, ephebe. But Phoebus was
> A name for something that never could be named.

Reality is purer than our interpretations:

> . . . The sun
> Must bear no name, gold flourisher, but be
> In the difficulty of what it is to be.

This is obviously a poetry of extreme subtlety and learning, full of Alexandrian delicacies—witness the interplay of sound and idea in the word "ephebe" that echoes "Phoebus" as if to express a filial relationship between the lost primal reality and modern man who tries to rediscover it. But the consummate knowledge operating in the poem refuses to remain satisfied with itself. It longs for a condition of *docta ignorantia* beyond itself, because it knows that reality always exceeds its definitions, and the human word's proper function in that regard will be to illuminate, not circumscribe.

Reality as essence is not simple, it is unseizably complex, and if the poet succeeds in approaching it, his verbal creation will partake of that mystery ("The poem must resist the intelligence/ Almost successfully," Stevens had said in "Man Carrying Thing"). Man's mistake has been to impoverish the real by inventions of anthropomorphic deities, all of them transitory and inadequate to the inspiring source, the impersonal "first idea." The central attitude of "Esthétique du Mal" re-emerges here, particularly if we remember the anti-Christian polemic of stanza III, which seems to echo Nietzsche's *Menschlich, allzumenschlich:*

> . . . now both heaven and hell
> Are one, and here, O terra infidel.
> The fault lies with an over-human god. . . .

and the open Nietzschanism of stanza VIII, where Satan's death is declared a "death of the imagination," and Stevens' Satan shows his resemblance to Nietzsche's Dionysus, the dynamic principle. Satan has been killed by a simple logical negation, but even under this act of the realist, Stevens concludes, there lurks an irrepressible Yea, the *ja sagen* of *Froehliche Wissenschaft*'s author. And actually a dialectic of man and superman, already anticipated by "Paisant Chronicle," appears in the three last pieces of "It Must Be Abstract," where the "major man" is contrasted with "McCullough" and with the "commonal," as a form of the first idea, which, however, will ultimately find its embodiment in the common man.

The second poem in the first section of the series emphasizes further the situation of exile from the primal idea, which we cannot even touch because any possession would contaminate it; hence the Platonic *eros* of the "priest" and thinker (or, to follow Stevens' deeper intention, of the poet, since the only religion and the only knowledge are, for him, those of the eye). Because the artist, that higher manifestation of man, desires truth without obfuscating it, "the first idea becomes/ The hermit in a poet's metaphors," in an otherwise alienated world, and desire as *philo*sophy, as the essence of the whole man in his creative efforts, "knows that what it has is what is not."

The third poem brings a moment of grace, the momentary reward of *eros,* in the advent of poetry, which

> . . . refreshes life so that we share,
> For a moment, the first idea . . . It satisfies
> Belief in an immaculate beginning
>
> And sends us, winged by an unconscious will,
> To an immaculate end. . . .

The lyric concludes on three images that symbolize the utter gratuitousness and naturalness of poetry: the Arabian singing in a dream, the remembered cooing of the turtledove, and the rhythmical surge of the ocean, which apparently imitates those other sounds. Particularly momentous, the last line clinches the whole with a perceptive statement that scores at the same time a poetical success:

> Life's nonsense pierces us with strange relation.

Poetry, so to speak, shuttles between idea and actuality, discovering the hidden nexuses between seemingly incongruous things. One could not restate more concisely Baudelaire's theory of "correspondences."

The fourth lyric formulates the theme of Paradise lost, lamenting that

> The first idea was not our own. Adam
> In Eden was the father of Descartes[10]
> And Eve made air the mirror of herself, . . .

Primitive man, that is, already harbored the nasty germ of geometrically analytical, and narcissistic, intellect (this is not the only place where Stevens expresses his distrust of the impoverishing order formal logic imposes on things). Nature anyway has a primacy on art, on human imitations:

> But the first idea was not to shape the clouds
> In imitation. The clouds preceded us. . . .
>
> There was a myth before the myth began,
> Venerable and articulate and complete.

Poetry, then, finds its function as a precarious attempt to bridge the chasm of this exile, to heal man's estrangement from pure reality:

> From this the poem springs: that we live in a place
> That is not our own and, much more, not ourselves. . . .

We might say, by way of comment, that poetry is the daughter of loss, the consequence of Paradise lost, rather than the boundlessly creative original power many Romantics made it out to be. Our destiny is that of imitating reality, platonically, under a lashing irony that unmasks the puniness of our achievements:

> We are the mimics. Clouds are pedagogues
> The air is not a mirror but bare board
> Coulisse bright—dark, tragic chiaroscuro

And comic colour of the rose, in which
Abysmal instruments make sounds like pips
Of the sweeping meanings that we add to them.

(In "Less and Less Human, O Savage Spirit," it was said that "It is the human that is the alien,/ The human that has no cousin in the moon./ It is the human that demands his speech/ From beasts or from the incommunicable mass.")

Thus we see how Stevens, after extolling poetry as the highest form of human activity (poem No. 3), now degrades it in sheer irony. It is as if he were saying that poetry is the poor relation of reality, and poverty our permanent lot. He has an ingrained tendency to see everything in a plurality of perspectives, and every vision becomes a paradox to him. Later on we shall focus on this dialectical structure of his poetical thinking; now suffice it to remark that the myth of the Fall serves his purpose by symbolizing the estranged human condition and outlining the dramatic trajectory of poetry as the endeavor to conquer such estrangement.

Going on to the fifth lyric, we find a closely related contrast in three impressive children of nature (lion, elephant, and bear) whose vitality, colorfulness, and freedom Stevens dramatizes as a foil to the degeneration of man, brooding in urban ennui on his impotence to create (the piano in the garret). The final tercet sarcastically epitomizes the whole:

These are the heroic children whom time breeds
Against the first idea—to lash the lion,
Caparison elephants, teach bears to juggle.

Man has not learned to live fruitfully with innocent creatures; the dream of Crispin in "The Comedian as the Letter C," symbiosis with the real, has miserably failed.

But Stevens never dwells too long on the same mood, whether it be one of abandon or irony, for he looks at reality as if through a prism and the game of refractions is his delight. The sixth poem of the series, therefore, passes on to present another aspect of alienation: the beauty of nature seen as transcendence, invisibility, imperviousness to passion and word, for Nature is a proud Venus who has only loosened, not discarded, her "ceinture." One is reminded of Schelling's conception of beauty as supreme "indifference" in its plenitude. The element of color, here particularly emphasized and connected with the name of the painter Franz Hals, itself appears as verbal inexpressibility, almost as a foil to the invisible. As a result, we get another paradox of the "first idea" and of man's attempt to reach it by a "supreme fiction":

> It must be visible or invisible,
> Invisible or visible or both:
> A seeing or unseeing in the eye.

This is followed by one more hint at the undue anthropomorphic constructions man superimposes on the purity of natural "first things;" in the course of our religious history we have personified the sky into many fictitious gods like Zeus, Ouranos, Varuna, Jupiter, or Thor, without realizing that to personify the sky is to impoverish it, to falsify its essence:

> The weather and the giant of the weather,
> Say the weather, the mere weather, the mere air:
> An abstraction blooded, as a man by thought.

"Abstraction blooded" here reads as "living and unadulterated essence," the result of phenomenological reduction.

This cue is immediately picked up by the ensuing poem:

> It feels good as it is without the giant,
> A thinker of the first idea. . . .

A personal God would spoil the purity and freedom of original reality by introducing there his iron law. And Stevens hates any dogmatically imposed truth, because

> . . . Perhaps
> The truth depends on a walk around a lake,
>
> A composing as the body tires, a stop
> To see hepatica, a stop to watch
> A definition growing certain and
>
> A wait within that certainty, a rest
> In the swags of pine-trees bordering the lake.

Once again, hope penetrates the alienated world, and it is a mere hope in the fortuitous: "Perhaps there are times of inherent excellence. . . ." We understand this scant grace is dearer to Stevens than any bliss secured by prayers to what he considers man's theological fiction. Truth visits us when we are least prone to the arrogant logic of the academies, and the privileged moment cannot be foreseen, it can only be recognized and accepted (the wind bloweth where it listeth). If the revelation comes, "extreme, fortuitous, personal," our consciousness will experience an "awakening" but "on the edge of sleep," an utter heightening that sharpens our every perception and enables us to look down from "an elevation" on "the academies" lost "in a mist." This contempt for institutionalized doctrine and logical formalism, which Stevens equates with political fanaticism of the revolutionary sort, recalls stanza XIV of of "Esthétique du Mal," where he says that "The cause/ Creates a logic not to be distinguished/ From lunacy . . . ," and concludes on what sounds like an antiphon to the present lyric:

> One wants to be able to walk
> By the lake at Geneva and consider logic:
> To think of the logicians in their graves
> And of the worlds of logic in their great tombs.

Much indeed "depends on a walk around a lake."

In the last three compositions of this first section, as we saw, the theme of the "first idea," having developed through the stages of the alienated human world and of a transcendent nature that poetry strives to rejoin with its precarious illuminations, modulates into a new phase containing a promise of redemption: the embodiment of the unattainable "first idea" in man as a superior being, as "major man." The first of these three last lyrics, with its deliberately ironic start, says that no artificially elaborate mansion, even if it has the grandeur of a palace designed by Viollet-le-Duc himself, can confer on its ordinary and pretentious inhabitant ("MacCullough") the stature of a great man. Not extrinsic grandiosity, which becomes a prison because it is the architectural equivalent of abstract logic and political fanaticism, but communion with the elements can elevate man, and it will do that through a renewal of language in spontaneity. Man should not wall himself in, but open himself to the instructive voices of nature, in the salvation of receptivity:

> If MacCullough himself lay lounging by the sea,
>
> Drowned in its washes, reading in the sound,
> About the thinker of the first idea,
> He might take habit, whether from wave or phrase,
>
> Or power of the wave, or deepened speech,
> Or a leaner being, moving in on him,
> Of greater aptitude and apprehension,

As if the waves at last were never broken,
As if the language suddenly, with ease,
Said things it had laboriously spoken.

Nature, conceived as a Bergsonian continuity and not as a Cartesian order, is the great pedagogue, the inspirer of a "greater aptitude," the awakener of our spiritual ("leaner") self in a new power of "apprehension." The theme has been stated in poem No. 2 of the present section and it will recur throughout. Whenever man's arbitrary order (whether as thought, as political and religious dogma, or as architecture) clashes with the free order of nature, the confrontation is decisive against the former—not, certainly, in the sense that man should renounce his intelligence, but that he can find a solution to the dilemma only by refreshing his mind and his whole being in a new contact with untainted reality, by "becoming ignorant again." The "ignorance" of poem No. 1 is here revealed as a condition of utter openness to life. To be sure, while examining the philosophical import of the poem, one should not overlook its artistic accomplishment, which may be skeletally described as a movement from the name-studded irony of the beginning to the lyrical release of the end. The diction could hardly be more effortlessly sustained.

And yet it rises to an even higher pitch of song in the next piece of the series. This one is, in a way, antithetical and complementary to its immediate predecessor, because it sings the spiritual idea of superman or "major man" as something to be attained not by romantic apotheosis but by the assiduous effort of reason, in the art of self-transcending thought:

. . . He comes,

Compact in invincible foils, from reason,
Lighted at midnight by the studious eye,

Swaddled in revery, the object of

The hum of thoughts evaded in the mind,
Hidden from other thoughts . . . .

The effect of lyrical heightening by comparison with the previous poem depends to a great extent on the fact that this one progressively takes shape as an intimate address, something wavering between invitation and prayer (unlike the former piece, which relied from beginning to end on an objective, third-person rhetorical structure):

My dame, sing for this person accurate songs.

He is and may be but oh! he is, he is,
This foundling of the infected past, so bright,
So moving in the manner of his hand.

Yet look not at his coloured eyes. Give him
No names. Dismiss him from your images.
The hot of him is purest in the heart.

If the previous lyric formulated the theme of man's regeneration as an advent fostered by rejection of artificial closures and total exposure to the voice of untainted nature, here instead that very advent is envisaged as eventually crowning the inwardly focused contemplation of the thinker, who can bring about the hoped-for "birth" of the superhumanly human by consuming in the fire of thought the "infected past;" once the miraculous advent has taken place, there will be no question of labels, names, or definitions.

The spontaneous dialectic we have already noticed at work in Stevens' poetry makes for a new progress-through-reversal in the thematic transition to the last poem of the series, "It Must Be Abstract;" for here we find, after the inner ascent of the ninth piece, a deliberate descent into bleak reality, to be best defined as a lay Incarnation and Transfiguration of man. The "major man" draws his strength from the common people, and the "abstract" idea of this non-Nietzschean superman merges with the idea of "man in the street" to produce the figure of the ragged tramp as pointing to a more human future. The reader cannot escape the surmise that Stevens here had in mind the ending of many a Charlie Chaplin movie:

> . . . in his old coat,
>
> His slouching pantaloons, beyond the town,
>
> Looking for what was, where it used to be?
> Cloudless the morning. It is he. The man
> In that old coat, those sagging pantaloons,
>
> It is of him, ephebe, to make, to confect
> The final elegance, not to console
> Nor sanctify, but plainly to propound.

Human values, and not supernaturally sanctioned ones, are the message of this lay prophet. The first dialectical phase of the "supreme fiction" thus ends by reversing itself into its opposite. The "first idea" is inaccessibly lost; we live in a strange world, and from the hell of this estrangement only poetry can save us with its intermittent flashes of epiphany, or else the self-questioning poverty of man denuded of any artificial superstructures. We find the same idea in "Paisant Chronicle," which turns on the problem of the superior man. The superior man is all men, the great leader is the choice of chance. But he is also a personage beyond reality, though compounded of real elements: the "fictive man created out of man." But instead of seeing him in the grandiloquent effusions of the baroque poet, we may well recognize him in the chance customer of a café, intent on ordinary things; indeed it must be so. Given the verbal complacencies of sophisticated Stevens, this plea for the "man in the street" takes on an additional value, indicating that our exquisitely aesthetical lawyer can see through and beyond the walls of his comfortable "tower."

And at this point, before passing on to the second section of the series ("It Must Change"), a further probable dimension suggests itself for *Notes toward a Supreme Fiction*. Many of Stevens' compositions, as we saw, exhibit a triadic structure, for instance "The Motive for Metaphor," examined above, "So-and-so Reclining on Her Couch," which takes its cue from the scene of a model posing for her painter only to sketch the three phases of artistic creation as progressive manifestations of the image, from "Projection A" (immediate visual apparition "without lineage or language") to "Projection B" (haloed idealization of the former) through "Projection C" (dynamic rapport between idea and reality, creator and object). The elegantly skeptical conclusion of this phenomenological poem consists in a gesture of courteous dismissal to the posing lady and of acceptance of the world as bare reality ("unpainted shore") rather than work of art. Then we have, along similar lines, stanza XIX of "Chocorua to Its Neighbor":

> To say more than human things with human voice,
> That cannot be; to say human things with more
> Than human voice, that, also, cannot be;
> To speak humanly from the height or from the depth
> Of human things, that is acutest speech;

and we have stanza XII of "Esthétique du Mal," "The Comedian as the Letter C," "Owl's Clover," and "Paisant Chronicle" as above discussed.

It would be unforgivably pedantic to constrain our subtle artificer's work within some prefabricated pattern, yet the triadic movement revealed in so many typical poems of Stevens might justify us in considering a Dantesque analogy at least subliminally present to shape, or concur in shaping, the threefold structure of *Notes toward a Supreme Fiction*. We have seen how all of its first section unfolds the theme of the estranged human condition and finally looks for a prospective redemption to the man in the street who comes to question our world ("to propound"); now the second section, whose very title ("It Must Change") provides an antiphon to "It Must Be Abstract," may well represent, after the "Inferno" of alienation and exile from the "first idea," a suitable "Purgatory" in the world of metamorphosis, being the intermediate stage, the insistent quest for a perfection still to come while metaphor revolves around a reality not yet fully possessed. Finally, the third section, which posits for the Supreme Fiction the requirement of pleasure ("It Must Give Pleasure") as if to climax the two previous ones (primal purity and liveliness of change), can be said to crown the whole sequence with a vision of Paradise—a terrestrial one, of course, since Stevens would never admit a transcendent heaven. How could we otherwise account for the presence, in that third section, of the "Canon Aspirin," of the angels, and of the beloved woman as utmost wholeness of being? Isn't there in the last poem of "It Must Give Pleasure" a clear embodiment of the eternal feminine, a kind of earthly Beatrice who has led our poet to the only fulfillment he knows?

Many other traits could be stressed to support this interpretive proposal: the didactic stance of language, where doctrinal words appear to advance an anti-theology for the sake of the "ephebe" 's instruction; the ironic-dramatic conception of the artist, to be traced back to the explicit Dantesque allusion of "Crude Foyer," where stanza 3 states that "we read the critique of paradise/ And say it is the work/ Of a comedian, this critique;" Stevens' predilection for symbolic or learned reference; the emphasis on the number three (three sections, three-line stanzas, albeit unrhymed) and on architectural symmetries (each section has ten poems and each poem consists of seven tercets). Besides, we could point to the avowedly polemical intent of a "human comedy" as antithetic yet structurally analogous to the *Divine Comedy*—and "Esthétique du Mal" would supply some cue. The Dantesque archetype, at least as a general pattern, seems not uncommon in modern English and American writers; James Joyce is a case in point, and so is Hart Crane with his vision of the New York subway as an Inferno from which one finally emerges to the paradise of "Cathay."

The entrance to the second section of *Notes toward a Supreme Fiction* is guarded by an "old gilded seraph"[11] who watches in tedium the perpetual alternation of seasons and generations, that change being really but the mask of repetitiousness. Bees, girls, and doves keep returning as if they had never departed; therefore the universal inconstancy of our world is mere illusion. The only refuge from this peculiar sense of the vanity of all things is, according to Stevens, the rawness of immediate sensation, preferably an "erotic perfume" (the scene seems set in a garden), something unmistakable and compact. Whenever reality threatens to dissolve, our poet reverts to the certainty of a brutal testimonial to reassure himself that something exists beyond and outside, something undefinable but reachable and present. And one should not miss, in this first poem of "It Must Change," the negative approach to what Stevens considers the second basic postulate of his "supreme fiction." The apparent change ever present in nature is no real change, only a static pattern of cycles. We shall see how subsequent lyrics resume this theme to discover its positiveness.

It is, in fact, inverted at once by the following poem, a contrived apologue that ironically contrasts human authority (the "President") with the ephemeral creature (the bee). The President "ordains the bee to be/ Immortal" because instead of wanting change he would like to fix reality, to make it absolutely stable and secure; but the bee cannot exist in that artificial immortality. Neither decreed "immortality" nor sheer repetition, but renewal, is the highest good, to be had only from love, which makes new every seasonal return by redeeming it from mechanical cycle:

> . . . Why, then, when in golden fury
>
> Spring vanishes the scraps of winter, why
> Should there be a question of returning or
> Of death in memory's dream? Is spring a sleep?
>
> This warmth is for lovers at last accomplishing
> Their love, this beginning, not resuming, this
> Booming and booming of the new-come bee.

Every love is, then, a new beginning; and love is nature in the finest sense, nature ever ready to mock the pretentious apparatus of human authority, politics, or construction. The bee is also a discreet Sophoclean symbol of poetry, which eludes any command and repetition, because it lives in creative metamorphosis.

Poem No. 3 of this section celebrates the revenge of time on the ambition of man, who wanted to stop it by a negative metamorphosis. The great statue of an important man, General Du Puy, which freezes into physical perpetuity the moment of solemn obsequies, is reduced morally to "rubbish" by the criticism of the intelligentsia. The great statesman is not exempt from the law of change; whether President or General, he is destined only to die: from flesh he may become bronze or marble, and from that—absurdity and nothingness. This is negative metamorphosis, the reverse of love, and appropriate punishment of man's refusal to accept creative change. If Plato presided over the section "It Must Be Abstract," Ovid is the presiding genius of this second section; and Stevens is never very far from Ovid anyway, with his predilection for each thing's secret metamorphoses. Even the frequency of the word "change" in his poetry speaks for this.

But after all this phenomenology of change, poem No. 4 rises to a philosophical grasp of the process, which is explained as the complementary relation of opposites and mutual participation of what is different. It has the tone of a Dantesque doctrinal passage, with the further analogy of an instructive trip undertaken by two persons who are respectively guide and disciple—the guide doing all the talking here, unlike Dante's. The journey is through the world of changing phenomena:

> Two things of opposite natures seem to depend
> On one another, as a man depends
> On a woman, day on night, the imagined
>
> On the real. This is the origin of change . . . .
>
> The partaker partakes of that which changes him.
> The child that touches takes character from the thing,
> The body, it touches. The captain and his men
>
> Are one and the sailor and the sea are one.
> Follow after, O my companion, my fellow, my self,
> Sister and solace, brother and delight.

The "greenest body" of the fourth tercet (omitted here) echoes the "green's green apogee" of "Credences of Summer" and anticipates the "green, fluent mundo" of the last poem, Part 3, which sings the completeness of woman as earthly happiness. O'Connor is right in emphasizing Stevens' green as a concrete symbol of earth and everything it stands for.

This emerges also from the next lyric (No. 5 of the second section), where we are introduced to the planter as an example of change. The planter died on his island, but he transfused himself into his orange trees gone wild, into the green glory of vegetal growth. Once again, we have Crispin's dream of symbiosis with nature, the love of earth that somehow reconciles death. The planter disappears in the luxuriance of a friendly nature, while the politician or the military man dies utterly, despite and through his pompous monuments.

Tropical vegetation, so congenial to Stevens' sensuous mind, evokes Shelley's nature cult, and the result is, in poem No. 6, a bizarre parody on one cut from "Ode to the West Wind" 's[12] final part: Shelley's prayer to the brisk air element, "Be thou me," becomes a sparrow's insistent chirping, "Be thou me"—another variation on the theme of metamorphosis. Yet this song is static and exhausts itself in monotony, as befits "minstrels without minstrelsy;" therefore "it will end." Maybe Stevens here implies that Shelley's hymn to nature is naïve, and he ironizes it; maybe instead he reaffirms the value of what is direct, unspoiled, and transitory, of unadorned nature, even while ironizing it. A sparrow's song is not comparable to the skylark's or to the west wind's, though it may be no less genuine, as far as it goes.

In any case, irony does not prevent Stevens from believing in the intact happiness of nature, and he reminds us of it in the next poem (No. 7) by saying that

> After a lustre of the moon . . .
> We have not the need of any paradise,
> We have not the need of any seducing hymn . . . .

because

> . . . the ever-ready love
> Of the lover that lies within us

makes us breathe

> An odor evoking nothing, absolute,

and yearn for

> . . . accessible bliss . . . .

since, conclusively,

> . . . easy passion and ever-ready love
> Are of our earthly birth and here and now
> And where we live and everywhere we live . . . .

so that happiness is not beyond the reach of "the ignorant man" or the scholar either,

> . . . who writes
>
> The book, hot for another accessible bliss:
> The fluctuations of certainty, the change
> Of degrees of perception in the scholar's dark.

This means that Shelley, that pantheistic worshiper of nature, is entitled to a symbolic rehabilitation after the witty parody; lyric No. 8 gives us his Ozymandias as resurrected from the oblivion of desert sands to receive the self-offer of "Nanzia Nunzio," a girl who came to him in pilgrimage to bring reality in its fullness, the living, fruitful present that revives the past. She will reappear in the series as "virgin Bawda" and finally as the bride of the poet himself, in the last lyric. The choice of an Italian name for this persona undoubtedly serves to reinforce her intended aura of earthly loveliness, her sense of physical presence; Stevens may also have thought of the meaning of *nunzio* (the good messenger or message, the accredited ambassador). Be it as it may, Part V of another poem, "Repetitions of a Young Captain," helps us to understand better "Nanzia Nunzio" 's identity:

> On a few words of what is real in the world
> I nourish myself. I defend myself against
> Whatever remains. Of what is real I say,
> It is the old, the roseate parent or
> The bride come jingling, kissed and cupped, or else
> The spirit and all ensigns of the self?

The desire of that poem's speaker is, predictably, to

> . . . discover
> A civil nakedness in which to be,
> In which to bear with the exactest force
> The precisions of fate, nothing fobbed off, nor changed
> In a beau language without a drop of blood.

This thirst for reality and paradoxical repudiation of poetry as literary language is a recurrent attitude that perhaps bespeaks Stevens' self-criticism. To return to "Ozymandias," we have no trouble recognizing in his episode a central concern of Stevens' poetry, the restless interaction of nakedness and fiction, reality and imagination, myth and history, that summarizes the manifold activity of the human spirit or "Man with the Blue Guitar":

On her trip round the world, Nanzia Nunzio
Confronted Ozymandias. She went
Alone and like a vestal long-prepared.

I am the spouse. She took her necklace off
And laid it in the sand. As I am, I am
The spouse. She opened her stone-studded belt.

I am the spouse, divested of bright gold,
The spouse beyond emerald or amethyst,
Beyond the burning body that I bear.

I am the woman stripped more nakedly
Than nakedness, standing before an inflexible
Order, saying I am the contemplated spouse.

Speak to me that, which spoken, will array me
In its own only precious ornament . . . .

At this point Ozymandias is more than the resurrected prince; he is the poet, who can crown the bride (Nature) with "the spirit's diamond coronal" and make her "precious" through his "perfecting." And he answers her passionate request by saying that "the bride/ Is never naked;" she is arrayed in a "fictive covering," the sacred beauty that emanates from love and rapt mind.

This is such a dance as Salome might have danced if holiness and not perversity had been her motive force. In the realm of unceasing metamorphosis, it anticipates the final fulfillment of "paradise" by harping with shining diction on the theme that poem No. 7 of "It Must Give Pleasure" will thus resume:

. . . To find the real,
To be stripped of every fiction except one,

The fiction of an absolute . . . .

The "supreme fiction" is possible, provided we renounce all external beautifications of reality, provided, that is, we exercise our aesthetic powers in an uncompromising concentration on the "first idea," on the inner fire of Being. For poetry, Stevens says in his prose work, is a heightening of reality, a purified perception, rather than a hortatory act or a passive copy of things. His realism, so energetically proclaimed at every step, has nothing naïve, nothing gross or documentary about it: it is a longing for essence, a poetical phenomenology. As such, it is a "revelation," an unveiling; for what Nanzia Nunzio does by performing the dramatic action of the poem now being discussed is clearly theorized on the level of explicit poetics by "Description Without Place," stanza VI (italics mine):

Description is revelation. It is not
The thing described, nor false facsimile.
It is an artificial thing that exists,
In its own seeming, plainly visible,
Yet not too closely the double of our lives,
Intenser than any actual life could be,
A text we should be born that we might read,
More explicit than the experience of sun
And moon, the book of reconciliation,
Book of a concept only possible
In description, canon central in itself,
The thesis of the plentifullest John.

As John's Gospel said, "in the beginning was the Word," and for the poet the word is all, it is world-creating:

Thus the theory of description matters most.
It is the theory of the word for those

For whom *the word is the making of the world. . . .*
It is a world of words to the end of it.

Thus the *Wesensschau* of revelatory perception raises, of necessity, the problem of language; and words are a precarious medium, though man can no more dispense with them than he can refuse the pitfalls of love. Language both unveils and veils reality, for it comes between us and the world as a "fictive covering," as a partition and an illumination, as a lens and a prism. This paradoxical situation underlies all of Stevens' work, and unless we take it into account we shall not be able to understand the existential motivation of that ceaseless brooding on poetry that constitutes so much of his exquisite Alexandrian verse. In a more or less mystical form, we find the same attitude in Hart Crane and in William Carlos Williams; the former hymns the Word in *The Bridge* (though he antiphonally rejects it in "A Name for All"), the latter devotes much of *Paterson,* including the final cadences, to the crisis and salvation of language. Similar themes were also present in Whitman and Dickinson.

But in Stevens the formulation of language as its own problem—such is the extreme stance of a poetry that has pushed to the limit its critical consciousness—always starts from a gesture of irony. Contempt is the mask of love, and it is only to counteract his obsessive love for language and his own verbal art that Stevens indulges in mockery, as he does in poem No. 9 of "It Must Change":

The poem goes from the poet's gibberish to
The gibberish of the vulgate and back again.
Does it move to and fro or is it of both

At once? Is it a luminous flittering
Or the concentration of a cloudy day?
Is there a poem that never reaches words

> And one that chaffers the time away?

Stevens concludes that the poet does not seek an escape, for he is the mouthpiece of mankind "at the most opaque barriers," the orator who makes the "vulgate" (the language sanctioned by social convention) his own speech, compounding universal and particular (convention and idiom) in his "lingua franca et jocundissima." This, of course, only at the risk of insubstantiality ("luminous flittering") and thick opacity ("concentration of a cloudy day"), since poetry faces the extremes of what is too airily sublime to be expressed and what is too trivial to redeem an all-too-facile expression.

The laborious meditation of *ars poetica* brings Stevens back to the central theme of this section: metamorphosis. And in the last lyric, metamorphosis appears as "trope," as liberating metaphor, which is the miracle of language, because:

> . . . The casual is not
> Enough. The freshness of transformation is
>
> The freshness of the world. It is our own,
> It is ourselves, the freshness of ourselves,
> And that necessity and that presentation
>
> Are rubbings of a glass in which we peer.
> Of these beginnings, gay and green, propose
> The suitable amours. Time will write them down.

The initial attitude, then, has reversed itself into one of hope; poetry, the "Theatre of Trope," has succeeded in raising change from the monotony of a repetitious cycle to make it the privileged chance of release for the human spirit. And now we are ready to enter Stevens' "paradise," the zone of happiness ("It Must Give

Pleasure") where it is given to relish the certainty of enlightened reality.

Poem No. 1 of this third section appropriately proposes the rarest exercise of joy, which attains its highest form when, instead of singing directly from the heart for the crowd in conventional ritual, one reaches out to seize the pre- or supra-rational genesis of the world as pure image:

> As when the sun comes rising, when the sea
> Clears deeply, when the moon hangs on the wall
>
> Of heaven-haven. These are not things transformed
> Yet we are shaken by them as if they were.
> We reason about them with a later reason.

Stevens' poetics has shifted again to the pole of intact "first idea;" the purity of things is immune to change, for our word cannot touch them; and yet, when we discover them in their virginality, we start as if at the magic of a metamorphosis. The ideal journey begun in the valley of exile with "It Must Be Abstract" has traversed the purgatorial realm of mutability, and is now reaching the goal of fullest reality. There has been a kind of dialectical inversion; things are no longer remote in impervious fixity, nor do they change shape in the former elusive dance, but they offer themselves to the eye in such a rich identity as to suggest inexhaustible metamorphosis in their variety, and that is why they "give pleasure."

No wonder, then, if the "blue woman" of lyric No. 2 (according to O'Connor, the color blue connotes whatever in Stevens pertains to the imagination) wants creatures exactly as they are, without fictitious transformations: for her, the clouds must be clouds and not foaming surf, the "argentine" birds must be just birds and not silver as their name would indicate; flowers must be acknowledged as the erotic organs they are and not falsified into idealized decoration. Imagination craves for the real; it looks out of the window and names

> The corals of the dogwood, cold and clear,
> Cold, coldly delineating, being real,
> Clear and, except for the eye, without intrusion.

Here the "blue guitar," as it were, sings "things as they are," and that affords utter fulfillment.

The herma of a red Dionysus cryptically dominates the next lyric as a provisional reality that eventually yields to a richer one. As far as this poem can be safely deciphered, we would see here a re-enactment of the Orpheus-Christ myth. Orpheus returns from hell to bring a powerful music; has this something to do with the poet who emerges from the unconscious to affirm life, as against the petrified reality of a statue? Or must we assume a painting as the source of this poem, since Stevens is so very visually minded that he often does take a pictorial work of art as the springboard for his poetry? Be that as it may, the hermetic lyric strikes us as an exercise in color delight, with red suggesting blood, wine, and fire, as if to stress, in antiphon to the previous poem, how rich and intense reality can be once we let it release its dynamic potential.

The following composition (No. 4) celebrates the wedding of the "great captain" and "virgin Bawda" at Catawba. They have married not so much from a mutual personal fascination as to fulfill a mystical harmony with the *genius loci;* children of the earth, they loved each other as children of earth and sun, and he saw in his bride the Catawba hill, she in him the sun. The poem seems to echo the Ozymandias one from the previous section, and it emphasizes once again that paradise is here on earth; there are no such things as heaven and hell, and love is terrestrial.

But earth is deep; sleep, the rest of the flesh, is a heaven where we rediscover ourselves in a new, richer guise. Poems No. 5 and 6, which introduce us to the "Canon Aspirin" and his female relatives, have something of what the old Provençal troubadours would have called *trobar clus,* not in the sense that the poet withholds important information, but that he hides many a logical nexus between the several parts of his discourse and assumes our familiarity with the more secret nuances of the theme. And this may be regarded a paradisal trait too, if we remember that *Paradiso* is the learned canticle par excellence. Doctrinal overtones can be heard even in the ironic name of the persona; if Aspirin inevitably reminds us of a commercial medicine, it also sends us back to the aspiring or desiring priest of poem No. 2, Section I. The Canon is a kind of Swedenborg, another mask of the poet who longs for incorrupt reality. He finds it in sleep (his own and his little nieces'), where

> . . . he was the ascending wings he saw
> And moved on them in orbits' outer stars. . . .
>
> Forth then with huge pathetic force
> Straight to the utmost crown of night he flew.
> The nothingness was a nakedness, a point
>
> Beyond which thought could not progress as thought.

Shortly before, we had been told that the mystical effacement of self in sleep was a climax "beyond which fact could not progress as fact." This is, then, the mystics' *nada, nada,* conceived as an infinite heightening of reality; and the Canon ends up embracing reality in all of its aspects, overcoming any antinomies or exclusions.

Such paradisal bliss, says the next poem, dwarfs to the point of ridicule the ordering activities of constrictive intellect. The political builder, whom we have already met in the guise of President and of General Du Puy, "imposes order" as the fox and the snake do, by surreptitious trickery, and in the parliaments he erects he installs "statues of reasonable men,/ Who surpassed the most literate owl, the most erudite/ Of elephants." Neither statesmen nor academicians are spared, it seems, by our newfangled Aesop, who polemically opposes to their form of knowledge his own "description as revelation;" this is what he had called "invention" in the very first poem of the whole series, thereby reviving a Latin source word (*invenire*) which meant "to discover." The contrary of this true knowledge is the arbitrary knowledge reached by intellectual distortion in a Procrustean act:

> . . . But to impose is not
> To discover. To discover an order as of
> A season, to discover summer and know it,
>
> To discover winter and know it well, to find,
> Not to impose, not to have reasoned at all,
> Out of nothing to have come on major weather,
>
> It is possible, possible, possible. It must
> Be possible. It must be that in time
> The real will from its crude compoundings come,
>
> Seeming, at first, a beast disgorged, unlike,
> Warmed by a desperate milk. To find the real,
> To be stripped of every fiction except one,
>
> The fiction of an absolute—Angel,
> Be silent in your luminous cloud and hear
> The luminous melody of proper sound.

Thus Stevens' earthbound poetics, faithful though it may be to its terrestrial matrix and to its skeptical irony, does not exclude the horizons of mysticism. The reason is that, inasmuch as mysticism is perception, it provides an experience no skeptic can deny; besides, mystical perception grasps precisely that irrational moment of reality which escapes any logical analysis—and the first lyric of "It Must Give Pleasure" has made it clear that for Stevens this is the goal of poetry's quest.

Indeed, poem No. 8, taking up the angel motif, will help us to account for such an unexpected soaring into the transcendent. The angel is probably no reality independent of his singer, yet he is real as a projection of the latter's inner experience, when reality emerges in its nocturnal aspect. Thus human poetry fills the spaces of the unknown, and even if they are mere "escapades of death," it still knows fulfillment as a "Cinderella" under her own roof, because no doubt can abolish the fact that the visionary mind rises to the point of discarding the category of "having" for that of "being":

> I have not but I am and as I am, I am.

On the strength of that certainty, the poet can then say in poem No. 9:

> Whistle aloud, too weedy wren. I can
> Do all that angels can. I enjoy like them,
> Like men besides, like men in light secluded,
>
> Enjoying angels . . . .

Talking to a tiny bird, he urges it to continue its love song, which loses nothing through being repeated. The implications widen so much that one cannot dispense with extensive quotation:

> . . . . These things at least comprise
> An occupation, an exercise, a work,
>
> A thing final in itself and, therefore, good:
> One of the vast repetitions final in
> Themselves and, therefore, good, the going round
>
> And round and round, the merely going round,
> Untill merely going round is a final good,
> The way wine comes at a table in a wood.
>
> And we enjoy like men, the way a leaf
> Above the table spins its constant spin,
> So that we look at it with pleasure, look
>
> At it spinning its eccentric measure. Perhaps,
> The man-hero is not the exceptional monster,
> But he that of repetition is most master.

This is a clear antiphon to poem No. 6 of Section II, where the sparrow's song became a senseless monotony. Here the concrete symbol of the circle, polemically related to Yeats' ineluctable "gyres" and to Eliot's Karma-like cycle in the *Waste Land,* expresses Stevens' acceptance of the cycle, his return to Nature, that cyclical goddess, and his discovery of happiness as the art of repetition.

The importance of such a solution stands out in sharper relief when we reread poem No. 1 of Part II, which stated the problem with neat urgency. Stevens' answer, after all his dialectical excursions into the glittering realms of the possible, had to consist in a reassertion of immanence. Believing as he does in the value of sensory experience and of aesthetic life as a whole, he coherently solves the dilemma in opposition to Kierkegaard's alternative of escaping the prison of "repetition" by a qualitative leap into transcendence. Stevens takes shelter in the "rock of summer," he seeks endless variations of his immanent single theme *within* and not without the circle of earthly existence. He had already said it elsewhere, in "Adult Epigram," apropos of

> . . . the ever-never-changing same
> An appearance of Again, the diva-dame.

Neither romantic vagueness nor Kierkegaardian anguish, born of dissatisfaction with this world, can thus beset our poet, who finally reaches his "heaven-haven" in the beloved. She is the quintessence of reality, to repudiate which would be folly; she is the triumph of earth in its richness, and that includes the experientially given and the possible. Though a familiar form, she reveals herself at every step as an unforeseen apparition; she well deserves to incarnate that first idea, that longed-for Eden where the poet will be able to find fulfillment. He gravitates around her with the affection of a thirsty planet, eager to discover as many facets as possible of his inexhaustibly prismatic "X":

> Fat girl, terrestrial, my summer, my night,
> How is it I find you in difference, see you there
> In a moving contour, a change not quite completed?

We notice how her epithets recapitulate the many sides of reality as experienced through the stations of our hedonist pilgrim's progress in *Notes toward a Supreme Fiction:* "terrestrial" links her to Mother Earth, "summer" to the rock of summer (later on, in the last line but one, she will be called "green, . . . fluent mundo"), "night" to the mystical flights of "Canon Aspirin" as well as to the sheltering function that is properly hers, "difference" and "change" to the second aspect of that "supreme fiction" she embodies. Though irrefutably present, she is in a way unknowable, because she unites in herself the contrary sides of existence:

> You are familiar yet an aberration.
> Civil, madam, I am, but underneath
> A tree, this unprovoked sensation requires
>
> That I should name you flatly, waste no words,
> Check your evasions, hold you to yourself . . .
>
> . . . You
>
> Become the soft-footed phantom, the irrational
>
> Distortion, however fragrant, however dear. . . .
>
> The fiction that results from feeling. . . .
>
> Thcy will get it straight one day at the Sorbonne:
> We shall return at twilight from the lecture
> Pleased that the irrational is rational,
>
> Until flicked by feeling, in a gildered street,
> I call you by name, my green, my fluent mundo.
> You will have stopped revolving except in crystal.

A touch of elegant irony, of course, tempers the earnestness. This earthly Beatrice appears to be a benevolent Sphinx, a boundless reservoir of vision that reconciles her poet to the paradox of existence and of language. She "revolves" like the green world that she is, a reality possessed but never in its entirety; inescapable and elusive as she is, she may one day be captured in the "crystal" of accomplished art, but that is the "supreme fiction" toward which we have been moving all along, and which she keeps eliciting. She is the real and ideal person to whom Stevens addressed his short prologue to *Notes,* saying of her that

> The vivid transparence that you bring is peace.

The foregoing analysis should throw some light on the paramount significance of *Notes toward a Supreme Fiction* as a grand rehearsing of Stevens' main themes, and therefore as a milestone in modern American and Western poetry. Even though we take into account the flaws an exacting critic like Yvor Winters[13] points out in Stevens' poetry (whimsical abstruseness of diction, preciosity, slightly gratuitous word play, exotic complacencies in foreign vocabulary, decadent languor), we have to acknowledge that here the "hedonist" has achieved a valid formulation of his own problems.

Favorable critics like O'Connor or Randall Jarrell also resent the involved style of some unfocused writing of his, examples of which could be gleaned even from *Notes,* however overwhelming his stylistic accomplishment may here be in general. Yet Stevens is the kind of hedonist who has succeeded in understanding himself, and his ingrained intellectual narcissism can therefore make room for the shining irruptions of reality. His starting point has to be identified with the predicament of an intelligence divorced from external reality and endeavoring to recover it through language. His itinerary is the reverse of that of Rimbaud, Hart Crane, or Dylan Thomas, who cry out for verbal release from an inner fiery tumult, while he reaches out toward reality from an embattled rhetoric. Exiled from reality, he undertakes a pilgrimage to find it, and in so doing seeks to make his expressive medium as transparent as possible. That medium, aptly symbolized in the crystal image at the end of Part One and Part Two of *Notes,* does not necessarily make for direct contacts with experience—and this is why he so often invokes them.

His is always a form of questioning or visual contemplation, rather than dramatic participation; his personae are always caught thinking, prying, and debating, they do not act; the only fire he knows is of the eye. Uprooted, he endeavors to root himself in Being through language, and if sometimes the belabored word frustrates his attempt, as happens in "Analysis of a Theme" or "Two Tales of Liadoff," the operation is generally successful. Thus we can say he often breaks through to poetry from rhetoric, being one of the most self-conscious writers we know, one who recurrently needs the literary *donnée* for a starting point. In a sense, he could be defined as a civilization facing its diseases, with the elegance civilization alone can afford. His quest for the enlightening word, from paradox to paradox, may remind us of Martin Heidegger's last phase of thought. Crispin of *The Comedian as the Letter C* is, indeed, a Heideggerian "shepherd of Being,"[14] and a shepherd of Being is what the poet should always be according to Wallace Stevens, since he by definition makes language his home.

Four / *Hart Crane's "The Bridge"*

IN[1] THE TERSE pages of *Exile's Return,*[2] which are really an autobiography of the *entre-deux-guerres* generation of American writers, Malcolm Cowley throws into significant relief the figure of Hart Crane as the symbol of an age. Crane's sensual and spiritual orgies, his devotion to poetry, his alienation from the family, his ceaseless search for an absolute value, his self-destructive fury could be called the tragic portrait of the jazz era. Cowley's words evince affection, and they help the reader to realize what the "roaring boy" 's presence must have meant to his fellow artists, and what consternation must have seized them at the news of his suicide in 1932.

In poetry and in life, Hart Crane had pushed to a point of no return the experience of uprootedness, frenzy, and restless search that was common to his contemporaries of the "lost generation." While most of them had found it possible to survive their rebellious turbulence, he burned himself out in ecstasy and despair; and he died with the age he had endeavored to perpetuate in a unique poetical testament. Decades after, Allen Tate—temperamentally so unlike him, so composed and self-controlled—still remembers him sadly, and sees in his troubled life an example of literary heroism.[3] In Tate's own life—as well as in the life of many others who happened to meet him and share something with him

—Hart Crane flashed by like an unforgettable, if perplexing, meteor; and to some extent this is also true of his poetry.

For whether we extol it as Waldo Frank does in the preface to Crane's *Collected Poems*[4] and as Henry Wells also does in *The American Way of Poetry,*[5] or whether we consider it with all the reservations advanced by a scrupulous critic like Yvor Winters,[6] by a conscientious biographer like Brom Weber,[7] by discriminating readers like Babette Deutsch[8] and Horace Gregory,[9] we shall find it hard to escape the fascination of its hermetic fire. Matthiessen[10] and Karl Shapiro[11] are likewise struck by this quality of his expression, which seems to reflect the brief but intense drama of his life; and the poems that have been written about him contribute to the aura of myth.

Nor is this strange, if we think of the poetical venture on which Crane staked all of himself. Pound, Joyce, and Eliot, though masters of style and models of artistic integrity, represented for the "lost generation" rather a desert to cross than a road to follow; in *Exile's Return*[12] Cowley says that even though he and his contemporaries did not yet see their own way, they instinctively repudiated Eliot's, whose undeniable accomplishment as both poet and critic offered an image of reality they could no longer accept for guidance. As to Joyce, Cowley finds his genius unbearably cold, while by the same token Pound seems to indulge in a literary game of "chimera hunting" to the perpetual frustration of readers. The autobiography of William Carlos Williams,[13] another important source for the history of that generation, records the moral blow that the publication of *The Waste Land* in *The Dial* inflicted on him as well as some of his brethren. Though he could not bring himself to discount Eliot's achievement and its subsequent impact on American writers, Williams felt at the time that this was a desertion of the concerted effort to raise the American idiom to lasting power and dignity. *The Criterion* had no place for the values of the Rutherford poet-doctor, who henceforth had to go on by himself without the helpful advice of the man they all looked up to for effective support in the battle under way. Williams' picturesque rage, of course, documents in the language of dated polemic how the void Eliot left in American literary circles could be filled by nobody else, and fortunately spares Ezra Pound, who in a sense was above any U.S.-Europe quarrel because from wherever he happened to be he knew how to act as the ideal mentor to all courageous artists, American or other.

Yet the alternative was real enough to dedicated writers who felt America had to "come of age" on her own terms, rather than defer to mother Europe. Waldo Frank[14] along with Gorham Munson[15], close friends of Hart Crane as his letters amply show, undertook to "rediscover America" just when Harold Stearns, with his wholesale indictment of her civilization, was disgustedly pointing the way to Paris for a number of temporary or permanent fugitives. With the publication of *White Buildings* in 1926, and even more of *The Bridge* in 1930, Crane meant to answer Stearns' gesture of rejection, hoping to satisfy the strongly felt need for a native American art that would be sophisticated enough to rise above the slough of provincialism, yet so committed to its matrix as to avoid the hothouse of mere aesthetic complacency. As a consequence, his own poetry is a continuous dialogue with Eliot, whose greatness Crane frankly recognized from the start; he tried to turn Eliot's lesson to account by vindicating what life source there was to tap in the midst of the waste land. Perhaps more subtly than Williams, Crane reacted to Eliot with a strong will of affirmation against the threnody of sterility and doom. This ambitious commitment accounts for some of the naïvetés and obscurities that mar his work; Crane is not a flawless writer, yet it will not do to exploit the obvious vulnerability of part of his poetical endeavor in order to deny or minimize his breakthrough. The glow of a powerful, if strange and at times private, vision is certainly there for eyes that want to see.

How significant that, while he was working at *The Bridge,* striving to transform a monument of industrial power into one of symbolic unification bridging different worlds and eras, a poet of the Russian revolution, Vladimir Mayakovsky, should have likewise written a hymn to Brooklyn bridge,[16] without, however, spiritualizing his theme. In those days of pre-Stalinist fervor Russia was looking to America for inspiration in its revolutionary program of constructive activity, and the subsequent suicide of Mayakovsky marks the disappointment that overtook a generation of Soviet intellectuals at the grim tightening of the screw. On the other hand, the tensions inherent in a fast-growing industrial society are enough to account for the spiritual dislocation that drove Crane, Lindsay, Yesenin, and Mayakovsky to suicide. Extremism is—or was—indigenous to both Russia and America. Crane wanted to be the rhapsodist of industrial America with its paradoxes of brutality, commercialism, and creativity; and it is as a rhapsody in the original sense of the term that we should consider *The Bridge,* which critics (except Waldo Frank) have generally proclaimed a failure as regards formal unity, acknowledging its validity only as a series of independent lyrical pieces. Despite the flagrant flaws in the texture, which Brom Weber imputes to the eventual wavering of Crane's faith in his chosen myth, a thick network of thematic links, recurrences, and developments connects the various parts of the poem, so that its true physiognomy seems to be definable as one cycle of closely related compositions—which is what a rhapsody should be. Moreover, *The Bridge* resumes or climaxes intrinsic motifs of all of Crane's antecedent poetry; one way to look at "For the Marriage of Faustus and Helen," "Recitative," "Possessions," "Lachrymae Christi," and

"Wine Menagerie" is as sketches, prefigurations, or variants of *The Bridge,* which would be too narrowly understood as a mere nationalist myth. If genetically considered, this relation of the shorter poems to the longer-winded effort will help to focus it in a broader perspective, relevant to the development of modern Western poetry as a whole.

Under the influence of Poe's theory, French Symbolist poets in the latter half of the nineteenth century had come to restrict poetry to the moment of illumination allusively expressed. With Verlaine, Rimbaud, and Mallarmé the "alchemy of the word" yielded a highly concentrated or "pure" poetry that strove to eliminate any discursive, i.e., logical and narrative, element; and this became the gauntlet of challenge for the new poets all over the West. In the English-speaking countries, that gauntlet was picked up by the Imagist group, with Pound redefining the moment of illumination as the emotional-perceptual complex in a unit of time, and translating it from psychological into stylistic terms as the concrete image shorn of any superstructure, as language reduced to the purely presentational. Imagism became the rallying cry of the new American poetry, with such diverse figures as Pound himself, William Carlos Williams, H.D., Amy Lowell, John Gould Fletcher, T. S. Eliot, Vachel Lindsay, and Wallace Stevens each interpreting it as unofficially and heretically as possible; but it did mean the final rejection of narrative plot and explanatory comment from the body of modern verse. Whether allusive or presentational, poetry tended to emphasize personal vision, rather than public myths, by isolating its own essence from rhetoric, factual information, and discursive argument in the very act of composition. But this ultimate purity could become a bottleneck or a dead end, for it threatened to supersede language itself by the wordless experience of the mystical, the irrational, or the self-sufficiently visual. Aware of the risk, in *fin-de-siècle* France poets schooled to

Symbolism, like Corbière and Laforgue, strove to restore a tangible dimension to poetry by reimporting into it the nonpoetical in the guise of irony; hence their frequent reliance on the folksy, the shocking, the drably quotidian.

So when American experimenters like Eliot, Stevens, or Crane assimiliated the inspiration of French symbolism, they took their Laforgue along with Rimbaud, Mallarmé, and Valéry, as René Taupin[17] so well shows; this meant the possibility of conversational developments in a poetical discourse that would have been limited to fleeting atoms of expression if it had confined itself to the high-strung instant, the privileged epiphany. Ironical conversation à la Laforgue rescued poetry from that hieratic rigidity and restored to it the flexibility of tone that Pound admires in Browning. Thus Pound's theory of Imagism could broaden to include the three dimensions of *phanopoeia* (imagery), *melopoeia* (music), and *logopoeia* (referential meaning) without sacrificing the exacting standards of the original quest. Eliot's early verse, from "Prufrock" to "Preludes" and "Gerontion," is the best illustration of this.

Image, music, and meaning, however, were still a very exclusive trinity, for not only did they abhor the obvious and the conventional, but they left no room for narrative poetry. The basic unit remained the essentially short, tightly organized, carefully focused lyric. So what was the new poet to do when he felt the urge to sing with more sustained breath? Medallions, cameos, piercing notations, concise satires or epigrams would not do. They could not accommodate the resurgent epic impulse, the need to formulate encompassing poetic statement under the peremptory promptings of a convulsed age. Politics, economics, history, religion, thrown out of Poetry's castle window by the exclusive pride of the Symbolist Narcissus, kept knocking for readmission, hoping that an inclusive form of poetry might take the place of that aristocratic arrogance. At this point the resourcefulness of the new poets met the challenge. The doors of Axel's castle—of the modern poem—were thrown open without shameful compromises or repudiations. Narrative plot and discursive rationalization were out; the inclusive form had to arise from the inherent potentialities of non-discursive verse. These potentialities were contained in the metaphoric nexus purified of explanatory intermediaries, and capable of relating a wide range of caught perceptions in a direct way that was presentational as much as allusive. This short-circuit of images could be expanded at will by resorting to thematic variations without comment or link; a dimension of sustained continuity was furthermore provided by the conversational-ironic mode. There is no other way of understanding the remarkable transition from *Personae* to the *Cantos,* from "Preludes" to *The Waste Land,* from *White Buildings* to *The Bridge,* from *Spring and All* to *Paterson.* The poems of St.-John Perse would be a French equivalent of this American development, and Rilke's *Duino Elegies* a German one. Cinematic sequence and montage, as pointed out by Sergei Eisenstein, no doubt contributed to their development, but only as a stimulant, not as a begetter.

We can now see that *The Bridge* was germinally contained in the earlier lyrics of Hart Crane; it was, so to speak, their destiny, just as his whole work constitutes an episode in the modern attempt to proceed from the "exclusive" to the "inclusive" mode of poetry. Despite its unevenness, *The Bridge* is a document of great aesthetic and spiritual importance in our time; and we would question the ultimate validity of the judgment passed on it by such a sensitive critic as R. P. Blackmur,[18] who denies Crane a real epic disposition and regrets that he should have betrayed his native vein of Dickinsonian lyricism for the Whitmanic equivocation of his major effort. Emily should have been his Beatrice to the end, according to Blackmur; Whitman was an unfortunate seducer. Actually the inclusive gesture of Whitman was necessary to the fulfillment of Crane's genius as a complement to the "exclusive" inspiration of Emily Dickinson, who was in many ways an American Mallarmé. That Crane should have developed such a polarity, with the catalytic mediation of Eliot, is evidence of his insight rather than of muddleheadedness. And it is important to observe that his use of Dickinson and Melville, along with Whitman, enabled his poetry to respond to the French Symbolist models without rejecting an earlier American tradition, indeed, establishing an intimate relation with it. *The Bridge* cannot be ignored if we recognize the brilliancies contained in *White Buildings,* to which it is contiguous.

As to Yvor Winters, who puts Crane among the "decadent" poets (those marred by vices of form and feeling) while admitting that he occasionally soared into memorable achievement, I find myself unable to accept his moralistic decree. In Winters' evaluation, the personal tragedy and what seems to him the artistic failure of this poet become a didactic apologue, for he believes that confusion and suicide inevitably cap a life devoted to romantic pantheism. Woe to the followers of Emerson and, worse, of Whitman! Henry W. Wells' argument that the idea of *The Bridge* temporarily redeemed Crane's disorderly existence may counteract Winters' pronouncement. In *The American Way of Poetry*[19] the reader will find a passionate vindication of what the myth of America did for the self-excruciating poet so long as his energies were absorbed in the challenging task. Wells may tilt the scales too far the other way with his frank Americanism, which leads him to underrate the shorter poems by comparison with *The Bridge;* yet he is right in assuming that the objective myth was a fruitful choice for Crane, who needed a moral support and reference in his state of chaotic restlessness. And even if the actual achievement fell short of the ambitious project in perfection and unity, the positive results were enough to justify the undertaking. Anyhow, Blackmur, Winters, and Southworth[20] (who reduces Crane to an example of tragic immaturity) fail to take into account the value of Crane's gesture in striving to go beyond the "waste land" with a vital Yea, by embracing the world, the machine, and his own psychic disintegration. From the literary point of view he should not be considered a mere victim any more than Rimbaud, Dylan Thomas, or Trakl, or than anyone else who, in our difficult age, unhesitatingly staked all of himself in the game of poetry.

An objective analysis should not overlook the element emphasized by Hyatt Howe Waggoner,[21] namely, the attempt to find a new agreement between truth and faith, science and poetry, in a world claimed by a practically omnipotent technology and subverted by the intellectual revolutions of pure science. Several American poets, along with Crane, are surveyed by Waggoner as champions of this struggle; and like Weber he traces in Crane the influence of Einstein's ideas as a powerful concurrent impulse toward a new conception of the world—a factor Whatmough does not seem to value adequately in his lively article on "One Use of Language: Literature."[22] Whatmough maintains that in Crane and in other writers of our time the imaginative potential of the new cosmic structures offered by science has been exploited only sporadically. But in Crane's work, as in that of Pound, Eliot, and Joyce, the formal organization itself evinces a new sense of space and time, of personality and memory, of matter and energy.

This development is parallel to, rather than a consequence of, the new cosmology of relativity, which has acted as a catalyst on the poetical imagination only because the latter was working in a similar direction. Once the framework of logical narrative continuity has been exploded, and expanding association of themes becomes the sole source of form, the poem can take shape only as an "expanding universe" (à la Eddington), unanchored to a particular time and place, but hospitable (potentially) to all time and all space. Pound's *Cantos,* like *The Bridge,* move backward and forward in history, to and fro in geography, to obey the law of creative analogy that supersedes the rigid identity of a given time, a given place, a given hero. Chaos threatens this dynamic form, but the breakthrough to be scored compares with the Romantic (really neo-Elizabethan) exhilaration in liberating the theater from the three Aristotelian unities. Relativity replaces any binding absolutes within this expanding universe. Any given moment or theme can be the *center;* moreover, each motif is perennially redefined, and therefore changed, by its relation to others. Metamorphosis operates from within, not just as a dissolving, but even more as a unifying force. The action of the poem, inevitably, extends to all space, all time, namely, takes place in "space-time"—in a contemporaneity made perceptual. The proper locus of action is thus the objectified consciousness of the poet, who only in this way can break through the monad-walls of his romantic self. The poem is an act of infinite expansion of the self, equaling its infinite negation; the dialectic should be clear to readers who remember what Tiresias stands for in *The Waste Land,* or Ulysses-Zagreus-Pound in the *Cantos.* In *The Bridge,* as we shall see, the very forms of perception—time and space—become objective themes interwoven in shifting relation.

The germinal idea of this rhapsody may be found in two repudiated poems[23] published in 1921, but it took shape as a conscious project somewhat later, as witness Crane's letter to Allen Tate dated February 6, 1923. There he says that he has already started working on "a new poem, *The Bridge,*" which continues the tendencies of *The Marriage of Faustus and Helen* but is still too inchoate. Three years later, on March 18, 1926, he sent his patron Otto Kahn an account of his progress in writing the poem, for which Kahn had advanced him an initial sum of one thousand dollars; at the same time he outlined the general plan of the work.

This is a document of exceptional interest for the light it throws on the poet's own conception of the structure, detail, and symbolism of his *oeuvre:*

There are so many interlocking elements and symbols at work throughout *The Bridge* that it is next to impossible to describe it without resorting to the actual metaphors of the poem. Roughly, however, it is based on the conquest of space and knowledge. The theme of "Cathay" (its riches, etc.) ultimately is transmuted into a symbol of consciousness, knowledge, spiritual unity. A rather religious motivation, albeit not Presbyterian. The following notation is a very rough abbreviation of the subject matter of the several sections:

I Columbus—Conquest of space, chaos
II Pokahantus—The natural body of America—fertility, etc.
III Whitman—The Spiritual body of America
(A dialogue between Whitman and a dying soldier in a Washington hospital; the infraction of physical death, disunity, on the concept of immortality)
IV John Brown
(Negro porter on Calgary Express making berths and singing to himself (a jazz form for this) of his sweetheart and the death of John Brown, alternately)
V Subway—The encroachment of machinery on humanity; a kind of purgatory in relation to the open sky of last section
VI The Bridge—A sweeping dithyramb in which the Bridge becomes the symbol of consciousness spanning time and space

The first and last sections are composed of blank verse with occasional rhyme for accentuation. The verbal dynamics used and the spacious periodicity of the rhythm result in an unusually symphonic form. What forms I shall use for the other sections will have to be determined when I come to grips with their respective themes.

In view of what was said above on the analogic-inclusive form of the poem, it is pertinent that its last part should have been written first. We can also see that the plan underwent significant changes, for the sections on John Brown and on Whitman's dialogue with the dying soldier never materialized; other motifs instead worked their way into the rhapsody. Enthusiasm and depression alternated in Crane's mind, for a few months later, on June 20, 1926, he confessed to his friend Waldo Frank that he now doubted the objective validity of the symbols on whose loom he had been weaving the glowing verse of *The Bridge.* The industrial America of his time now seemed to him vulgar, flat, and noisy with commercial advertising (we shall see the repercussion on the final draft of the poem); his own symbols appeared too ideal and private to afford a grip on his world's objective reality, even if "darkness" was part and parcel of the preliminary reckoning. Emotionally, he said, he wanted to write *The Bridge,* while from a coldly intellectual point of view the whole theme and project now seemed absurd.

Hence Weber concludes that Crane brought the poem to completion only by an act of will, to honor his obligation to Otto Kahn, but without achieving an intimate fusion between chosen subject and formal expression; hence social pessimism clashes with the ecstatic climaxes, and sections like "Cape Hatteras," "Quaker Hill," and "Indiana" slip into bathos. Instead of mastering his theme Crane was often mastered by it, according to Weber, partly because of his faulty intellectual background; but where he did master it, the result was outstanding. In a sense we might say that Crane failed to unify his poem thoroughly because he had not succeeded in integrating his own personality; conversely, if he had achieved a more profound critique on the paradoxes of the world in which he lived, he would perhaps have achieved complete unification of the poem and the salvation of his own moral self. To Yvor Winters, who urged on him the necessity of an ethical system as a requirement of human wholeness, Crane replied on May 29, 1927, that he had a certain ethical code, although he had not tried so far to reduce it to an exact formula, in view of the endlessness of such a task. It was clearly much harder to save oneself when one happened to be Harold Hart Crane instead of Yvor Winters or, say, Malcolm Cowley or Allen Tate; and this alone should make us appreciate the struggle Crane conducted with himself in his relentless pursuit of life and of expression.

In its final shape as licensed by the author, *The Bridge* consists of eight sections, some of which in their turn divide into subsections. The main parts follow this sequence: "Ave Maria," "Powhatan's Daughter," "Cutty Sark," "Cape Hatteras," "Three Songs," "Quaker Hill," "The Tunnel," "Atlantis." Part Two ("Powhatan's Daughter") comprises five subsections: "The Harbor Dawn," "Van Winkle," "The River," "The Dance," "Indiana;" Part Five ("Three Songs") modulates into "Southern Cross," "National Winter Garden," and "Virginia." Instead of telling a conventional story, these sections present in alternating and telescoped order different moments of American history, grasped in their mythical and human significance; the real unity, as has been observed, is given by the poet's own consciousness, omnipresent in time and space throughout the rhapsody.

The proem ("To Brooklyn Bridge") stands somewhat apart, with its compressed quatrains hymning the main symbol, New York's well-known landmark—

> O harp and altar, of the fury fused,
> . . .
> Terrific threshold of the prophet's pledge,
> Prayer of pariah, and the lover's cry,——

which finally reveals itself as the divine archetype of poetical consciousness, soaring to span in its sleepless curve river, sea, and prairie, namely all of the world in space, all of time's order:

> O Sleepless as the river under thee,
> Vaulting the sea, the prairies' dreaming sod,
> Unto us lowliest sometime sweep, descend
> And of the curveship lend a myth to God.

In the poem's epilogue ("Atlantis") the image of the bridge reappears consumed in a mystical fire that destroys its materiality, transfiguring it into a harp of light, into ecstasy. From the viewpoint of structure (and of genesis, as we saw) truly *The Bridge* can say of itself "In my beginning is my end." Some critics have found difficulty with this symbolization of a mechanical object which was ill equipped to bear such an investment of transcendental attributes; Crane, however, saw in that iron structure a dynamic form instead of a static thing, for he felt, condensed in it, the whole fury of a Faustian epoch. Besides, Brooklyn Bridge lived in pictorial iconography; the painter, Joseph Stella, used it in a famous Futurist-Cubist work which also brings out the formal suggestion of a harp and of a Gothic cathedral, and he explained in writing the reasons for his visual treatment, arousing Crane's warm response in a letter now accessible in published form. Mayakovsky's ode has already been mentioned, and that too goes to show that if Brooklyn Bridge stimulated Crane's imagination, it was no purely private event, despite his contrary misgivings. The wealth of symbolic connotations he discovered, or poured out on it, may at times be disconcerting, for it tends to clutter the page with baroque redundancies; but this means that Crane's problem was a crisis of richness rather than of poverty. And, finally, a bridge *bridges;* the poet's imagination suffers no restriction when it comes to feeling a suitable object as pure action.

The proem epitomizes the whole poem with subtle anticipations. It gives us the chaotic energy of the city, the breath of oceans, the mystical afflatus, the linguistic violence that pervade the whole work; and it rises to striking beauty, for instance, in the first two quatrains, where the vision of seagulls circling the Statue of Liberty in weird whiteness against the iron-gray background of the harbor dawn, with the Bridge itself as a perpetual apparition to counterpoint it, evokes to the inner eye such a New York as might have been painted by the demonic brush of Oscar Kokoschka. The strength of these lines results from a tense balance between the stability of the bridge, full of arrested motion, and the frenzy of the city culminating in the (autobiographically prophetic) suicide of the madman:

> Out of some subway scuttle, cell or loft
> A bedlamite speeds to thy parapets,
> Tilting there momently, shrill shirt ballooning,
> A jest falls from the speechless caravan.

The violent atmosphere, swaying between outcry, dithyramb, and prayer, parallels very closely the most characteristic work of certain German expressionists, particularly Heym, Stadler, and Werfel.

As to the poetical validity of the bridge symbol, Sonia Raiziss makes the best case for it in *The Metaphysical Passion,*[25] where Crane is placed, along with other significant moderns, in the perspective of twentieth-century metaphysical poetry. Quoting from Henry Wells's *New Poets from Old,* she sees all of metaphysical art as a *bridge* spanning the finite and the infinite, the many and the one, past and future, the apparent chaos and the essential harmony of existence. This kind of poetry, according to her, rises as a mirror of, and response to, ages of climactic ideological conflict, like our century and the seventeenth. Paradoxical imagery seeks to hold together, without muffling them, the centrifugal pulls of an explosive reality; it is the crisis and the effort to overcome the crisis on the level of imagination. Thus the bridge does not appear in Crane's poem merely as its literal protagonist (despite the invocations he addresses to it), but because it concretely expresses the inner structure of the world Crane set out to explore. For the bridge, when we think of it as analogic form released from the weight of steel, is the metaphor, the linguistic and cognitive act of poetry as such—the only kind of unification Crane knew. This much remains true even if we feel that the bridge, in Crane's fiery addresses, is at times on the verge of becoming an idol. On one level, the poet extols in the language of worship a man-made thing, while endeavoring on the other to capture in it the human source of energy from which it arose, and the self-transcending drive of that energy. The simultaneities are enticingly precarious.

After this astonishing proem, which Waggoner and Wells agree in considering one of the most important lyrics in American literature, the poet's camera eye turns back four centuries and a half to enter the mind of Christopher Columbus on his first return trip to Spain from the newly discovered shore. The navigator is thinking of hardships met so far and of those he will still have to face at the hands of his royal patrons; of Ferdinand's greed, of the thirst for gold that may spoil the fruits of his conquest; he lifts his thought to the God Pneuma, manifested in the ocean wind, and to the Virgin Mary, protector of ships; he envisions the future crops of golden wheat and "pendant seething wheat of knowledge" that may posthumously crown his fondest hopes, and finally soars with prophetic imagination beyond any earthly reach, into the fiery heart of God:

> Thy purpose—
> still one shore beyond desire!
> The sea's green crying towers a-sway, Beyond
> And kingdoms
> naked in the
> trembling heart—
> Te Deum laudamus
> O Thou Hand of Fire.

This section, drawn from Columbus's diary through the splendid mediation of William Carlos Williams' *In the American Grain,* shows to great advantage Crane's mastery of language, his inspired sincerity, his musical and painterly sensibility. The sea—a recurrent theme in his poetry, from *The Bridge* itself to "Voyages" and *Key West*—lives in these lines with dazzling force:

> Here waves climb into dusk on gleaming mail;
> Invisible valves of the sea,—locks, tendons
> Crested and creeping, troughing corridors
> That fall back yawning to another plunge.
> Slowly the sun's red caravel drops light
> Once more behind us. . . . It is morning there—.

The marine rhythm, the brilliancy of that image of the sea as the armor of a cataphract, which stresses the basic situation of struggle against men and elements alike; the effectiveness of the alliterations and internal echoes ("climb . . . gleaming;" "invisible valves"; "crested . . . creeping . . . troughing . . . corridors"); the movement of thought from imminent European dusk to the sunrise Columbus' ship left behind in the New World, which thereby receives its proper connotations as the Land of the Morning, the Orient he believed he had reached, and, at the same time, as the new dawn of history to be found in the West, the world of the new beginning; the subtle metaphor transforming the sun into a heavenly caravel that analogically repeats Christopher's light-bringing voyage to the new empires—everything contributes to make these lines a tight, radiant tissue. We have already pointed out the affinity of Crane's exuberant, exclamatory poetry to Expressionism; and it would be no contradiction to add that his problem can best be defined by the critic as *grandeurs et misères du baroque,* if we keep in mind Eugenio d'Ors's definition of baroque. For this is perhaps the truest stylistic portrait of Hart Crane as it emerges from failures and successes alike: a melter of forms, sensually and mystically effusive, forever spinning coils of thought and sound, vaulting sensory concreteness into abstraction and back again, from "Faustus and Helen" to "The Broken Tower." The incidental mannerism was well worth risking.

Many motifs in the Columbus section are interwoven with other parts of the rhapsody. They generate a kind of unity by interplay: for instance, the "white birds" of stanza 4 directly echo the seagulls of the proem and anticipate the eagles and airplanes of later sections. A closer look, however, shows deeper implications. The phrase "The Great White Birds!" is uttered by the natives of San Salvador at the approach of the majestic white-winged vessels, toward which they "came out . . . crying;" thus the passage fuses the seagull of the proem, stanza 1, with the "apparitional sails" of stanza 2. But the synthesis, chromatically based on the whiteness of birds and sails and spontaneously proposed by the animistic imagination of the primitive gazers, creates a new level of reality by raising Columbus' ships, crew and all, to the status of angels—which they certainly are as messengers of European civilization and, more specifically, of the Christian God. It is impossible to dismiss the suggestion that Crane here kept an eye on the sacramental etymology of the Genoese admiral's names: "Christ-bearer" (Christopher) and "Dove" (Colombus). However that may be, he did consciously enhance the angelic overtone of the sail imagery toward the rapturous end of the section, where he transfigured the ships into choirs of angels circling God:

> Elohim, still I hear thy sounding heel!
>
> White toil of heaven's cordons, mustering
> In holy rings all sails charged to the far
> Hushed gleaming fields. . . .

This imaginative climax anticipates the "white choiring wings" of "Atlantis," stanza 10, and reverberates on the beginning of the proem, where the seagull analogically circles the Statue of Liberty and conjures the fleeting memory of a remote, but still available, past: the "apparitional sails" of Columbian discovery, the great beginning, not to be lost.

The Virgin Mary with her "ageless blue" reappears in "Virginia" as blue-eyed Mary the typist, as Eternal Feminine in Pocahontas ("The Dance"), and in "Indiana" 's pioneer mother; the Divine Hand of Fire re-emerges as erotic yearning in "The Harbor Dawn," then as a human guide at the end of "Cape Hatteras" ("My/ hand in yours, / Walt Whitman—/ so—"), and finally at the end of "The Tunnel":

> How far away the star has pooled the sea—
> Or shall the hands be drawn away, to die?
> Kiss of our agony Thou gatherest,
> O Hand of Fire
>   gatherest—

Cathay, of course, runs through the whole poem to the climax of "Atlantis," where it blends with the informing idea of the bridge, with the mythical submerged continent and with the fire of God:

> One Song, one Bridge of Fire! It is Cathay. . . .

Since Columbus thought he had reached China by inverting the customary route, this most provocative of historical mistakes allows Crane to identify the reality of geographic discovery with the driving force of vision, paradox with evidence, actual America with the America to be.

"Atlantis" becomes thus more understandable as the attempted consummation of the rhapsody—a consummation that seeks to achieve itself not merely on the sweeping plane of general idea, but through the intimate innervations of language. Comparison of "Atlantis" with "Ave Maria" will show how accurately the stanzas of the concluding section rehearse those of the opening one, merging the latter with the proem in one final thrust of prophecy. One capillary example: the "cordage tree" of "Ave Maria," stanza 7, line 5, in addition to being a fruitful vegetal pun in itself, visually supported by the essential shape of a ship-mast, develops into a different "cordage" in "Atlantis," "stanza 2, line 1, where it summarizes the "bound cable strands," the "flight of strings," the "telepathy of wires," the "transparent meshes" that, in stanza 1, dynamically describe the design of the bridge as such. But since in the universe of expanding-interweaving metaphor the center is everywhere, this thematic relation is finally resolved in the ultimate theme of the poem; it is far more than clever word play, if we think that it projects the "cordage" or rigging of Columbus' ship into the lithe metal structures of Brooklyn Bridge, and thereby epiphanizes the idea that Columbus was himself a "bridge" between two worlds, while the present-day construction resumes, on another level, the same function as an actuality, yet also as a symbolic possibility.

To follow the ramifications of that "cordage tree" means, therefore, to trace the entire nervous system of Crane's ambitious poem. A pivotal echo rings in the last stanza of "Ave Maria":

> White *toil* of heaven's *cordons,* mustering
> In holy rings all sails. . . . [italics mine—G.C.]

Thus the metamorphic impulse transforms the tree-like image of the ship's mast and rigging into a net (compare the "transparent meshes" of the bridge in "Atlantis"). It is, however, a net of circles ("holy rings"), and this opens up a whole gamut of further possibilities, the more immediate one being directly exploited a few lines below:

> —The kindled Crown! acceded of the poles
> And biassed by full sails, *meridians reel* . . . [italics mine—G.C.]

The circular network of meridians and parallels mathematically defines the globe around which Columbus was sailing, and at the same time manifests in its inclusive form the completeness of God, the Bridge of Bridges, spanning all distances, as the last line of stanza 9 had proclaimed:

> Te Deum laudamus, for thy teeming span!

Besides, meridians and parallels are mere abstractions of map geometry; they become perceptible by analogy, for a navigator, as the shifting horizon line that determines his position on the sea and that he, in his turn, determines by his course; thus the mystical-geometric metaphors of "Ave Maria" 's last stanza bring us back to the vividly pictorial experience of stanza 6:

> Series on series, infinite,—till eyes
> Starved wide on blackened tides, accrete—enclose
> This *turning rondure whole,* this *crescent ring*
> Sun-cusped and zoned with modulated fire
> Like pearls that whisper through the Doge's hands
> —Yet no delirium of jewels! [italics mine—G.C.]

We note the symbolic inherences: man's eyes (a recurrent leitmotif of the rhapsody) enclose and are enclosed by the like shape of macrocosm in the act of exploration, or knowledge, that acquires in itself a round shape; and roundness connects, in the chain of being, pearls, eyes, horizon, earth, planets, sun, and the heavenly vault. This manifests the full potential of the bridge, which, at the end of the proem, had been implored to "of [thy] curveship lend a myth to God"; the curvature of four-dimensional space, for Crane, who absorbed Einstein's ideas through the visionary mediation of Ouspensky, embodying as such the godlike experience of totality.

But we are not yet done with the interlocking analogies that sprout up in every direction from the initially chosen point: those "pearls" and "jewels" start another chain reaction in stanza 9, with "Teneriffe's garnet," and in stanza 10, where we find

> This disposition that thy night relates
> From Moon to Saturn in one sapphire wheel. . . .

"Teneriffe's garnet," a vivid metaphor for the volcano Columbus met on his way to America, takes up the imagistic cues of "jewels" and "modulated fire" from the previously quoted passage of stanza 6 to merge them into one, and transcends both again by resolving the achieved crystallization into the concrete sight of a volcanic eruption:

> And Teneriffe's garnet—flamed it in a cloud,
> Urging through night our passage to the Chan; . . . .

The metaphoric impulse never stands still, and relates the volcano to the pillar of fire that guided the Hebrews by night and the cloud that guided them by day, while the tactical appearance of the Chan, Cathay's emperor, picks up in its own right the jewelry cue; two stanzas below, fire, smoke cloud, kingly attributes, stars, and jewelry will blend into one flash of telescoped images that gives us God in the act of full revelation or, so to speak, "unclouding":

> . . . —round thy brows unhooded now
> —The kindled Crown!

The real King supersedes his earthly counterparts: Ferdinand of Spain, avid for earthly jewels, and the Khan of Cathay, reigning over fabled riches; the Crown (astronomically, Corona Borealis) has become the "rondure whole" of the ultimate "Curveship," and echoes directly the "sapphire wheel" of stanza 10, with its immediate development:

> The orbic wake of thy once whirling feet. . . .

It may also be worth noticing that the sapphire's canonic attribute with regard to splendor and purity is "oriental," so that in this context it would seem to connote the shining kingdom of Cathay, while on the other hand, as Crane may have seen in Webster's dictionary, the word "sapphire" itself is etymologically related to Saturn. "From Moon to Saturn": heavenly bodies are important to a navigator even if he has, like Columbus, a compass to rely on; but then, the "true appointment" yielded by the magnetic needle of line 2 in this stanza becomes a multivalent "disposition" in line

5, thereby acquiring an astrological connotation that suggests the bridging of lunar femininity and saturnine masculinity, as well as the conjunction of good and bad luck (the moon's phases being used in astrology to determine by calculation propitious and unfavorable days, while Saturn was considered "infortune" or malevolent). Astronomically speaking, Saturn has a ring that would not be ignored in this context, and apart from that, it derives its name from the Roman god of time, of the golden age, of harvest, thus relating to the "pendant seething wheat" and "hushed fields" of the following stanza, and by the same token to the "ripe fields" and "harvests" of "Atlantis," stanza 9. Taking into account the function of the moon as ageless time-measurer and Saturn as time god, we may find the "amplitude that time explores" of line 1 locally echoed in the line that conjoins the two planets, with a possible overtone of the week pattern ("from Monday to Saturday") to introduce the idea of a cycle to be crowned by "Sunday," the day of the Sun and of the Lord, who appears as Elohim two lines below. Whichever way we look, we get the idea of completion, of what Dickinson would have called "circumference," and a spatial aspect can be added to it by recalling that, in ancient cosmology, the moon was the closest and Saturn the farthest of the planets: thus the "sapphire wheel" encircles the solar system itself.

The endlessly intertwining ramifications of the "cordage tree" have branched out into the cosmos, but always with a bearing on the central idea of "bridges." One particularly felicitous development takes place, as has been pointed out before, in the proem as well as in "Atlantis," where that "cordage" vibrantly shades into the strings of a harp. In those privileged moments, without losing sight of the visual object before him (the bridge), Hart Crane can project man's music (his own as well as the shriller one of his culture as a whole) into the music of the spheres, because the harp at that point epitomizes the entire cosmos. Columbus, the man of science and faith, provides the particular focus in "Ave Maria," yet as navigator he reappears in the sailor of "Cutty Sark," as explorer in the tramps of "The River," and in the Larry of "Indiana," as embodied yearning for knowledge in Walt Whitman ("Cape Hatteras"), and in Crane himself. Columbus had been a natural archetype in American poetry long before Williams and Crane dramatized him; Joel Barlow's *The Vision of Columbus* is an especially poignant antecedent because it shows the Genoese seafarer contemplating, from a hilltop where he has come to rest and die, the great future of America, but Philip Freneau's "Pictures of Columbus" should also be remembered, along with Washington Irving's copious volumes on Columbus and on his companions. Finally, Whitman's "Prayer of Columbus" has to be taken into account, given Crane's affinity for Walt, in a perspective focused on *The Bridge*. Undoubtedly Crane responded felicitously to this theme because he felt it from the inside, aided by a sustaining American tradition. Columbus spontaneously became in his hands a focal symbol of the human mind venturing into new horizons—something comparable to the Ulysses archetype in Ezra Pound's *Cantos,* whose very beginning is deftly varied in the cadence of "Ave Maria" 's fourth stanza.

With the following section ("Powhatan's Daughter") the poet resumes his travel from present to past and from New York to the rest of the continent. "The Harbor Dawn" introduces us to a characteristic world of fog, wailing foghorns, reawakening bustle, restless signals, but the poet surrenders to a hypnotic sleep, confronts a mysterious woman who is the first avatar of Powhatan's daughter (namely Pocahontas as America and Mother Earth) and, while the fog lifts, gazes at a drowsy star. Thus a powerful spell is cast on Time: the next subsection ("Van Winkle") centers on the Irving hero who spanned twenty years in one long sleep to awake to the baffling changes of post-revolutionary America. Rip Van Winkle is, once again, the poet returning to the memories of childhood under the spell of the hurdy-gurdy; he is also modern America feverishly growing from year to year without realizing the extent of its growth, lunging to devour space with a thousand highways ("Macadam, gun-grey as the tunny's belt . . ."); and he is finally Crane's own poetry, committed to the exciting game of jumping backward and forward in time with a continuous change of perspective: another projection of the bridge as a spanner of time. The hurdy-gurdy song, activating the mechanism of memory much as the juke-box does in "Cutty Sark," gives the clue to an autobiographical identification of Rip with the poet, who teeters between past and present without a lasting chance to root himself, since all he has is the grey road—and from this tormenting memory of his unstable family life he will be released at the end of "The Tunnel."

But his personal story broadens into a panoramic view of the contemporary American scene; "The River" brings us from the subway to the Twentieth Century Limited, to leave us eventually in the company of three tramps who are following the tracks. Snatches of random talk in the cars, a kaleidoscope of sensations, voices, advertisements, the din of urban America: from this the tramps flee toward the heart of the continent. "SCIENCE—COMMERCE and the HOLYGHOST/ RADIO ROARS IN EVERY HOME WE HAVE THE NORTHPOLE/ WALLSTREET AND VIRGINBIRTH. . . ." We have come a long way from Columbus' use of science and commitment to faith; that strident mixture of religion and publicity is a well-known trait of American life, with its Salvation Army campaigns, its modernized revivals, its loudly advertised Christianity that strains itself at times to compete with the roar of industrialized commerce and be heard above it. In New York it is not difficult to find, printed in huge capitals on a blind wall, some religious warning like "The Wages of Sin Is Death" or to meet in the tumult of the subway an improvised prophet who preaches Christ to blank faces and deafened ears.

Crane's heart is all for the tramps, who adumbrate his pioneer ancestors; they are childlike and thus remind him of his infancy in Garrettsville and Cleveland, when he first approached in tenderness the body of Mother Earth. Between early memories and bits of folksong—"Kentucky Home," "Casey Jones," "Some Sunny Day"—one heads for the Mississippi, the central vein of America's body, which absorbs in its flow all the voices because it is the river of time. Toward the end of the episode the pulse of poetry rises from loose rhapsody to a rare concentration of expressive power; Winters, Tate, and Weber agree on rating this part among the great things of English poetry. Flowing into the Gulf of Mexico, the river carries with itself all the life of the continent and its past, to rear in the mind's eye like a heraldic snake. It is a climax of lyrical accumulation; the expansion of individual identity into the ceaseless flow of all life is admirably grasped:

> The River, spreading, flows—and spends your dream.
> What are you, lost within this tideless spell?
> You are your father's father, and the stream—
> A liquid theme that floating niggers swell.

And let us listen to the snake motif:

> The River lifts itself from its long bed,
> Poised wholly on its dream, a mustard glow
> Tortured with history, its one will—flow!—
> The Passion spreads in wide tongues, choked and slow,
> Meeting the Gulf, hosannas silently below.

It had been foreshadowed in "Van Winkle," and it will soon recur in "The Dance," to clarify its symbolic nature. The snake is Time, as the eagle (or hawk, or seagull, or airplane) is Space; and the two motifs punctuate the whole poem, finally to combine in the last lines of the epilogue ("The serpent with the eagle in the leaves . . .")[26]

In the "Dance" section we invert the itinerary; the poet paddles and portages a canoe upstream, crosses the Appalachian mountains, and takes part in an Indian ritual, a sacrificial dance honoring Pocahontas, the blossoming earth-bride; at the climax of the sacred orgy he is killed to blend with her, and Time fuses with Space:

> Dance, Maquokeeta! snake that lives before,
> That casts his pelt, and lives beyond! Sprout, horn!
> . . .
> O, like the lizard in the furious noon,
> That drops his legs and colors in the sun,
> —And laughs, pure serpent, Time itself, and moon,
> Of his own fate, I saw thy change begun!
>
> And saw thee dive to kiss that destiny
> Like one white meteor, sacrosanct and blent
> At last with all that's consummate and free
> There, where the first and last gods keep thy tent
> . . .
> We danced, O Brave, we danced beyond their farms,
> In cobalt desert closures made our vows . . .
> Now is the strong prayer folded in thine arms,
> The serpent with the eagle in the boughs.

Time is change, like the skin-sloughing snake; space is eagle wing and eagle eye, it is flight, dominion, comprehensive presence, perennialness. The plumed serpent, then, is reality in its highest expansion and power, it is immortality reached through an overcoming of life and death, which explains the memorable address to Maquokeeta:

A cyclone threshes in the turbine crest,
Swooping in eagle feathers down your back;
Know, Maquokeeta, greeting; know death's best;
—Fall, Sachem, strictly as the tamarack!

Pocahontas, Earth, buds periodically in maize, and this underlies the ritual. No mere folklore digression, however, this is also the ritual of the poet, who in his vision seeks to master time and space, death and life. We think in this connection of "Atlantis," the grand finale that fuses in white-heat compression all the main strains of the rhapsody.

The tone sinks considerably in the following subsection ("Indiana"), which sentimentally tells the disappointment of a pioneer couple who came back empty-handed from the 1849 gold rush. The woman meets a squaw with her papoose, and feels a sisterly closeness to the latter-day Pocahontas, representative of a vanishing race. The white woman, old and stony like the southwest desert, is herself a decrepit incarnation of Pocahontas, while the frustrated quest for gold instead of wheat and corn is a thematic variation on the Columbus passage with its prophetic emphasis on the gold of wheat and knowledge versus material wealth. When the old pioneer wife says farewell to the son who goes to sea to try a better fortune, the previously followed route is inverted again in the imaginative shuttling between land and water. This affords an antiphonal transition to Part III ("Cutty Sark"), where the departing Larry of "Indiana" returns provisionally to dry land to have a drink and swap a few words, counterpointed by juke-box songs, in a South Street bar. The songs, "Stamboul Rose," "Atlantis Rose," subtly anticipate the "Atlantis" finale, where the rose will blossom into an "anemone," "whitest flower," "answerer of all," "Atlantis," into the continent of flowering light to which the poet entrusts his soul. At the same time, the songs of "Cutty Sark" prelude the "Three Songs" section as such. The interweaving process does not end here, for the repeatedly inverted passages from land to water and back throughout the sections and subdivisions analyzed so far are a dynamically invisible presence of the bridge, and to clinch the point we only have to turn to "Atlantis," stanza 1, line 3, which appropriately describes it as "taut miles of *shuttling* moonlight . . . ," with a later imagistic corollary in the "towering *looms*" of stanza 4 (italics mine).

"Cutty Sark" brings us back to New York, and gives us the first direct mention of Brooklyn Bridge after the proem ("I started walking home across the Bridge . . ."). The sailor is a poetical reincarnation of Columbus, so that the theme of land exploration prevalent in "Powhatan's Daughter" yields now to maritime exploration with his broken reminiscences of voyages in the Orient. Names of winged clippers, punctuating his talk, conclude the episode on an airy note:

> *Thermopylae, Black Prince, Flying Cloud* through Sunda
> —scarfed of foam, their bellies veered green esplanades,
> locked in wind-humors, ran their eastings down;
>
> *at Java Head freshened the nip*
> *(sweet opium and tea!)*
> and turned and left us on the lee . . .
>
> Buntlines tusseling (91 days, 20 hours and anchored!)
> *Rainbow, Leander*
> (last trip a tragedy)—where can you be
> *Nimbus?* and you rivals two—
>
> a long tack keeping—
> *Taeping?*
> *Ariel?*

Thus the inlay work deftly modeled on Joyce, Pound, and Eliot is resolved in a climbing movement, with additional propulsion from the very names of the ships, so musically light and culminating in the unimprovable *Ariel*. These ships really existed, of course,[27] and for his song quotations Crane drew from the folklore of American chanteys. Melville's name aptly ushers in this section, so full of emblematic motifs. The green of eyeglasses and eyes sparkles at the beginning and returns at the end as the color of the sea; the rose carries the imagistic seed of "Atlantis," as we have seen, and the juke box is likewise full of echoes and intimations, for by inserting a coin in the slot one enters the mazes of memory, one races the oceans again on the nimble clipper ships, one also dives in the hell of time lost:

> interminably
> long since somebody's nickel—stopped—
> playing—
>
> A wind worried those wicker-neat lapels, the
> swinging summer entrances to cooler hells. . . .

If Crane insists so much on the coin-in-the-slot motif, as shortly before:

> in the nickel-in-the-slot piano jogged
> "Stamboul Nights"—weaving somebody's nickel—sang—
>
> O *Stamboul Rose—dreams weave the rose!*

and shortly after:

> *Sweet opium and tea, Yo-ho!*
> *Pennies for porpoises that bank the keel!*

he has his good reasons. For this is a leitmotiv, to be heard in "Van Winkle" ("Keep hold of that nickel for car-change, Rip"), then in "Virginia":

> Out of the way-up nickel-dime tower shine,
> Cathedral Mary,
> shine!—

and then in "The Tunnel":

> —Quite unprepared rush naked back to light:
> And down beside the turnstile press the coin
> Into the slot. The gongs already rattle.

and again, in the same section:

> O caught like pennies beneath soot and steam,
> Kiss of our agony thou gatherest. . . .

It is Charon's coin, for passage to Hades, and the poet uses it to gain access to the hell of the subway, of modern urban life, of his own subterranean despair. Money, besides, has something to do with the gold that attracted the pioneers to frustration in "Indiana" and that aroused the greed of Ferdinand of Spain in "Ave Maria." Yet, since the poet must needs descend to hell if he wants to sing with authority, whether that hell is the alienated world of the city, or the unconscious, or his own threatening alienation, that coin is not just infernal; it is also the symbolic tribute exacted by poetry, of which one gets an ironic adumbration in the mechanically reproduced music of "Cutty Sark."

This section's conclusion, where the ethereal parade of sailing vessels makes for a movement of ascension, is offset by the contrary movement of "Cape Hatteras," so heavily descensional:

Imponderable the dinosaur
sinks slow,
the mammoth saurian
ghoul, the eastern
Cape . . .

After Ariel, the dinosaur; after the rise, the descent. But this too issues from the pivotal mention of Melville, whose typical animals had appeared in "Cutty Sark" with the shark tooth worn by the sailor and his "murmurs of Leviathan." Melvillian animals are not lacking indeed in Hart Crane's poetry elsewhere, as witness the ending of "Voyages II":

O minstrel galleons of Carib fire,
Bequeath us to no earthly shore until
Is answered in the vortex of our grave
The seal's wide spindrift gaze toward paradise.

See, again, the "mammoth turtles climbing sulphur dreams" of "Repose of Rivers," which recall the "Encantadas" prose; or the "huge terrapin" of "O Carib Isle;" or finally, the white albatross of 'Voyages IV." But with Melville Hart Crane shares another motif, far more dominant, as we shall see later.

The initial movement of descent in "Cape Hatteras" is immediately followed by another one, of ascent:

While rises in the west the coastwise range,
slowly the hushed land—
Combustion at the astral core—the dorsal change
Of energy—convulsive shift of sand. . . .

Such a beginning might presumably give the cue to another celebration of earth; instead, this failure of an episode, marred by the heaviest extravagances and the worst taste in all of the poem, attempts to sing the intoxication of space, the airplane, therefore the element of air (after the previously exploited earth and water). The fourth element—fire—will appear at the end of the rhapsody as "Bridge of Fire" (which in a work-sheet draft, appended by Weber to his monograph, was a "Bird of Fire," a spatial symbol). If "Cutty Sark" was under the constellation of Melville, "Cape Hatteras" invokes Whitman for brotherly guidance. "Cutty Sark" embroiders crafty variations on the theme of time and memory:

> "It's S.S. *Ala*—Antwerp—now remember kid
> to put me out at three she sails on time.
> I'm not much good at time any more keep
> weakeyed watches sometimes snooze—" his bony hands
> got to beating time . . . "A whaler once—
> I ought to keep time and get over it—I'm a
> Democrat—I know what time it is—No
> I don't want to know what time it is—that
> damned white Arctic killed my time . . ."

but "Cape Hatteras" keeps hymning space and the conquest of space:

> The captured fume of space foams in our ears—
>
> . . .
> But that star-glistened salver of infinity,
> The circle, blind crucible of endless space,
> Is sluiced by motion,—subjugated never.
>
> . . .
> Now the eagle dominates our days, is jurist
> Of the ambiguous cloud. We know the strident rule
> Of wings imperious . . . Space, instantaneous,

Flickers a moment, consumes us in its smile:
A flash over the horizon. . . .

. . .
Stars scribble on our eyes the frosty sagas,
The gleaming cantos of unvanquished space. . . .

. . .
This tournament of space, the threshed and chiselled height. . . .

. . .
Taut motors surge, space-gnawing, into flight;
Through sparkling visibility, outspread, unsleeping,
Wings clip the last peripheries of light. . . .

. . .
While Cetus-like, O thou Dirigible, enormous Lounger
Of pendulous auroral beaches,—
. . .
—Hast splintered space!

. . .
. . . thy stilly eyes partake
What alcohol of space. . . ! Remember, Falcon-Ace,
Thou hast there in thy wrist a Sanskrit charge
To conjugate infinity's dim marge—
Anew. . . !

And the airman finally falls spinning to his death in a vortex, a contemporary Icarus, a sacrificial eagle.

His symbolic resurrection is celebrated by Whitman:

O, upward from the dead
Thou bringest tally, and a pact, new bound,
Of living brotherhood!

in the fraternity of a new people, and in such capacity the singer of American democracy will be invested with magic attributes (the rod):

> Past where the albatross has offered up
> His last wing-pulse, and downcast as a cup
> That's drained, is shivered back to earth—thy wand
> Has beat a song, O Walt,—there and beyond!

Thus another ascension succeeds the descent, resurrection the vortex:

> ... Ascensions of thee hover in me now
> As thou at junctions elegiac, there, of speed
> With vast eternity, dost wield the rebound seed!;

and the intermediary of miracle is poetry, understood as fecundity magic (hence that *seed,* which reverberates on the rod imagery to make it phallic) but also as necromancy (hence the *wand*). Therefore, if "Cutty Sark" recalled in many ways "Rip Van Winkle," "Cape Hatteras" somehow sends us back to "The Dance;" for the Indian dancer is the poet, and the sacrificial victim, the aviator. Toward the end of the episode we find the curious attribute of "Panis Angelicus" in the rhetorically impassioned address to Whitman; probably Crane meant it as a pun with ecclesiastical connotations (to make Walt into the "bread of life" for us, like a newfangled Christ), yet that Latin salutation three times ritually repeated would seem to bring out Whitman's pagan mysticism, his resemblance to mythic Pan, the Greek god of pastures and of the cosmic All. We should also note a brief reference to the literal bridge, soon to be metamorphosed into the "spanning" open road of Whitman.

Needless to say, this is the worst section of the rhapsody, the one where Crane's innate baroque style degenerates into noisy, opaque, strained externalities, worthy of third-rate futurists who think that to be modern means simply to enthrone Energy and Machine in rhetoric. On the other hand, these lamentable faults of execution should not obscure the many nexuses with the other parts of the poem and with its germinal conception. For instance, the theme of the airplane and its American inventors, the Wright brothers, develops from a much better passage in the Van Winkle episode:

> The grind-organ says . . . Remember, remember
> The cinder pile at the end of the backyard
> Where we stoned the family of young
> Garter snakes under . . . And the monoplanes
> We launched—with paper wings and twisted
> Rubber bands . . . Recall—recall.

From the Van Winkle subsection, then, there fork out the dance episode, the "Cutty Sark" section, and "Cape Hatteras" itself; for what we have throughout is basically the same ritual, namely, an endeavor to kill Time (the snake) and to master Space (through a bird or airplane.) The fusion of highest temporal intensity with utmost extension of space is pure energy, which accounts for the thing Crane tried to accomplish in his unreadable aeronautical hymn (he hoped to convey the spiritual aspect of energy here, but it remained untransfigured). Cape Hatteras, near the scene of the Wright brothers' momentous experiment, protrudes from an island off the eastern coast of North Carolina, very dangerous to navigation, hence the threatening animistic nature of the dinosaur metaphor at the outset. And when Crane defines the dirgible by the name of the constellation of Cetus, he is merely raising to the sky, in tune with the dominance of the air element here, the Melvillian leviathan or whale of "Cutty Sark," and in a way the dinosaur itself.

Official sentimentality, vulgarity, dated excesses have ruined the whole thing, without quite concealing the occasional marks of the lion's paw, as in the majestic attack with its surprise of inverted movement in the seascape, like a scene shot by a movie camera aboard a sailing ship (but all of *The Bridge* somehow relates to cinematic language, with its sequences, montage effects, sudden transitions, and fadeouts). And here and there, some isolated line flashes out from the junk heap. Crane, an admirer of Hopkins, sometimes rivaled that poet's spastic, tactile sonority, and there are hints of that power even in this most unfortunate part of *The Bridge,* though the best example of his kinetic synaesthesia would possibly have to be sought in the jazz rhythms of "For the Marriage of Faustus and Helen," Part 2:

> O, I have known metallic paradises
> Where cuckoos clucked to finches
> Above the deft catastrophes of drums.

Part 3 of the earlier poem, having to do with air warfare and death, was of course seminal to the ambitious attempt of "Cape Hatteras," where incidentally we would note, toward the end, the spiritualization of the bridge into a rainbow:

> And see! the rainbow's arch—how shimmeringly stands
> Above the Cape's ghoul-mound, O joyous seer!

This rainbow, intermittently shining elsewhere in the rhapsody (particularly in "Cutty Sark" in the guise of a ship name), will overarch the last lines of "Atlantis." Its symbolic value rests on its visual shape, contextually exploited by our cunning seer, and it acquires further meaning when we consider that the rainbow is the totality of the spectrum in its diffracted form, which Crane then gathers to extreme concentration in the "Whitest Flower" of the climaxing ecstasy. Sometimes Crane supplies the clue to his symbols, sometimes instead he lets their recurrence hypnotically work on the reader. For the basic leitmotiv of the Time serpent and Space eagle the clue is explicitly offered in "The River," shortly after the middle:

> . . . But I know her body there,
> Time like a serpent down her shoulder, dark,
> And space, an eaglet's wing, laid on her hair.

We have now come to "Three Songs," an afterthought interpolation that somehow breaks the continuity of our rhapsody, yet is firmly anchored to its Eternal Feminine motif. This is a threefold avatar of Pocahontas, herself a reincarnation of Helen, with whom, in the form of Faustus, the poet had earlier consummated a symbolic wedding; and in this regard it is pertinent to remember that, just as the dance section of *The Bridge* rehearses "Faustus and Helen," Part 2, the whole idea of that mythical marriage foreshadows the informing Gestalt of the later and longer poem. Love is a kind of "bridge," as "Atlantis" explicitly tries to show in its fiery hymnal. The remarkable triptych gives us woman in her different manifestations: Eve, Magdalen, and Mary, the mother of the race, the seducer, and the redeemer; sea, earth, and air.

In the first Song ("Southern Cross"), sung on a ship deck, there are memorable lines, like these:

> O simian Venus, homeless Eve,
> Unwedded, stumbling gardenless to grieve
> Windswept guitars on lonely decks forever;
> Finally to answer all within one grave!

Or these:

> I wanted you . . . The embers of the Cross
> Climbed by aslant and huddling aromatically

> It is blood to remember; it is fire
> To stammer back . . . It is
> God—your namelessness. And the wash—

The Southern Cross, setting in the ocean, symbolizes a twilight of Christianity, to be immediately followed (in the poem) by a rebirth of Eve from the sea as Venus Anadyomene:

> All night the water combed you with black
> Insolence. You crept out simmering, accomplished.
> Water rattled that stinging coil, your
> Rehearsed hair—docile, alas, from many arms.

The "stinging coil" of Eve's hair, "rattled" by water, evokes in a flash of simultaneity the reptilian Tempter, which will writhe in the burlesque sinuosities of dancing Magdalen in "National Winter Garden":

> Pearls whip her hips, a drench of whirling strands.
> Her silly snake rings begin to mount, surmount
> Each other—turquoise fakes on tinselled hands.
> We wait that writhing pool, her pearls collapsed, ...

Apart from the mastery of verse, Crane should be complimented here for having so effectively projected a scene drawn from a peculiar item of American marginal mores into the Gospel archetype. The result is a strange, irresistible poetry.

The third avatar of woman ("Virginia") is the commonplace New York typist, managing to maneuver her life between routine work and week-end temptations. She achieves a sudden transfiguration into the Virgin Mother, and as "cathedral Mary" and "blue-eyed Mary" she certainly echoes Columbus' vision:

> . . . O Madre Maria, still
> One ship of these thou grantest safe returning;
> Assure us through thy mantle's ageless blue!

Like Joyce, Crane seeks epiphany, the paradox illuminating the quotidian with a lightning from other skies; and that in itself is a "bridge" between workaday reality and the purest dream. This does much to connect the particular passage with the total network of the poem; and we have no trouble realizing that the sequence of the three feminine incarnations rehearses in a capsule the rhythm of human history as birth, sin, and redemption, from terrestrial paradise to exile on earth and final transfiguration. Faded as it is, there still lurks a spark of the spiritual archetype in degraded modern life; the Eliotic pattern of mythic-historical echoes is used with a Whitmanian faith in the possibilities of common man. Crane has overlooked no structural device to impart consistency to the three pieces and unify them with the rest of *The Bridge*; thus the final movement of "Virginia" inverts the process sketched by "Southern Cross," retrieving the sunken Cross from the depths of the sea to enshrine it as shining "Cathedral Mary." After the victory of flesh on vanished religion, the apotheosis of woman; and once again, woman is America.

"Quaker Hill," the sixth section, brings us back to earth and grazing cows, "awkward, ponderous and uncoy": we have thus another alternation effect comparable to the transition from "Cutty Sark" to "Cape Hatteras." Like "Cape Hatteras," this section is a letdown in terms of poetry, though much less blatant. In a sentimental tone mostly masked as tough satire, Crane voices concern for the degeneration of his America under the encroachment of ruthless speculators. Partial successes are still scored by lines like:

> This was the Promised Land, and still it is
> To the persuasive suburban land agent

In bootleg roadhouses where the gin fizz
Bubbles in time to Hollywood's new love-nest pageant.

The triumph of banality, the advertising noise of a nation converted to the cult of Mammon, offend our poet, who, with accents borrowed from Prufrock and Gerontion, is here denouncing the spiritual entropy of his world; and he mournfully invokes the shades of erstwhile inspiring presences:

In one last angelus lift throbbing throat—
Listen, transmuting silence with that stilly note

Of pain that Emily, that Isadora knew!

The mention of Emily Dickinson, vestal of poetry, echoes the previously discussed references to the Virgin Mary, while Isadora Duncan directly recalls the motif of Pocahontas's dance, subsequently vulgarized by the burlesque artist of "Three Songs," and thus makes us think of America's violated body. The wailing whippoorwill of the conclusion sings a nocturnal elegy to agrarian and pioneer America. Sadness and despair are the keynote of the section, and by frankly facing them Crane succeeds in passing on, with "The Tunnel," to one more stretch of valid poetry.

The descent described by "Quaker Hill" could find its conclusion only in the infernal world of New York's subway, where we meet the crowds of anonymous faces, the jumble of meaningless talk, the dehumanization of mass society. And here, like a new Dante, the poet, after paying his coin to Charon by dropping a dime into the turnstile slot, will get the phosphorescent epiphanies of hell: Poe's ghost. Poe is the infernal counterpart of Whitman, and also an implicit self-portrait of Crane in his revulsion from the daily life of business and professional copy writing. The demon that hurled Poe to death threatens also the humble Italian washerwoman who is returning home from her day's work; the shade of Columbus instantly appears behind her, evoked by a tactful adjective:

> And does the Daemon take you home, also,
> Wop washerwoman, with the bandaged hair?
> After the corridors are swept, the cuspidors—
> The gaunt sky-barracks cleanly now, and bare,
> O *Genoese,* do you bring mother eyes and hands
> Back home to children and to golden hair?
> [Italics mine—*G.C.*]

Thus the descent to hell, prepared by seminal hints in the proem, "Cutty Sark," and "Three Songs," redevelops with antiphonal contrast the central motifs of the whole poem; Crane's private despair becomes a dominant climate, and the subway is revealed as the mind's inferno:

> The phonographs of hades in the brain
> Are tunnels that re-wind themselves, and love
> A burnt match skating in a urinal— . . . .

The sorcery of analogy conjures Poe's apparition in a place that is at the same time of the city and of the mind:

> Whose body smokes along the bitten rails,
> Bursts from a smoldering bundle far behind
> In back forks of the chasms of the brain,—
> Puffs from a riven stump far out behind
> In interborough fissures of the mind . . . ?

The metaphysical fusion of thought and reality, of psychic and urban physiognomy, achieves here its own kind of perfection and enables us to claim for Hart Crane a place with great poets of the century, in these intermittent climaxes of his; has Eliot given us a more convincing image of hell?

Eliot has approached hell with detachment, and perhaps with greater consistency, by rendering it in a portrayal of total sterility; Crane instead, in his own more uneven way, has entered it by direct participation, and he feels it rather as chaotic turmoil (in the style of Blake) than as dead barrenness. Both Eliot and Crane bear witness to a struggle against the alienation they sensed in and around themselves; but each gets the hell he deserves and uses his own kind of weapons, and the difference is important. Crane attempts a resurrection from his seething variety of Hades at the end of "The Tunnel," envisaging himself as a Lazarus of the industrial world. Through wavering faith in the power of his own poetry ("shrill ganglia/ impassioned with some song we fail to keep") he knows the worst agony, but finally manages to re-emerge to the free air of the harbor. The concluding lines belong to his achievement, with their tactile sensibility:

> I counted the echoes assembling, one after one,
> Searching, thumbing the midnight on the piers.
> Lights, coasting, left the oily tympanum of waters;
> The blackness somewhere gouged glass on a sky.
> And this thy harbor, O my City, I have driven under,
> Tossed from the coil of ticking towers. . . . Tomorrow,
> And to be. . . . Here by the River that is East—
> Here at the waters' edge the hands drop memory;
> Shadowless in that abyss they unaccounting lie.[28]

It is now midnight, the rhapsody having completed its cycle from the "harbor dawn" in a way that rehearses and expands the analogous movement of the proem; the poet is looking for light and a guidance, and knowing himself to be in direct competition with that inspiring model, Eliot, he caps the section with lines echoing "Death by Fire":

> Kiss of our agony Thou gatherest,
> O Hand of Fire
> gatherest. . . .

In the same way, "The River" paid tribute with a rapid allusion to the Phlebas of "Death by Water":

> . . . sliding prone
> Like one whose eyes were buried long ago.

Crane's avowed enthusiasm for Eliot's mastery of non-narrative poetry went hand in hand with his reaction against the Wasteland image of reality to produce an ambivalent response to the older writer's lines. It is interesting indeed to see Eliot's technical lesson so profitably received by such a temperamentally different artist.

The resurrection of the word through love, which was Crane's desperate yearning throughout his life, is then the real theme of "Atlantis," *The Bridge's* epilogue. Aesthetically speaking it exhibits both his visionary power and his strained verbal excesses; the several reworkings, which Weber documents in the worksheet facsimiles appended to his monograph, did not quite manage to purify this language of accumulated paroxysm. It certainly speaks for Crane's commitment to his theme; he fought with all his strength to retain something comparable to Columbus' faith in the future of America in the face of harrowing doubts. And it shows a powerful effort to master a formidable subject; the mark of genius is to be found, unmistakable, in this forest of baroque exclamations. By a chain-reaction process we have been tracing all along, the title object of the rhapsody becomes an "unspeakable . . . Bridge to Thee, O Love," and, as in the proem, a personified presence invested with divine attributes. Indeed, when we review the epithets and addresses ("whitest Flower," "Giver of all answers," "Anemone," etc.) we clearly see that the bridge is meant to be taken as God, the All-encompassing. Since, however, the poet keeps a marked initial focus on the metal structure as such, that exaltation may remain a bit gratuitous, and the new god risks degenerating into an idol, despite all the reasons to be pleaded for this supreme metaphorical expansion. We have no trouble understanding how the bridge can become the act of bridging, and by symbolic implication the experience of spiritual totality; but when this experience in its turn is hypostasized into a divine Interlocutor, the original iron bridge has or should have been left far behind. It should have been used as a bridge, i.e., really transcended, but Crane does not make that clear. At any rate, one of its manifestations is Atlantis, the mythical counterpart of Cathay, the never-never America that, by disappearing into the depths of the ocean, cleared the way to the real America. Atlantis also connotes death by water and an ideal resurrection of the poet in his song for future America, and it supplies an apt name for the "American Dream" as the dream of all mankind. Finally, America is a geographic bridge between two oceans, between Asia and Europe, between past and future.

To this crowning vision the poet immolates himself in one more ritual death, which closely recalls the love-death[29] complex of "Voyages" and thereby forecasts that final leap into the sea from the deck of the *Orizaba*. From a personal angle, Atlantis, Cathay, the East are all geographic symbols of the paradise Crane craved for, and this paradise was to be sought not in the concrete realities of America, but in his own private experience of destruction as fulfillment, of death as love and vice versa. This, however, does not easily blend with the public prophecy of the poem, even though we are supposed to connect the Columbus-echoed vision of future glory and abundance and human accomplishments in America with the sacrificial death of the singer, who was here trying to confess and transfigure, by relating it to a promise of increased happiness for his fellow men, his own tragic disintegration. He saw himself as Dionysus, and by recapitulating in a wheel of incandescence the main leitmotivs of the rhapsody he projected beyond time and space the solution of his personal and social problems. The actual relevance of this ecstasy to the historical aspect of his theme, America, is dubious, yet the climax brings to a forceful consummation the earlier dionysian thrusts of Columbus, Maquokeeta, the crashing airman, Poe, and the subway traveler:

> So to thine Everpresence, beyond time,
> Like spears ensanguined of one tolling star
> That bleeds infinity—the orphic strings,
> Sidereal phalanxes, leap and converge:
> —One Song, one Bridge of Fire! Is it Cathay,
> Now pity steeps the grass and rainbows ring
> The serpent with the eagle in the leaves . . . ?
> Whispers antiphonal in azure swing.

The individual poet committed to the myth of America as the next creative leap in human history felt, after all, the need to go beyond history; he expressed this paradox by repeating the gesture of Melville's Taji, who leaves Mardi behind to venture into the ultimate ocean, with strong accruing echoes of Whitman's "Passage to India." But even though all the "many twain," the rending conflicts of vision and life, are supposed to be finally *bridged* here, we have persisting doubts. Crane's intoxication with the myth at times merely seems to cover disappointment and despair instead of resolving them.

Certainly the American cult of experience, brought by Crane to the point of paroxysm, counts for something in his repeated striving for ecstasy through orgy, and the dream of deliverance from time, memory, and the "curse of sundered parentage" has a deep existential motivation that helps us to understand his interest in Ouspensky's cosmology. Time can be consumed by dionysian Faustus to such an extent that it will be annulled into permanence, at the ultimate cost of death. One of the important aspects of *The Bridge* is the effort to perceive time spatially, for space is the realm of permanence; an apt comment on Crane's poem might be furnished by the intense pages that Charles Olson devotes to Melville's (and America's) sense of space.[30] Olson, without referring to Crane, even goes to the extent of saying that the basic act of this civilization, externally taken, is "a BRIDGE." In many American writers besides Melville and Crane the spatial expansion of consciousness as an imaginative endeavor to include most of available reality in a sphere of co-presence to be ranged at will finds recurrent expression in the myth of the Orient. Emerson, Thoreau contemplating the "confluence of Walden and Ganges," Ezra Pound seeking in the Chinese ideogram the visual-literary means of spatializing thought, have all provided antecedents to the "Ever-presence" of "Atlantis."

Thus the bridge is grasped from the very start as a *voyage,* a spatially realized and ever-present act of *spanning*; a dynamized object, an arrested, perpetuated temporal gesture. The serpent-eagle heraldry that permeates and caps the rhapsody points to its four-dimensional setting: *The Bridge* takes place in Einstein's space-time, which is used throughout as a form of perception. It would be hard to conceive of a more interesting ambition for the modern rhapsodist.

As for the existential anguish that sought deliverance in this fulfilling perspective through an imaginatively rehearsed ritual of death and resurrection, it is easy to find its counterparts in much modern Western literature, but it is even more important to consider it as the germinal link between *The Bridge* and the rest of Crane's work, lest we be tempted to discount the major effort as an unacceptably "official" undertaking severed from the genuine roots and interests of our poet. If *The Bridge* is such a ritual, the same is true of most of Crane's other poems, in which its dominant motifs are clearly discernible. The incisive lines of "Legend" are a preface to all of Crane's career:

> It is to be learned—
> This cleaving and this burning,
> But only by the one who
> Spends out himself again.

"Chaplinesque," a lyric whose sentimental ending cannot obscure the culminant epiphany, is aptly defined by its own author as a "pantomime"[31] that represents the frustrations of the poet in contemporary society, particularly American. The pantomime reflects the Grail legend; if the Grail is an "empty ash-can" illuminated by the moon, and the Pure Fool engaged in its quest a sentimental clown à la Laforgue, this shows our world's degeneration. At the same time, it is a brave clown who fights the entropy of values; while Eliot's analogous linkages of past and present, myth and chronicle, in his *Waste Land* phase invariably stress the irreversible deterioration of Western society, Crane fights back and tries to recapture the elusive glow in the very thick of our scrap-heap. In Crane's poem, the eerie light of the moon does much more than unmask the hopelessness of our culture, for it enacts a transfiguration:

> . . . but we have seen
> The moon in lonely alleys make
> A grail of laughter of an empty ashcan. . . .

That laughter is dionysian, not satirical; it flares up from the imagination's moonlight chemistry, forever striving to transmute opacity and ugliness into transparence. But it begins where it should, at the very bottom of our moral abyss. Despair and counterbalancing recovery are thus joined in a uniquely vivid flash of vision, which the knightly clown cannot yet share with his fellow men. The effort to broaden that painful privacy into achieved communion accounts for Crane's lifelong suffering and frenzy, as well as for the writing of *The Bridge,* the hoped-for final resolution.

"For the Marriage of Faustus and Helen," as has been observed before, is a first sustained embodiment of *The Bridge,* celebrating the desire of modern man to consummate a new union with lost beauty in a world impervious to it. Crane's letter to Gorham Munson of January 14, 1923, gives the main clues to the difficult paean, whose triadic movement seeks a final ecstasy beyond love, dance, and the destruction of war:

> Distinctly praise the years, whose volatile
> Blamed bleeding hands extend and thresh the height
> The imagination spans beyond despair,
> Outpacing bargain, vocable and prayer.

In this somewhat tortured and cluttered epilogue the focal verb "span," predicated of the imagination, cannot escape our notice, for it recapitulates the entire poem and foreshadows *The Bridge.*

The ritual of liberation or redemption motivates many other outstanding poems in *White Buildings*: "Possessions," "Lachrymae Christi," "Passage," "The Wine Menagerie," and "Recitative," all directly related to central aspects of *The Bridge* itself and sometimes marred by the obscurities of a strained language, but also illuminated by lightnings of concentrated vision. "Possessions" condenses the materiality of blood in an emblematic "stone of lust" that the poet holds up to the light in order to make it transparent. This transparency will come at the end in the form of a

> . . . pure possession, the inclusive cloud
> whose heart is fire . . . , —the white wind. . . .

as the advent of poetry, but incandescent vision will have to be paid for by a ritual sacrifice of the poet himself:

> Tossed on these horns, who bleeding dies,
> Lacks all but piteous admissions to be spilt
> Upon the page whose blind sum finally burns
> Record of rage and final appetites.

The poet must give all he has, and then, instead of just "possessing" his amulet, he will be possessed by the fire of illumination and thereby "possess" a shared gem surpassing all material rubies. The Dionysian transfiguration of animal desire and violence into pure vision involves him in an act of self-donation that is *inclusive* despite its privateness. The relation of the artist to his fellow citizens of a smoky and turmoiling town resembles that of Columbus to his loyal patrons and to his envisioned posterity; the acrobatic play on jewel imagery clinches this affinity between "Possessions" and "Ave Maria."

"Lachrymae Christi," one of Crane's most hermetically powerful statements in its convoluted mannerism, sings the triumph of the Nazarene on the sphinx-like opacities of our factory world. The resolving image is a vertical outburst à la El Greco: Christ raises the Grail of the earth, thereby developing in cosmic dimension the key motif of "Chaplinesque," and by converting his tears into a demonic, but redemptive, smile identifies himself with Dionysus and indeed with the whole force of self-transcending life. Since Lachrymae Christi is a wine, the identity was of course implicit from the start in the title itself. The Redeemer, who has fire along with "tenderness" in his "Nazarene and tinder eyes. . . ," has absorbed in his figure the Parsifal-clown of the thematically related poem, and thus projects the identity of the poet into that of a sacrificial god. But in the process the person of Crane has been submerged in the godlike persona, who appears as an Interlocutor conjured from the depth of his own soul. Life, capable of immortality through death and rebirth, is set over against the undying-unliving stoniness of a manufactured reality. A rare imaginative thrust identifies the sinister imperviousness of the factory by night with the finally cracked secrecy of the Sphinx, of the Pyramids (connected with the Christlike Osiris) and of Christ's own sepulcher. A strange animistic touch closes the circuit by attributing to the ominously quiet machinery crouching inside the factory the "smile" we inevitably associate with the (later mentioned) Sphinx, and when this smile lightens the face of Dionysian Jesus, it has been transfigured. The continuity of the metaphor suggests that the Redeemer's victory can be achieved not by ignoring evil, but by transforming its negativity into the positive. Few poets, to be sure, have attempted so much without indulging in the concessions of rational comment. A further trait to be observed in "Lachrymae Christi," "Possessions," and "Chaplinesque" is that the dreamed transfiguration takes place by night; the rights of the imagination in our busy world can be asserted only in secret, waiting for a more propitious chance.

"Passage" celebrates, in coded language, the struggle with time, the release from memory, that we have seen to occur in *The Bridge* from the Rip Van Winkle episode onward. The initial stanza gives us the clue to this, as a rebirth of innocence:

> Where the cedar leaf divides the sky
> I heard the sea.

> In sapphire arenas of the hills
> I was promised an improved infancy.

We have then the passage of Lethe:

> My memory I left in a ravine,—

The poet longs for release from the "chimney-sooted heart of man" and meets a hostile other self in the person of a thief holding his own book. An utterly cryptical conversation ensues, having somehow to do with man's predicament in transitoriness; catharsis takes place when time is annulled in the sun of ecstasy, in symbols familiar enough to the reader of *The Bridge*:

> A serpent swam a vertex to the sun
> —On unpaced beaches leaned its tongue and drummed.
> What fountains did I hear? what icy speeches?
> Memory, committed to the page, had broke.

The mystical breakdown of memory is rendered in a line strangely akin to Dante's "All'alta fantasia qui mancò possa" in the conclusion of *Paradiso,* where the spiritual context is not dissimilar from Crane's own in the present poem; and the over-all analogy with Dante's *Purgatorio,* involving a purifying process and release from the memory of sins, is as remarkable as the modern poet's use of a hieratically emblematic language that in itself makes the parallelism with the *Divine Comedy*'s second and third Canticles worth stressing, even though we know from Crane's letters that his direct acquaintance with Dante's work dates from a later stage of his life. It was hardly possible for Crane to respond to Dante as he did, and to write a poem titled "Purgatorio" with autobiographical intention, if something like an elective affinity had not been there from the start—an affinity that Eliot's writing and Allen Tate's friendship surely did everything to strengthen. The non-Dantean side of Crane, his orgiastic pantheism, is so obvious that it needs no emphasis, and yet it did not prevent his major work, *The Bridge,* from articulating itself in a Dantesque structural sequence of hell-purgatory-paradise.

Dionysian redemption through orgy and ecstasy informs "The Wine Menagerie," which connects with "Lachrymae Christi" by stating that "wine redeems the sight." The demonic nature of this process is revealed by the hallucinatory animals inhabiting the poem, the first of which was notoriously hitched by Greek myth to the chariot of the wine god:

> A leopard ranging always in the brow
> Asserts a vision in the slumbering gaze.

After the Bacchic leopard, we shall find in this strange zoo also the familiar snake of Time:

> What is it in this heap the serpent pries—
> Whose skin, facsimile of time, unskeins
> Octagon, sapphire transepts round the eyes; . . .

Intoxication brings about the discovery of new spiritual worlds:

> New thresholds, new anatomies! Wine talons[32]
> Build freedom up about me and distill
> This competence—to travel in a tear
> Sparkling alone, within another's will.

Blackmur praises the metaphysical boldness of "new thresholds, new anatomies" and the ensuing projection of macrocosmic movement into a tear, but he objects to the verbal straining of ideas involved in an expression like "wine talons." Crane loved composite imagery, and most of his poems are built on a progressive condensation of initially heterogeneous elements to achieve a finally heightened perception, but in so doing he sometimes fell into obscurity or artifice, despite the sincere motivation of each poem. We must admit that this happens locally in "Wine Menagerie," however amenable we may be to the higher degree of violence that accrues to words and images from the theme of Dionysian hallucination. The idea of "wine talons," like others in this poem, verges on abstraction; it finds a partial support in the title itself, in the previously introduced leopard, in the eagles implied by the expression "feathered skies," but remains dangerously close to verbal jugglery even if we accept it as a telescoped synthesis of former motifs, to be taken psychologically and tactilely rather than visually. The introduction of "distill" in the immediate context does not help, because it tilts the scales too much toward an overflowing liquidity.

It is not easy to descry each thematic nexus in this Cubist-like poem, but it seems to find a focus in the idea of deliverance from worldly passion through poetry. This liberation is achieved first by surrendering to the promptings of visionary drunkenness, then by passionate participation in other lives, and then by detachment, since the poet, parading like a Petrushka who recalls closely the delicate clown of "Chaplinesque," finally walks out of the ambiguous trap of love and jealousy to resume his "exile" at the suggestion of his own inner voice. Crane's devotion to art combines with his homosexual urge in portraying his male friend as the victim of an imperious woman (stanzas 3 and 5), endowed with cruel eyes ("mallets"), who ends up symbolically beheading the man, since in stanza 10 specific mention is made of Holophernes and John the Baptist. The inner voice's exhortation to "walk away, stepping over Holophernes' shins" sounds like a clear warning to the speaker of the poem about the destiny that threatens him if he refuses to disentangle himself from the equivocal situation, and this might throw some further light on the role of Judith-Salome. Not all the animals of the "wine menagerie" are favorable and Dionysian; some may well be boarlike victims of Circe (woman as such), whose charms are insidious:

> Between black tusks the roses shine!

The ambiguity parallels the one of "Lachrymae Christi," where both Christ-Dionysus and his enemy the Sphinx smile. But "Wine Menagerie," interesting as it is for psychological insight and experiment in diction, fails to achieve the strength and consistency of the other poem.

"Recitative" tells the intimate split in the poet's soul between joy and sorrow, darkness and light, in an alienated world; here Christ and Dionysus are not reconciled, Crane is "Janus-faced" in unhealed doubleness, and he feels the need to leave the Babel tower of New York's industrial world:

> The highest tower, —let her ribs palisade
> Wrenched gold of Nineveh; —yet leave the tower . . . .

This deliverance from the world of chaotic sterility and greed, which Crane probably identifies with his father, is glimpsed in the sight of a bridge—and we need not stress its central relevance to the rest of Crane's work:

> The bridge swings over salvage, beyond wharves;
> A wind abides the ensign of your will.

After this, a real release will occur in the form of time condensed and spatialized:

> In alternating bells have you not heard
> All hours clapped dense into a single stride?

A victory over time, obtained by sheer intensity of spiritual experience, means a temporary overcoming of death and materiality.

Often the prismatically angular language of these poems betrays the effort of exercise. "Voyages," also included in the *White Buildings* collection, evinces more abandon, in a medium on the whole less contrived though not entirely untainted by mannered affectations like "fragrance irrefragibly." It has been closely discussed by H. C. Morris and others, and its connection with *The Bridge* resides in the general theme of love, death, and the sea, best focused in parts No. II, III, and VI; in the last one a memorable vision of sea-born Aphrodite as crown of the cosmos and luminous Word reminds us more particularly of "Atlantis." Purification through death by water motivates the hermetic "At Melville's Tomb," one of Crane's best-known poems, where the sharply contracted imagery works in a magic way, sustained by a majestic amplitude of diction. The *Key West* group contains noteworthy pieces, of which the title poem plays autobiographically on the theme of alienation, accusing father and mother:

> Here has my salient faith annealed me.
> Out of the valley, past the ample crib
> To skies impartial, that do not disown me
> Nor claim me, either, by Adam's spine—nor rib. . . .

The conquered freedom from oppressive or unresponsive parents is exercised in a travel to "Heaven or Hades," tropically embodied, but the concluding note is one of despair, for apparently the industrial world of Father is taking over the world:

> O, steel and stone! But gold was, scarcity before.
> And here is water, and a little wind. . . .

> There is no breath of friends and no more shore
> Where gold has not been sold and conscience tinned.

In "O Carib Isle!" the alienation appears as sun-hot sand ranged by poisonous or carapaced animals, and the poet tries to conquer it by a magic of fertility:

> To the white sand I may speak a name, fertile
> Albeit in a strange tongue.

Naturally it will be the magic of the word, the only wizardry a poet can really trust, but the outcome is negative, for the wind dies down, syllables fail, and the only thing left for him to do is to invoke Satan, destruction:

> You have given me the shell, Satan, —carbonic amulet
> Sere of the sun exploded in the sea.

This is a tightly woven composition, couched in a more direct and relaxed diction than most of Crane's poems exhibit, and its alliance of depth with visual vividness recommends it to the exacting reader.

"The Mermen" repeats the motif of the first of "Three Songs": the Cross sinking into the sea, but here rising again from the waves with the face of Christ:

> This Cross, agleam still with a human face!

"A Name for All" rejects the distorting labels of human language to sanctify in a Franciscan vein the non-human existences, supposedly in closer touch with an indwelling God. "Royal Palm," thickly constellated with religious images, rivals Valéry's analogous poem in dramatizing the slim desert tree as a triumph over sterility and an ascent into light, and we would consider it as a triumph of poetry, unjustly ignored by almost every critic so far. The address to Emily Dickinson deserves likewise more attention than it has received, and "The Air Plant" shows Crane's baroque vein to its best advantage. Here we have a dionysian plant, conjurer of hurricanes and demonic in shape, to contrast the complementary vision of the palm tree as an Apollonian dramatis persona; and if "Royal Palm" recalls Valéry in some respects, "The Air Plant" parallels both theme and style of García Lorca's "Agave."

"Imperator Victus" drastically restates a tragic alternative ("the Dollar and the Cross"); "The Broken Tower" once again presents, in baroque language, the ritual of the poet who conquers hell by effusing himself in the word:

> . . . —to wander the cathedral lawn
> From pit to crucifix, feet chill on steps from hell.

"The Phantom Bark" contains an intimation of death by drowning:

> So dream thy sails, O phantom bark
> That I thy drownèd man may speak again. . . .

but the boat of death will allow the poet to be resurrected in the word, past all shame and disappointment (the "breath of males/ imprisoned never. . . ."). "A Traveler Born" identifies memory with hell and sin; "Enrich My Resignation" invokes the destruction of time under the sign of Dionysus, longing for the "peace of the fathers":

> Die, oh, centuries, die, as Dionysus said,
> Yet live in all my resignation. . . .

"The Circumstance" likewise dreams of stopping time; "The Visible the Untrue" is an elegy on caducity ("And it is always the day, the day of unkind farewell") even though it envisages an "eternal rainbow" that hints at the emblematic values of the bridge; "Reliquary" and "Purgatorio" struggle once more with time and exile; "The Return" yearns for re-immersion in the "natal bosom" of the sea.

From the analysis and summary that I have essayed here so far it should be possible to trace in the body of Crane's verse certain recognizable constants and variables (sometimes bordering on idiosyncrasy) that mark it as his own; but others remain to be pointed out, and their ubiquity makes them indispensable for a fuller understanding of the nature of his language. We have seen how Melvillian motifs permeate Crane's poetry: the sailor figure, the emblematic animals, the erotically mythicized sea, the whirlpool that appears as "calyx of death's bounty" in "At Melville's Tomb" and as "vortex of our grave" in "Voyages II." But a more capillary motif predominates to the extent of becoming obsessive, infused as it is in the minutest tissues of Crane's verse both as a sheerly pictorial and as a vastly symbolic element: the note of whiteness.

We might say it is lacking in none of Crane's poems, as witness the bewitchingly white albatross of "Voyages IV," the ecstatic "Whitest Flower" of "Atlantis," the "antarctic blaze" of "Paraphrase," the consuming "white wind" of "Possessions," the lunar "white rinsings" of "Lachrymae Christi," or the repulsive, funereal whiteness of *White Buildings.* The vision of Helen, in the first section of "Faustus and Helen," is lily-white, and a turn of verbal inventiveness effectively contrasts it with the sepulchral whiteness of cities:

> White, through white cities passed on to assume
> That world which comes to each of us alone.

Strange white shadows haunt the dance of "Faustus and Helen II;" white is the color of love in "Atlantis," white the purity of

Magdalen's skin in "National Winter Garden," white the Arctic, and white the juke box in "Cutty Sark." And again, the sails of evoked ships are heraldically white; the poet himself becomes a white meteor in the instant of ritual death at the climax of the Pocahontas dance, and in the "Harbor Dawn" there gleam synaesthetic "white surplices of gongs." The quotations could go on for a long time to make an impressive list.

Now, without thereby making Crane's poetry derivative, we can find a clue to his chromatic idiosyncrasy in the much-discussed chapter of *Moby Dick* that dwells on "the whiteness of the whale." The color white, if one keeps in mind bones, shrouds, and gravestones, can have funereal connotations, or it can evoke the idea of purity, or again of light, of totality and joy. In all of these cases, however, it is the "objective correlative" of a threshhold-experience, the experience of absoluteness. Crane, through the language of paroxysm, repeatedly sought to cross that threshold, in a total experience that would annihilate sequential time and thus transcend history itself. Shipwreck was the foreseen price, as it was for Captain Ahab. Death is white, ecstasy is white, and so is the fusion of space and time in the final vision of the bridge that condenses in itself the whole gamut of possible experience. Crane lived at white heat, ultimately to be burned out in his own quest. God is also death.

Another pervasive unit of Crane's linguistic code is the eye. His lines are eye-ridden: Pierrot has "everlasting" eyes in the memorable "Praise for an Urn," the lover has "broken eyes" in "Stark Major," the Redeemer of "Lachrymae Christi" glows with "tinder eyes," "Wine Menagerie" exhibits eyes clarified by liquor and eyes destructively hammering away like "mallets," "Recitative" mentions restless "eyes at search." In "Faustus and Helen I" we find the "half-riant" eyes of Helen and the "million brittle, bloodshot eyes" of the crowd, next to the "lone eye" of the poet; in "At Melville's Tomb" there are magical "frosted eyes . . . that lifted altars," while "Voyages IV" mirrors in the eyes of the loved one the "blue latitudes" of the ocean, and "lost morning eyes" of vanished swimmers re-emerge from the surf in "Voyages VI." And again, the "buried" eyes of "The River," the seawater eyes of the sailor in "Cutty Sark," the agate eyes of Poe in "The Tunnel" next to the motherly eyes of the 'wop washerwoman," and the tactile eyes of hawk and worm in "Quaker Hill."

The eye is vision, and Crane assimilated Rimbaud's theory of the poet as seer, but it would be wrong to make it a matter of one-sided derivation. Emerson was no less congenial a source when he wrote that "the light of the body is the eye" and defined the (physical) power of vision as the most remarkable magic of man; indeed, when in a rapturous moment of contemplation he felt changed into a "transparent eyeball" reflecting and absorbing the universe, he gave additional nourishment to Crane's imagination, and the fruits are to be seen in the "glowing orb of praise" that caps "Faustus and Helen," Part I, with an abstract self-portrait of the poet. Matthiessen in his *American Renaissance,* and Feidelson in his *Symbolism and American Literature,* have elaborated persuasively enough on the importance of the eye in the nineteenth-century American classics, and I would like to recall in particular Feidelson's statement that Emerson and Thoreau "lived as eye," to clinch my point with regard to Crane. The point could be extended to include in an American scope the poetry of Wallace Stevens, which Crane also read with deep interest.

For the poet of *The Bridge,* the eye is the organ of spatial dominion, an attribute of the eagle, and it alternates with the hand, which recurs as an organ of close, tactile possession, although the eye itself at times comes to be invested with tactile powers, in the tendentially synaesthetic world of this visionary poetry. Besides, the spherical shape of the eye makes it a geometrically perfect microcosm that implies the rounded inclusiveness of the (Einsteinian) whole. But the organ of sight is capable of a further metamorphic surprise. It concentrates such an intense power that it becomes a star, symbolizing the transfiguration of the poet. We can follow this transformation through Crane's poetry, from the "tinder eyes" of Jesus to the "lone eye riveted" to Helen's "plane," and instantly enkindled into "one inconspicuous, glowing orb of praise," and the imaginative culmination is reached in the finale of "Atlantis" with the "spears ensanguined of one tolling star." The musical body of light in space is here the Word, the very essence of the poet, and it bleeds like Christ under Longinus' spear (the sacrifice of "Possessions" would provide a clear antecedent). Thus the image drawn from Blake takes on a special value in Hart Crane, for in terms of this climactic metaphor the seer's eye does more than encompass reality, it transfigures it by pervading it with a heavenly blood of light. The religious leanings of Crane's language are thus fulfilled in his own way, and the fulfillment is such that, once his shortcomings have been duly discounted, it warrants his literary resurrection in our memory from the waters into which he plunged to extinction, that April day of 1932.

Five / *William Carlos Williams' "Paterson" as the Drama of Integrity*

"SAY[1] IT, no ideas but in things." This recurrent motto announces from the very beginning of *Paterson* the "objectivist" poetics of Dr. William Carlos Williams, and it partly accounts for Ezra Pound's friendship, so unmistakably documented by the declarations of affectionate esteem to be found in the latter poet's *Cantos* and *Letters*. Pound's early influence on Williams is well known, and Williams himself makes no effort to disown his literary debt to the turbulent friend whose fruitful lesson is visible in both the structure and the style of the ambitious four-book epic that was completed in 1951. But this work which came to enrich a modern Anglo-American tradition that includes the *Cantos, The Waste Land,* Hart Crane's *The Bridge,* and Archibald MacLeish's *Conquistador,* cannot be explained as a simple derivative outgrowth of Pound's own experiments.

For the Rutherford, New Jersey, doctor owes his poetics and poetry primarily to himself. His lifelong experience as a practitioner of medicine counts for something in his development as a writer who puts directness and honesty first in his questioning portrayal of reality. Compare the characteristic bluntness of his style with Stevens' acrobatic subtleties, and you will realize that two different types of searching are involved, one aesthetically connected with the lawyer's verbal casuistry and the other with the doctor's concern for biological facts and diagnostic truth. Having grown up in New Jersey's industrialized environment, the

Rutherford poet-doctor has been able to scrutinize at ease an America afflicted by the strong growth fever that invited disquieting comparison with Europe's altogether different crisis. The author of *Paterson* is used to the courage of truth. His raw straightforwardness goes back to the same source that originated pragmatism and the New Deal. We see, then, how his postulate of integrity with regard to language reflects much more than an obvious indebtedness to Pound's imagism and its peremptory "don'ts," for it voices the virile attitude of pioneer America, a hatred for compromise, a will to face things squarely even at the price of forfeiting nuance. With such a background, which the medical profession did everything to enhance, Williams recognized an ally in vociferous Ezra; intolerance for literary frills and for the seduction of gratuitous music was their common battle cry and their heartfelt practice.

The cult of integrity is the very essence of the cultural heritage that the Puritan fathers bequeathed to modern Americans, even though thinned down through many generations; and without it we could not understand Pound's belligerence, Gertrude Stein's experimental daring, Hemingway's clipped style and tough philosophy, Faulkner's prophetic cruelty, Dos Passos' radical writing, Dewey's drastically reductive thought. It can impel its devotees to extreme gestures, including political repudiation—witness John Reed's involvement in a world-shaking experience, and his ancestor Thoreau's private secession; or see what Emerson had to say on the exploitation of slave labor in his essay on "American Civilization," and on the necessity for a functional art, stripped of decorative superstructures whether of words or of architectural ornament, in "Art and Criticism." Impatience is sometimes translated into suicide, more often into exile; the American rebel does not settle for compromise, either in life or in literature, and he may have to pay very dearly for it.

Rawness can be the price of such a violently sought answer, and its marks are clear in much of what Dr. Williams wrote; *Paterson* itself, and the two volumes of his *Collected Poems,* afford abundant evidence. Here blunt realism and dare-devil experimentation never make concessions to decadent aestheticism. Although Williams has visited France and breathed the heady air of Montparnasse, he has used the intellectual stimulation to strengthen his purity rather than to indulge in exquisite word play. The bluntness becomes easy to forgive when one realizes the underlying honesty.

If honesty is a starting point, integrity is a conquest; seen in this light, Williams' creative career takes on a dramatic quality, unfolding as it does from the early episodic or fragmentary lyrics to the expressionist acme of *Paterson.* After that massive, nearly chaotic, statement of crisis, *Desert Music* opens a calmer vein, almost a Franciscan idyll with nature (one of the last compositions is indeed dedicated to the Assisi saint, and another, provisionally titled "Work in Progress,"[2] tells the joys of living and of self-expression). *Paterson* therefore has a decisive value for us as the crucial phase of Williams' poetry, which happens to be one crucial attempt in modern American writing. *Paterson* constitutes the supreme endeavor of the poet at self-integration, after the vivid *aperçus* of so many short poems; one might say it is the enterprise to which he had pledged himself in lyrical statements like "A Sort of a Song":

> Let the snake wait under
> his weed
> and the writing
> be of words, slow and quick, sharp
> to strike, quiet to wait
> sleepless.
>
> —through metaphor to reconcile
> the people and the stones.

> Compose. (No ideas
> but in things) Invent!
> Saxifrage is my flower that splits
> the rocks.

For *Paterson* does try to "reconcile the people and the stones" by identifying man and city through a multivalent symbolism of Joycean type. Williams' admiration for Joyce is documented by the essay he contributed to an early symposium on *Finnegans Wake,*[3] and the latter book's use of topography to match the dramatis personae is reflected in the American writer's long poem. Just as, in *Finnegans Wake,* the hill of Howth is the hero H.C.E. and the river Liffey embodies his wife Anna Livia Plurabelle, in Williams' epic Paterson lives simultaneously as an individual man, as a city of New Jersey, and as a cliff on the Passaic river's falls, while his complementing antagonist is woman seen as the river's water. But Paterson is also the poet in his effort to redeem life through language, and in still another aspect he is industrial America ravaged by greedy latter-day generations, the land ravished and not married, deprived of language, of love, threatened by the material hypertrophy that prevents the harmony of an organic development. In the "hard core of beauty" the poet has compressed his anxious concern as an enlightened patriot, better, as a Westerner who cherishes no delusions about the dangers of power. Jeffers' historical pessimism comes here to mind.

But one should read *Paterson* also against the background of *In the American Grain,* the lively essays Williams published in 1925 to dramatize American history as the story of an unconsummated marriage between the land and its various conquerors, from the ephemeral Vikings to the all-too-sensitive Latins, whether Spanish or French, who failed to dominate the land because of their very sensitiveness, down to the narrow-minded, if virile,

Anglo-Saxon Puritans, who failed for the opposite reason, since their moral stubbornness prevented them from loving and understanding the country; they could merely impose themselves on it and fight its primitive inhabitants. This quarrel between the aesthetic and the ethico-pragmatic sense, as embodied respectively in Latins and Northerners, explains why America was either courted or raped by her several suitors, but never wedded—though Williams sees glimpses of hope in solitary figures like Franklin or Daniel Boone. Since Williams' approach accounts for Anglo-Saxon dominance in North America as a result of natural selectivity at the expense of "weaker," if more sensitive and imaginative, European stocks, it is easy to recognize in his mythology of American history another formulation of the dilemma that preoccupied and inspired such different predecessors as Melville, Hawthorne, and Henry James. The dilemma is indeed rooted in his personal existence, which he owes to the spark-striking combination of a typical English father and a lively Latin mother. American history, American problems, are thus identical with Williams' ideal autobiography; the accident of his birth afforded him a direct, shocking confrontation with the basic issues of American history, which, being a poet, he could not help translating into myth.

America as a civilization in the making, then, is the central theme of Williams,[4] who, after presenting in his mythological way what he considers the facts of the case in 1925, now asks the urgent question: Is marriage still possible between Americans and America? or, to paraphrase it unmythologically: Granted our pioneer start, is real civilization still attainable? Can we "integrate" with our land? And with ourselves? *Paterson* is this cry of alarm, and it springs from *In the American Grain* as directly as a whole section of Crane's *The Bridge* did before. In *Paterson* we see Dr. Williams taking the pulse of America, the perennial betrothed, whose (industrial) fever seems to have aggravated those early disabilities, Puritan asperity and pioneer crudeness. Aesthetically anemic, materially apoplectic; is this to be America's destiny?

It is, then, a problem of spiritual "opening up," of achieving ripeness, and this is where Williams focuses his inquiry, this is the center of his historical awareness. For America, the final reckoning has not yet come, or rather, it comes every day; the major hope lies in a victory of American man over himself and his own power —since the physical environment is by now safely conquered. *Paterson* voices this preoccupation in a way that reminds one of the concern of William Faulkner when dealing with the myth of the nemesis visited by history on the latter-day descendants of those who despoiled and alienated the land; though Faulkner's prejudice against Yankee industrialism does not quite check with Williams' critique. But we cannot help noticing how strongly history is felt by the polemically anti-historical writers of America, if by history one understands a living issue bequeathed to us by the past, a direct concern of our society, and not a simple matter of erudite knowledge. Nothing could be more American than Williams' passion to criticize America; when he questions the national heritage, with Puritan intransigence—though no Puritan himself but a lover of life—he really is "in the American grain."

In this light one may understand his aggressive plea for a literature based on American speech and not on British usage, and his shocking statement that a poem is "a machine . . . made of words."[5] Beyond the polemical shock of such functionalism we can feel the typically American need for expressive integrity; this will help us to see how *Paterson* finally developed from the seminal themes of an early work like *The Wanderer, a Rococo Study,* which was followed in 1936 by *Adam, Eve and the City*. But for some felicitous lines, like:

> The weight of the sky is upon them
> Under which all roof beams crumble. . . .[6]

or, to glean further on:

> Then the river began to enter my heart,
> Eddying back cool and limpid
> Into the crystal beginning of his days. . . .

or the part describing the Paterson strike (a telling choice), *The Wanderer* is watered down by a naïve rhetoric. Even so, it does reveal an important spiritual archetype. The poet-narrator humbles himself to a mysterious feminine entity, embodying the New Muse or the Womanhood Principle as an undeterred carrier of possible beauty, who appears to him in the midst of a teeming harbor and in the guises of a raven and a seagull takes him in flight over the monstrous city. From her he invokes an inspiration that will enable him to sing "modernity," to redeem the ugliness of the industrial metropolis; and she, after that airborne tour, dips him in the waste-soiled Passaic river to make him lose his old self and gain a new awareness. This ritual parallels by contrast the purifying action Dante undergoes in the Terrestrial Paradise (*Purgatory,* Canto XXXI) at the hands of sweet Matelda, who dips him in the Lethe river to wash his soul clean of the memory of sin. A spiritual rebirth is involved in both cases, and with striking similarity of details; the contrast lies in the fact that the Passaic, unlike Lethe, is a dirty river. By his immersion there the poet seems to announce a realist's intention not to elude the filth and ugliness in his native scene, since only by facing them may he eventually find a catharsis. What he sheds in the muddy river is aestheticism.

Stripped of its residual idealism, the archetypal idea reappears many years after in *Adam, Eve & the City.*[7] Adam is modern man, more specifically an Anglo-Saxon Puritan irremediably exiled from that Eden which is the life of the senses, and Eve is a wrecked myth, an old dame ready for death. Her face has motherly as well as wifely traits, which link her to a poem titled "An Eternity" where the poet thus addresses his dead mother: "Frankly, I do not love you;" while "Adam" for his part seems to have a lot in common with Williams' own British father. It is not strange to find the poet projecting his autobiography into a public myth, when we realize his constant involvement with America as a difficult love and an "estranged" mother. Nor do we see in this fact any reason to discount the public, historical relevancy of Williams' poetry in favor of an all-too-easy psychoanalytical reduction. A man's imaginative commitment to his world may well be rooted in the sexual-vegetative element, while expanding to encompass the social, historical, and political concerns of life. Who said that the root is more real than the branches?

Paterson resumes the great theme to develop it at epic length in four books, the first of which ("The Delineaments of the Giants") states the intertwined subthemes of the whole poem: the mythical origins (having something to do with Viconian giants), the present desolation of the city, the multiple characters of Paterson and of his woman correspondent, the quest for a redemptive communication, the drama of language, the shock of brute chronicle forever rehearsing man's fall, the unceasing rush of the cascades that submerges man as does the elemental fury of unformulated psyche in the downward trend of an "irreversible" human world that has become impervious to inner as well as social order.

After this grand overture, Book 2 ("Sunday in the Park") takes its cue from a walk in the park to show us all the frustrations of love in an industrial city, the disillusionment of modern man, the corrupting power of money and its repudiation on the part of a foreign-born Protestant minister, the myth of wealth and its tragedy, the poet's rebellion. Book 3 ("The Library") exposes the futility of inert knowledge stacked up in dusty bookshelves, in a way that makes one think of St.-John Perse's *Les Vents*. The creative spirit has left libraries and universities alike, and the poet dreams of a symbolic fire (an "inclusive flame") which may regenerate man by ridding him of that burden. Of course the poet does not have in mind another dubious "burning of the books" of the type that seals the abdication of culture to barbarism. He speaks of a Phoenix fire that destroys to recreate, and that burns above all in the soul. Book 4 ("The Run to the Sea") goes from an ironic pastoral interlude based on a strange triangle situation to the theme of atomic disintegration and entropy, to conclude on the resolving note of the sea that reabsorbs all, as in the famous ending of *Finnegans Wake*. The geographic and psychological river waters flow on forever to obliterate everything; time is irreversible, the age of pioneers is over, and we must begin a new cycle. The last lines emphasize the leitmotiv of the "fall" (and of the *falls*) with a catastrophic vortex:

> This is the blast
> the eternal close
> the spiral
> the final somersault
> the end.

That "somersault" immediately follows the report of a hanging, which Williams quotes from a nineteenth-century local chronicle having no immediately apparent connection with the actual theme. But all of *Paterson* is built like that, with a montage technique whose direct antecedents are to be found in Pound's *Cantos* and in Dos Passos' *U.S.A.* trilogy. By inserting in the body of his verse passages of local history or chronicle, Williams applies a special scansion to the theme; the raw documentary material arouses its own echoes, which reverberate on the "singing" lines in a stimulating way. Here and there the effect of this alternation weights the poem down, but it is a vital trait of its total physiognomy.

Variants of this "eccentric" structural device can be recognized in the insistent letters an unknown woman writes to the man Paterson to obey an urge of confession, frustrated communication, and misunderstood uplifting. Paterson methodically rejects this woman, and the result is an additional stress on the dominant note of estrangement throughout the poem.

If we, however, want to do justice to Williams' ambitious attempt, we must look more deeply into his reasons for using the raw document in poetry. Chronicle, direct observation of reality, is to him a prime source of modern poetry,[8] and he introduces it in the raw as a foil to the phases of lyrical fluency, which may thereby acquire a deeper dimension. We might say he keeps returning to chronicle as the giant Antaeus returned to Mother Earth during a fight—to draw from it fresh energy for a renewed assault. For the poet perhaps cannot keep away for very long from his matrix—unembellished existence—without incurring the risk of sterility. Besides, there is the quest for what André Breton calls *hasard objectif,* the fruitful chance for poetry that every chronicle contains in the exciting references the reader may detect in its unintentional cues. In a short poem Williams has said that the poet must draw from chaos itself if he wants to get a valid form; now he tries to introduce chaos in his pages as if to include in his literature the seething formlessness of contemporary American reality, in a dramatic confrontation of form with the formless. If successfully included, the formless becomes the nourishing element of form, the very leaven of poetry; if poetry manages to "include" it, instead of being included itself, as it physically is, we have a triumph of form on a new level.

Consequently, the discontinuity of our life's rhythm as woven in an industrial milieu penetrates the pages of *Paterson* to make it a tough poem. It is a far cry from the fluent melody of Conrad Aiken, who in his *House of Dust* (1916-17) essayed a complex analogy between the city as a living multicellular organism and the multicellular composition of human consciousness. It is a far cry also from Santayana's refined style, and the comparison becomes inevitable since Williams quotes a passage in Santayana's novel *The Last of the Puritans* as a proem to Book 4 of *Paterson.* The passage in question has to do with the organic nature of cities as works of art and nature at the same time; they are another body for the human mind, though Santayana's puritanical hero refuses to admit it. This thematic reference sends us to another, and implicit one, namely, Lewis Mumford's *The Culture of Cities,*[9] a book of wide scope that diagnoses the cancer of contemporary "megalopolis," condemned to become a necropolis unless it is radically restructured on an organic plan compatible with the requirements of life.

For the time being, indeed, the huge creature has got out of hand, and society is alienated from its body (the industrialized city) just as mind is alienated from life, psyche from language, and man from woman. In language, which is or should be a human act of communication, Williams desperately seeks the key to redemption for his estranged fellow men who

> because they neither know their sources nor the sills of their
> disappointments walk outside their bodies aimlessly
> for the most part, locked and forgot in their desires—unroused.

But by being "outside their bodies," that is, losing in alienation the intimacy of their own physical reality, men also lose their minds:

> They may look at the torrent in
> their minds
> and it is foreign to them.

The torrent of emotional life, like the muddy Passaic river with its falls, flows in an unredeemed time so as to become strange to its experiencing subjects, because

> the language is missing them
> they die also
> incommunicado.
> The language, the language
> fails them
> They do not know the words
> or have not
> the courage to use them.
> —girls from
> families that have decayed and
> taken to the hills: no words
> . . .
> —the language
> is divorced from their minds,
> the language . . . the language!

The recurrent theme of invoked "marriage" and actual "divorce" thus merges with that of expression. No ideas but in things: language must not be a flight from reality, vulgar though the latter may be, but an approach to its very heart. Tough realist though he may be, Williams ultimately envisages human problems in a spiritual dimension, since with an emphasis that would not displease his "enemy" T. S. Eliot he keeps saying that existence is to be redeemed by expression, that time is to be saved in the word, that the individual fulfills himself in action and communication, in love. If the modern city is monstrous it is because it is devoid of "marriage;" if "marriage" has "come to have a shuddering implication" and human relationships have been warped (Book 4), all the gigantic production that centers on the industrial city becomes a heap of wreckage, and man collapses in the river of 'blood" (blind instinct) that carries him drifting away toward the sea of death, the sea which "is not/ our home."

Unlike so many other writers, especially Hart Crane, Williams finds in the sea not a liberating symbol but a destruction of the forms man shapes in his own world; it is another facet of that threatening formlessness that the abnormal growth of modern industry presents. Williams wants the definite form, the clear work, the fruitful order; and so in the "boom" of anarchistic mass production he sees another virgin forest to be tamed, one made by and of men, yet really inhuman. It perverts or atrophies language itself, and on page 164 the typographical arrangement of lines on the page reproduces, in a welter of disconnected phrases or stumps of phrases, this Babelic menace to our world, while on page 219, at the beginning of the last section of *Paterson,* Book 4, the painful question re-emerges:

> Haven't you forgot your virgin purpose,
> the language?

But on page 234 the yawning ocean swallows "language," that is, the human world of history:

> But lullaby, they say, the time sea is
> no more than sleep is . afloat
> with weeds, bearing seeds .
>
> Ah!
>
> float wrack, float words, snaring the
> seeds .
>
> . . . .

I warn you, the sea is *not* our home.
                    the sea is not our home

The sea *is* our home whither all rivers
(wither) run

We catch in these lines a note of ambiguity not to be overlooked: the sea is and is not our home because it is a womb luring us to final peace in death—but there is no salvation in that for us as men who must build our world; the rivers run toward the sea and in some sense also "wither"; the formlessness of existence seeks to re-absorb us in the fascination of the open sea, yet this is a threat. Obviously, man cannot save himself either by closing himself up in the machine-haunted world of his own rigid making, or by regressing to the sea of blood and primal instinct; between the sterile mechanical form and the roiling formless there lies the true, the harder way, which for a poet consists in language—the definition of a world. One leitmotiv of the poem then clarifies itself: the *fall,* which appears in several guises as the Passaic falls, as Mrs. Cumming's accident (Book 1), and as the analogous mishaps of other figures periodically interpolated in the prose sections. The fall of so many beings is always the same: it is the fall of man from his creative commitment as a social articulate being.

Yet the river falls, at the end of Book 3, take on a positive meaning by embodying language itself as the mediator between past and future, visible and invisible:

The past above, the future below
and the present pouring down: the roar,
the roar of the present, a speech—
is, of necessity, my sole concern .

They plunged, they fell in a swoon .

or by intention, to make an end—the
roar, unrelenting, witnessing .
Neither the past nor the future

Neither to stare, amnesic—forgetting.
The language cascades into the
invisible, beyond and above : the falls
of which it is the visible part—

Not until I have made of it a replica
will my sins be forgiven and my
disease cured— . . .

Yearned-for integrity can be attained only at the price of suffering the present in its difficulty, the daily *fall* of man, to express it in words. Elsewhere (still in the "Library" book, the third) all those stacked books were said to be mute because devoid of humanity. And there the element of water was changed into the element of fire to signify annihilation and catharsis:

And for that, invention is lacking,
the words are lacking:

the waterfall of the
flames, a cataract reversed, shooting
upward (what difference does it make?)

The language,

Beautiful thing—that I
make a fool of myself, mourning the lack
of dedication
mourning its losses,
for you

Scarred, fire swept
(by a nameless fire, that is unknown even
to yourself) nameless,

drunk.

Rising, with a whirling motion, the person
passed into the flame, becomes the flame—
the flame taking over the person

—with a roar, an outcry
which none can afford (we die in silence, we
enjoy shamefacedly—in silence, hiding
our joy even from each other

keeping
a secret joy in the flame which we dare
not acknowledge). . . .

Thus the downward motion of the falls reverses itself into the ascending motion of fire, an "inclusive flame" which also contains a destructive consummation in the concrete symbol of the frantic rhythm by which modern man squanders time. As in Eliot's *Four Quartets,* the four elements—earth, air, water, fire—keep interwining, dissolving into each other or alternately superimposing. Book 1 of *Paterson* ends with an image of fabling Earth, mother of all speech; the "library" book is stirred by a fitful wind

For there is a wind or ghost of a wind
in all books echoing the life
there, a high wind that fills the tubes
of the ear until we think we hear a wind,
actual .

to lead the mind away.

Drawn from the streets we break off
our minds' seclusion and are taken up by
the books' winds, seeking, seeking
down the wind

until we are unaware which is the wind and
which the wind's power over us .
to lead the mind away

and there grows in the mind
a scent, it may be, of locust blossoms
whose perfume is itself a wind moving. . . .

Immediately after, the wind of memory is metamorphosed into the cascade roaring in the mind:

. . . something
has brought him back to his own

mind .

in which a falls unseen
tumbles and rights itself
and refalls—and does not cease, falling
and refalling with a roar, a reverberation
not of the falls but of its rumor

unabated. . . .

Then comes the passage to fire:

Beautiful thing,
my dove, unable and all who are windblown,
touched by the fire. . . .

And the return to earth's dark womb:

and unable,
a roar that (soundless) drowns the sense
with its reiteration
unwilling to lie in its bed
and sleep and sleep, sleep
in its dark bed.

The elements' vicissitudes, besides symbolizing man's perennial fate, ultimately refer to the phenomena of language, which can be dark, solid, and seminal like earth; fluid, confused, and thundering like water; thin and unstable or quickening (pneumatic) like air; intense and destructive, or purifying, like fire. But language is the whole man, whose integrated form Williams is seeking through all his complexities; and he, despite his belief in the solid reality of things, will have to accept their paradoxical contradiction in an existential climate that is not far from Eliot's mystical tension as stated particularly at the beginning of "East Coker":

For the beginning is assuredly
the end—since we know nothing, pure
and simple, beyond
our own complexities.

Yet there is
no return: rolling up out of chaos,
a nine months' wonder, the city
the man, an identity—it can't be
otherwise—an
interpenetration, both ways. Rolling
up! obverse, reverse;
the drunk the sober; the illustrious

the gross; one. In ignorance
a certain knowledge and knowledge,
undispersed, its own undoing.

* * *

It is the ignorant sun
rising in the slot of
hollow suns risen, so that never in this
world will a man live well in his body
save dying—and not know himself
dying; yet that is
the design. Renews himself
thereby, in addition and subtraction,
walking up and down.

Integrity is not to be retained or attained through false simplifications, but on the contrary by including the actual tensions of existence; it is the elements and their changing interplay, it is what Stevens would call "first idea," the sun to be perceived only at the price of becoming an ignorant man again, as the first of *Notes toward a Supreme Fiction* has it—and if Williams here speaks of "ignorant sun" it is not by accident. It is likewise not accidental that he should equate knowledge with the act of sowing. "Knowledge undispersed" neutralizes itself in sterility, and the open attitude of the poet finds a structural counterpart in the open form of the poem, which strikes us by rolling waves through repetition and progression. Open, and at times avalanching, rhythm reflects the openness of Williams to a dialogue with fellow poets like Eliot, Stevens, and Crane, even if sometimes the dialogue is a polemical argument; this, too, is unquestionably "in the American grain."

To write "stale poems" is a temptation particularly close, Williams feels, to contemporary American writers, and he warns against that with characteristic vigor (*Paterson* is also a poem in the making and an *ars poetica,* like so much of modern verse). To avoid the trap himself, he lends an attentive ear to living American speech, according to his own forcefully stated principles, and in a kind of running conversation with his brethren in art he comes to grips with the urgent issues, with our daily struggle in a tough reality. Thus on page 126 of *Paterson* he proclaims:

> Escape from it—but not by running
> away. Not by "composition". Embrace the
> foulness
> —the being taut, balanced between
> eternities.

To accept the precarious position of a tightrope walker "balanced between eternities" is the condition for making poetry and for saving one's integrity as man; this way nameless Beauty will appear, a "lover of flame." Note how this sudden illumination results from a chronicle cue the poet has picked and emblematically expanded. The passage just quoted follows the prose story of a tightrope walker of bygone days, who repeatedly defied the Passaic falls. And of course, the inclusive and not the exclusive gesture ("embrace the foulness"!) is what counts for Williams, grandchild of Whitman that he is. The above passage clearly shows his belief in the birth of elegance from the accepted impurities of life, since purity can be a goal or a result but not a departure.

Our poet's attitude to poetry, though, is not exempt from doubt and discouragement, as a provisional alter ego makes clear in a weary gesture that involves America as well:

> Doctor, do you believe in
> "the people", the Democracy? Do

you still believe—in this
swill-hole of corrupt cities?
Do you, Doctor? Now?
Give up
the poem. Give up the shilly
shally of art.

This reminds the reader of Williams' friend, Marianne Moore, whose well-known beginning of "Poetry" runs:

> I, too, dislike it: there are things that are important beyond
> all this fiddle;

but as the rest of the work abundantly shows, it is a lover's quarrel she has with poetry, the mask of an absolute devotion—and the same is true of Williams. As for his intermittent dialogue with Stevens, it will pay to read carefully the following lines:

The province of the poem is the world.
When the sun rises, it rises in the poem
and when it sets darkness comes down
and the poem is dark. . . .

an obvious antiphon to Stevens' *Man with the Blue Guitar*—

Poetry is the subject of the poem,

a statement of faith in the metaphysical autonomy of poetry to which Williams certainly cannot subscribe, no matter how provisional it may be in the context of Stevens' protean dialectics. And if he puts "the world," like the good realist he is, before and around "poetry," it is not because he discounts the latter, since on page 99 of *Paterson* he calls it

> the most perfect rock and temple, the highest
> falls. . . .

towering above the sterile erudition that threatens to crush the modern poet. This passage occurs at the end of Book 2, and it anticipates the "Library" theme of Book 3; if we go on to page 156, we find:

> . . . Texts mount and complicate them-
> selves, lead to further texts and those
> to synopses, digests and emendations. . . .

a weird perception of modern specialized culture as the unmanageable growth Flaubert made it out to be in his *Bouvard et Pécuchet.*

Language is not printed paper but continuous invention, and its enemy is usury; against that enemy the whole poem protests, especially in a section in Book 2 that clearly echoes Pound's "Usura" Canto in its cadence ("Without invention nothing is well spaced . . ."), while the Poundian linkage of economic with spiritual entropy becomes even more explicit in the episode of Klaus the preacher:

> Cash is mulcted of them that others may live
> secure
> . . and knowledge restricted.

Indeed, the alarming accusation "language is worn out" often rings out in *Paterson,* to unheeding ears; and in the last book the chemical entropy of uranium ceaselessly degenerating into lead is made to symbolize the spiritual degeneration man undergoes by resiging to the usury of language. As uranium loses its radiation power when it becomes opaque lead, so language, deadened by thoughtless usage, loses its radiance to become a repertory of inert forms, a debased currency. Ths is another variation on the theme of the fall.

But it is offset by the antiphonal movement of rising language that redeems itself in discovery:

> The descent beckons
>   as the ascent beckoned
>   Memory is a kind
> of accomplishment
>   a sort of renewal
>   even
> an initiation, since the spaces it opens are new
> places
> . . .
> No defeat is made up entirely of defeat— . . .

For language conquers time, and the form of its victory is memory, presence, the recovery of what was lost; we seem to hear again a note that would not jar in the music of Eliot's *Four Quartets.*

Williams' conscious fidelity to an American locale is not the same thing as a deaf provincialism, since it allows for an ideal convergence with the work of an Eliot, a Pound, a Crane, or a Stevens, different though each may be as a stylist. The meeting point of them all is in the drama of the word, which, existentially interpreted as a neo-Cartesian *loquor ergo sum,* constitutes the central theme of *Paterson.* With Hart Crane (whose "For the Marriage of Faustus and Helen" corresponds thematically to Williams' *The Wanderer*) it will be "Creation's blithe and petalled word," or the "incognizable Word/ of Eden." With Eliot, it will be a matter of "Speech without word" and "Word of no speech." With Stevens, there will appear "the theory of the word for those/ For whom the word is the making of the world" to bring about the tentative naming of the unnamable in *Notes toward a Supreme Fiction*. And in the case of Allen Tate, far though he may be from Williams in style and attitude, it is not inappropriate to keep in mind "Retroduction to American History" apropos of *Paterson*:

> Heredity
> Proposes love, love exacts language, and we lack
> Language. When shall we speak again? When shall
> The sparrow dusting the gutter sing? When shall
> This drift with silence meet the sun? When shall
> I wake?

The invocation to the redemptive Word, and the paradox of language struggling with the inexpressible in a "tightrope walker" situation, are a form of existentially religious consciousness that we can trace within the American literary tradition to Whitman and Dickinson alike. One climax of the "Song of Myself" is a hymn to the Word to be born (stanza 50), of which Whitman says that

> I do not know it—it is without name—it is a word unsaid,
> It is not in any dictionary, utterance, symbol,

and that

> To it the creation is the friend whose embracing awakes me.

Whitman's effusions stem in part from American revivalism, and they have become an essential legacy for Lindsay, Crane, and Williams himself. The originating form and impulse have to be seen in prophetic exclamation or mystical apostrophe. Even in introverted Dickinson, who never speaks out loud, we find the theme of language as necessary paradox:

Nature is what we know—
Yet have no art to say—

Elsewhere she says:

It is the Ultimate of Talk
The Impotence to tell;

and seems to echo in her own way the Whitman of "Song of Myself" where he says:

I hear you whispering there O stars of heaven,
O suns—O grass of graves—O perpetual transfers and promotions,
If you do not say anything how can I say anything?

E. E. Cummings was to embroider on that in poems No. 225 and 234.

Dickinson had formulated the paradox of poetry as a spiritual possession achieved through renunciation:

Perception of an
Object costs
Precise the Object's loss.
Perception in itself a Gain
Replying to its price;
The Object Absolute is nought;

and as an exhilarating discovery of things beyond the limits of habit-worn language:

Exhilaration is the Breeze
That lifts us from the ground
And leaves us in another place
Whose statement is not found;

> Returns us not; but after time
> We soberly descend
> A little newer for the term
> Upon enchanted ground.

Poetry as a temporary exile from existence to be followed by a fruitful return is a central attitude and topic in Emily Dickinson's verse, but the whole problem of language as a self-questioning confrontation of existence is inherent in the American "pioneer" tradition—and one might add that it has become particularly relevant to self-questioning poets all over the West in our crucial times. We need only recall Ungaretti's

> Have I torn to pieces my heart and mind
> To fall into slavery of words?

In Williams, however, there appears also another probable American strain, which can affect style in a more radical way. We have seen how *Paterson,* after the example of Joyce, Eliot, and Pound, is all woven as a "music of ideas," since it treats themes in a harmonic progression which is supposed to provide a unity for the poem without resorting to narrative continuity or "plot." Elsewhere Williams had said that poetry must not "represent" but "present" its object; hence the technique of the montage of images. As Left-Bank experimenters like Gertrude Stein or Hemingway can show, the secret of this evocative game is verbal iteration; here, a syncopated iteration, alternately distended in effusive spells and contracted into jumpy contretemps. The rhythmic suggestions of jazz music, so powerful in our century all over its native continent, may have affected these rhythm-conscious writers, and particularly a keen listener to the patterns of living speech like Williams.

Paterson, in fact, counterpoints its image recurrences with word recurrences, from which the poet elicits a heightened sonority that sharpens the edges of words while making them part of a developing fullness of utterance. To realize this, one only has to read the first sequences of Book 1, particularly pages 16-17; or the 'Library" book as above quoted, which affords rich examples of heightening repetition, sound-metamorphosis and syncopated rhythm; or the beginning of Part II, Book 1:

> There is no direction. Whither? I
> cannot say. I cannot say
> more than how. The how (the howl) only
> is at my disposal (proposal): watching—
> colder than stone .
>
> a bud forever green,
> tight-curled, upon the pavement, perfect
> in juice and substance but divorced, divorced
> from its fellows, fallen low—
>
> Divorce is
> the sign of knowledge in our time,
> divorce! divorce!
>
> with the roar of the river
> forever in our ears (arrears)
> inducing sleep and silence, the roar
> of eternal sleep . . challenging
> our waking—
>
> —unfledged desire, irresponsible, green,
> colder to the hand than stone,
> unready—challenging our waking:

Internal echoes (how-howl, proposal-disposal), alliterative chains (ears-arrears-roar-river) and later on inner rhymes set up a nervous counterpoint in staccato style, interrupted by "improvisations" like "Ain't they beautiful!" or "Indians!" We might even say that the frequent repetition of key words like breath, divorce, language, charges them with electricity as if they were pieces of amber rubbed by wool. Syncopation pervades Book 2, where Klaus the preacher appears and holds his revivalist speech, and it reaches a climax toward the end of this Book, on page 95:

> Look for the nul
> defeats it all
>
> the N of all
> equations .
>
> that rock, the blank
> that holds them up
>
> which pulled away—
> the rock's
>
> their fall. Look
> for that nul
>
> that's past all
> seeing
>
> the death of all
> that's past
>
> all being .
>
> But Spring shall come and flowers will bloom
> and man must chatter of his doom . . . . .

Counterpointed meanings in the rhymes (nul-all, seeing-being, doom-bloom) precipitating toward a dark tonality, convulsive shortness of irregular lines, and the abrupt switch to a longer measure in the final couplet, all contribute to the crisp effect.

Dante's *Inferno,* because it fits as a graphic allusion the subway world and more generally the frantic city above it, as Hart Crane saw, and Shakespeare's *The Tempest* for the sake of bitter irony, since the "sea change" here described is of the horrible kind, are contrapuntally present in another highly syncopated passage (pages 194-96) whose broken rhythm embodies the chaos and disruption of the scene it portrays:

> Condemned .
> But who has been condemned . where the tunnel
> under the river starts? *Voi ch'entrate*
> revisited! Under ground, under rock, under river
> under gulls . under the insane .
>
> . the traffic is engulfed and disappears .
> to emerge . never
>
> A voice calling in the hubbub (Why else
> are there newspapers, by the cart-load?) blaring
> the news no wit shall evade, no rhyme
> cover. Necessity gripping the words . scouting
> evasion, that love is begrimed, befouled .

I'd like to spill the truth, on that one.

Why don't you?

This is a POEM!

> begrimed
> yet lifts its head, having suffered a sea-change!
> shorn of its eyes and its hair

its teeth kicked out . a bitter submersion
in darkness. . . .

Since we pointed out before an archetypal affinity, not necessarily supported by direct influence, between Williams' early *The Wanderer* and Dante's *Purgatorio,* the explicit reference to Inferno in the present quotation acquires contextual value. There is no sweet lady to guide the poet here, no Matelda or Beatrice, there is only the underground hell of the tunnel, and above it, on the surface thick with skyscrapers, the more refined hell of the business world:

While in the tall
buildings (sliding up and down) is where
the money's made
up and down
directed missiles
in the greased shafts of the tall buildings .
They stand torpid in cages in violent motion
unmoved
but alert!
predatory minds, un-
affected. . . .

This vision of megalopolis is just as chaotic as Hart Crane's, but more desperate. We can recognize in the disfigured corpse surfacing from the harbor waters an image of what we ourselves are or may become in a world threatened by rapaciousness and emptiness. Hart Crane is evoked in the present context by a thematic affinity, and his name will appear in a letter on page 205 of *Paterson*, though he may be symbolically present also before, where a chronicle passage mentions Tim Crane, who built a slim bridge over the river and then fell into the water to his death (page 26). Anyway, if Crane saw a release from the city inferno in a mythical "Cathay" that stands for the image of a still incorrupt America, no such outlet is envisaged by Dr. Williams, who is the tougher realist of the two, as the following judgment amply proves:

> . . . a world of corrupt cities,
> nothing else, that death stares in the eye,
> lacking love: no palaces, no secluded gardens,
> no water among the stones.

A comparison between the young suicide of 1932 and the long-lived poet-doctor of Rutherford, N.J., despite the partial affinity of themes, makes a basic difference of approach stand out. Crane's Dionysian intoxication, with the extreme gesture of self-destruction that arose from it, contrasts with Williams' stubborn lucidity in facing a world threatened by spiritual entropy—the loss of love and the erosion of meaning. We easily see, at this point, how the drama of modern America and the drama of language are the same thing as Williams' drama of a man cast to live among men, who can hope for salvation and integrity only from an outspoken denunciation of the dangers besetting our world at large. It is the irony of literary history that makes him write something like a new edition of *The Waste Land* in the very teeth of his own avowed anti-Eliotism.

Historical relevancy and literary affinities or indebtedness bring us to the very threshold of the poem as a work of art, but the ultimate question to be asked is: "How good is it? How successful as poetry?" When we pose this question apropos of *Paterson,* we shall not find it easy to answer. The foregoing quotations selected for focal illustration or critical comment should certainly help in assessing the levels to which Williams' poetry can rise, yet a judgment of his major effort as a total accomplishment will have to be mixed. We are confronted by a strong effort to master contemporary disorder through the ordering power of language, but language itself seems to succumb partly to the disintegrating process, and the unity of the long poem is impaired by its own desperate boldness. This is the cry of a human heart that cannot afford the luxury of polished forms, and poetry springs in violent gushes, intermittently, from among the dross that could not be refined out of existence. The French might see in this an example of *art brut*. With the subsequent *Desert Music* we shall be borne on a long wave of felicitous song, but here we are jolted along by a fitful current punctuated by rapids and cataracts. Yet it is impossible to close this rough book without wanting to reread it sooner or later, for its words have been staked out against an ultimate goal of humanistic commitment that is the destiny of the poet as Williams sees it. Aesthetic complacencies are out of the question. Williams has always been a rather fragmentary poet, and it is no wonder that verbal anarchy should loom in this vast attempt of his; on the other hand, Williams' individualism accounts also for the specific weight, density, and rapidity that words can acquire in his uneven context.

Mr. Southworth[10] analyzed the texture of Williams' lyric discourse to bring out its rhythmical values, and Randall Jarrell[11] said that certain passages from *Paterson* and several poems from *The Collected Later Poems* belong to the finest achievement in English verse. The very unevenness of accomplishment is due, in Williams' case, to his persistent experimentation, whose attendant failure can be variously described as the result of polemical realism or of an all too tenuous impressionism learned perhaps at the French school. "Drunkard" and "Breakfast" of 1923 are sufficient examples of the former type of failure, while "The Locust Tree in Flower" illustrates the second:

Among
of

green

stiff
old
bright

broken
branch
come

white
sweet
May

again
(*The Collected Earlier Poems,* page 93)

Williams is not Verlaine, and this kind of rarefied verbal sensibility that reduces words to undimensional floating surfaces could not go very far, especially if one keeps in mind the utterly different type of sonority that precludes an English-writing poet from the musically sustained effects the French language puts at the disposal of its own native speakers and craftsmen. *Paterson* constitutes the quest for an appropriate dimension in language, away from the bodiless and the opaque alike, even if it is not a consistently successful quest.

Paterson, however, is an endeavor that has been made possible by the felicity of certain previous poems where words move in a crepitant air, with firm outline, in such a way as to set up a strong rhythm; for instance, "Burning the Christmas Green," "Dedication for a Plot of Ground" (a rhythmical triumph), "Approach to a City" (a neat etching), "The Words Lying Idle," "New Mexico," "The Seafarer," "Venus over the Desert," "Mists over the

River," "The Pause," "The Sound of Waves." The brilliant directness of "New Mexico" invites illustrative quotation in its entirety:

> Anger can be transformed
> to a kitten—as love
> may become a mountain in
> the disturbed mind, the
> mind that prances like
> a horse or nibbles, starts
> and stares in the parched
> sage of the triple
> world—of stone, stone
> layered and beaten under
> the confessed brilliance
> of this desert noon.
>
> (*The Collected Later Poems,* page 169)

Words, in such a rhythmic structure, retain a marked edge, a pronounced individuality, yet they reverberate on each other in a network of mutually strengthening sounds and meanings that make for a unified form. This form winds up, so to speak, on a conclusive ending, though it depends for unity on the instability of run-on lines, none of which is a self-sufficient unit because each sends us forward to the next, thereby creating an accumulative impetus that reaches an expressive climax in poems like "Dedication for a Plot of Ground." At other times, instead, Williams experiments with an even more open form by ending the poem on a note of final suspense that, as happens in E. E. Cummings, is typographically symbolized by the absence of a period. This is where he resembles an otherwise very different poet like Emily Dickinson, who often concludes her poems on a final dash, as if more were to follow when silence supersedes the singing voice. A poem thus becomes something utterly different from a self-contained structure; it is more like a moment of the mind, a temporary surfacing of the stream of consciousness, or perhaps just the beginning of an endless poem. Objectivist Williams meets the symbolists without meaning to, by giving us the poem that is not end-stopped just as his individual lines are not end-stopped.

Whether in the self-contained or in the open utterance, however, Williams has learned to endow single words with their proper specific weight, without weighting them into inertia and without dissolving their outlines; they can thus acquire a spontaneous life in the very simplicity of diction that he prefers:

> "Sweet land!"
> at last!
> out of the sea—
> the Venusremembering wavelets
> rippling with laughter—...
> ("St. Francis Einstein of the Daffodils,"
> *The Collected Earlier Poems,* page 379)

And here is an "exclamatory" poem that is both dimensional and airy:

> January! The beginning!
> A moon
> scoured by the wind
> calls
>
> from its cavern. A vacant
> eye
> stares. The wind
> howls.
>
> Among bones in rose flesh
> singing

wake the stormy
stars.

("Moon and Stars," from
The Collected Earlier Poems, page 462)

The reduction of statement to bare essentials, the isolation of words, and the use of concomitant short lines rhythmically connected by alliterative echoes, all contribute to beget wonder, and we are not very far here from the typical accomplishment of Giuseppe Ungaretti's[12] early phase, since he worked on his own language with the same deliberately reductive technique to elicit a new immediacy and mystery.

To sum up the conclusions our analysis has made at least provisionally possible, it would be unfair to deny that William Carlos Williams, in the honesty of his lifelong quest, has achieved a high degree of integration between the hard, masculine half of his spiritual world and the atmospheric, fluid, feminine one, which is of course the "marriage" *Paterson* invokes:

Sing me a song to make death tolerable, a song
of a man and a woman: the riddle of a man
and a woman.
What language could allay our thirsts,
what winds lift us, what floods bear us
past defeats
but song but deathless song?

The rock
married to the river. . . .

(*Paterson,* page 131)

In his poetics of unflinching integrity he has shunned any decadent complacency[13] to face reality wholesale and possibly master it. From the rock there could thus gush forth a frequent water of pure song.

Six / *Robert Lowell: History as Eschatology*

THE[1] POET stands in time, yet rises above it, like the philosopher; or at least his presence in time is not entirely timebound, if he is to fulfill his mission as a witness: "Lebe mit deinem Jahrhundert, aber sei nicht sein Geschöpf; leiste deinen Zeitgenossen, aber, was sie bedürfen, nicht, was sie loben" (Live with your century, but don't be its creature; perform for your contemporaries, yes, but what they need, not what they praise). This Schiller quotation from the ninth *Letter on Aesthetic Education* might be an apt commentary on the work and attitude of Robert Lowell, who is one of the most history-conscious American writers of our time precisely because he has a quarrel with history.

If history is the past, and the past is unchangeable, then Lowell's quarrel with it is futile. But his implicit philosophy is not Crocean;[2] it is closer to Bergson's conception of time past as impinging on time present in the dramatic duration of the experiencing mind.[3] Now his relation to this past is extremely tense, and also complex; to understand it is to see how his poetry comes *toward*[4] our history, and how our history painfully procreated it in its own inverted image.

As an American, Lowell is the heir of the New England past; this shows clearly in so many poems that, like "Quaker Graveyard in Nantucket," "In Memory of Arthur Winslow," and "Mary Winslow," project family history into public history. On the other hand, to inherit New England means to inherit a secession from Europe, from that older past and wider cultural horizon in which Lowell feels involved as a Westerner: 'I write the Wonders of the

Christian Religion, flying from the Depravations of Europe, to the American Strand. . . ." One way to acquire a greater intimacy with Lowell's poetry as a child and judge of history is to read it contrapuntally against the background of Cotton Mather's General Introduction to *Magnalia Christi Americana.* Only Lowell has reversed the position: what he flees from is not the "depravations of Europe," but the (to him very real) "depravations" of America itself.

His direct inheritance was a promise, but a disinheriting one. The Pilgrim Fathers were indeed "children of Light," but of a blighting light, the light of Lucifer:

> Our fathers wrung their bread from stocks and stones
> And fenced their gardens with the Redman's bones;
> Embarking from the Nether Land of Holland,
> Pilgrims unhouseled by Geneva's night,
> They planted here the Serpent's seeds of light;
> And here the pivoting searchlights probe to shock
> The riotous glass houses built on rock,
> And candles gutter by an empty altar,
> And light is where the landless blood of Cain
> Is burning, burning the unburied grain.

Between the benighted Calvin at Geneva, guilty of having contributed to the breakup of Christian Europe, and the hell fire that sprang from his message, the Mayflower pilgrims were in a bad way when they sailed from the infernal ("nether") land of Holland, for the seeds they brought from betrayed Europe were those of destruction, as the red men came to know; if they hoped to earn another garden of Eden, death and the snake soon penetrated it, and their very consciences, those searching lights, expose them as "landless blood of Cain," as accursed nomads doomed to sterility, not holy pilgrims sustained by a divine Covenant. Few people would miss here, as in so much else that Lowell wrote, the forceful way in which history begets poetry, and poetry in its turn accuses history, through the alchemy of metaphor: the puns on the Netherlands, on Lucifer, on the searchlights, on the "riotous" houses built on Biblical rock, but too brittle to stand the coming quake, are not clever word play, but a structural device bent on eliciting its fearful meaning from the landscape of history, down to our own time.[5] In the same way, the speaker of a later poem ("Mother Marie Thérèse") says of General Montcalm that he lies asleep "on Abraham's bosom," utilizing the geographic name of the famous battlefield near Quebec to bring out transcendent implications. In still another composition, "The Dead in Europe," we find the name of Maryland switched from its actual etymology to a religious one that has to do with the Queen of Heaven, not of seventeenth-century England. The moving epitaph for Santayana, from the 1959 volume *Life Studies,*[6] imaginatively connects the watchful nuns of Santo Stefano Rotondo, where the skeptical philosopher spent the last years of his life, with the Capitol geese that according to legend saved Rome's last stronghold from the nocturnally creeping Gauls. Humor is not absent from this flash of telescoped vision, or, for that matter, from all of *Life Studies* with its affectionate family sketches, or from its predecessor, *The Mills of the Kavanaughs.*

But the earlier volumes—*Land of Unlikeness, Lord Weary's Castle*—have little or no humor, being attuned to a mood of bitterness that might well make them offensive to whoever refuses to share Lowell's fiery conversion. Who is, after all, this New Englander who repudiates his spiritual lineage? Isn't he simply a renegade? If so, the poetry will have to be accepted as a merely private expression of troubled genius in a historical context to which it is irrelevant. A personal conversion to the long-abandoned dogmas of Papist Rome,[7] even if it results in magnificent verse, cannot have any bearing on the realities of Protestant Yankeedom: can you abolish three hundred years of history by a stroke of pen?

At this point the historical sense will intercede for the "unhouseled" poet by reminding us that his secession from his secessionist forebears actually continues their own attitude, whatever the motivating ideology. Rome is Lowell's Walden, as the impassioned poem on Concord reveals:

> Ten thousand Fords are idle here in search
> Of a tradition. Over these dry sticks—
> The Minute Man, the Irish Catholics,
> The ruined bridge and Walden's fished-out perch—
> The belfry of the Unitarian Church
> Rings out the hanging Jesus. Crucifix,
> How can your whited spindling arms transfix
> Mammon's unbridled industry, the lurch
> For forms to harness Heraclitus' stream!
> This Church is Concord—Concord where Thoreau
> Named all the birds without a gun to probe
> Through darkness to the painted man and bow:
> The death-dance of King Philip and his scream
> Whose echo girdled this imperfect globe.

The stream of Heraclitean becoming, history in the making, threatens to be our lost chance if we stake everything on "Mammon's industry," for the only forms with which that stream can be "harnessed," that is, with which time can be redeemed, are those of meaningful ritual, thought, and art, not the feverishly multiplied machines on which we pride ourselves. The "ten thousand Fords" will never carry us to what we most need—the fountainhead of a reliable tradition. What remains of America's promising start, here in the town that fired the Revolutionary War and then the revolutionary thought of Thoreau and Emerson, is just "dry sticks;" the landmarks are pitiful ruins, the local version of Christianity is powerless to counteract the creeping materialism of the "children of light," and what we hear in response to our devotion aroused by the well-known monuments is not the "shot heard round the world" of Emersonian memory, but the disquieting cry of a remoter war; murdered King Philip claims his long-due revenge, much as Ikkemotubbe summons the Sutpens, the Sartorises, and the Compsons to the earth of which he was defrauded by the white man, in Faulkner's Yoknapatawpha saga.

A perceptive sociological historian like Oscar Handlin emphasizes separation or "apartness" as the fundamental experience of the immigrant to America, therefore of America as such; it is easy to see how Lowell, like other American writers of note, stands apart from his native land within his native land, and thus takes up the posture of the prophet. It would seem that America is one vast community of "sinners in the hands of any angry God;" will it mend its way and avoid the threatening doom? The conscientious objector cannot tell; he sees what he sees, and he feels it is his mission to awaken, not to soothe. In "Where the Rainbow Ends," his native Boston swings dangerously between salvation and destruction:

> I saw my city in the Scales, the pans
> Of judgment rising and descending. . . .

In "At the Indian Killer's Grave," the head of the redskin chieftain announces nemesis to the descendant of his destroyers:

> "Surely, this people is but grass,"
> He whispers, "this will pass;
> But, Sirs, the trollop dances on your skulls
> And breaks the hollow noddle like an egg
> That thought the world an eggshell . . .
> . . . The Judgment is at hand. . . ."

The Indian killers are no "chosen people":

> ". . . Your election,
> Hawking above this slime
> For souls as single as their skeletons,
> Flutters and claws in the dead hand of time."

In "As a Plane Tree by the Water," Boston, and all of America by implication, are equated with Babel:

> Darkness has called to darkness, and disgrace
> Elbows about our windows in this planned
> Babel of Boston where our money talks
> And multiplies the darkness. . . .
> Our Lady of Babylon, go by, go by,
> I was once the apple of your eye;
> Flies, flies are on the plane tree, on the streets.

Postwar America of the middle and late forties feels secure within its still impregnable defenses, but, the poem concludes, they are just another German "Atlantic wall," likely to crumble as the walls of Jericho; conversion to the Spirit will be the only way to survival.

This plea for national soul-searching, which subsequent world events have partly borne out, takes its place with Robinson's "Cassandra" as a powerfully worded reminder to the prosperous republic not to yield to the temptation of *hybris;* but the hymning note of love is not lacking. Christ is envisaged as the liberating force behind the accusing violence of the prophet; Lowell is an apocalyptic believer, like Blake or Hopkins, and "Colloquy in Black Rock" embodies to perfection his imaginative thrust from the machine-like rhythm of an earthbound beginning to the transcendent lightning of the crowning line:

. . . —my heart,
The blue kingfisher dives on you in fire.

It is this moral tension, translated into a uniquely taut compactness of style, that enables Lowell to sustain a successful dialogue with formidable literary ancestors like Melville. "The Quaker Graveyard in Nantucket," one of the modern poet's highest achievements, is precisely such a dialogue. The sailor drowned at sea, Lowell's own relative Warren Winslow, surfaces ominously to stare his surviving fellows-at-arms out of countenance, and can be taken to repeat in the modern context the posthumous gesture of Fedallah in *Moby Dick,* for ill omens are gathering on America's might at sea:

Sailors, who pitch this portent at the sea
Where dreadnoughts shall confess
Its hell-bent deity,
When you are powerless
To sand-bag the Atlantic bulwark, faced
By the earth-shaker, green, unwearied, chaste
In his steel scales: ask for no Orphean lute
To pluck life back. The guns of the steeled fleet
Recoil and then repeat
The hoarse salute.

Poseidon, the "earth-shaker," the scaly sea god, shatters the Atlantic Wall of America; the *Pequod*'s fate is re-enacted (stanza 2). Life, imagination, spirit, not walls or steel, are the appropriate response to the challenge of present history. One could almost read Toynbee, along with Melville, between the lines. The apocalyptic vision of past and future doom expands to a Melvillian climax when the fifth stanza develops the whale symbol to encompass the decay of modern civilization culminating in a shipwreck like the *Pequod*'s:

Gobbets of blubber spill to wind and weather,
Sailor, and gulls go round the stoven timbers
Where the morning stars sing out together
And thunder shakes the white surf and dismembers
The red flag hammered in the mast-head. . . .

But the harpooned, hacked, rotting whale is not just a source of corruption; it is life, and can harbor Jonah-Christ in its huge body:

. . . Hide,
Our steel, Jonas Messias, in Thy side.

Thus the harpoon of the old Quaker whalemen becomes the spear of Longinus, and the symbolic killing of the whale an act of sui cide, since it is a crucifixion of our own culture, without a guaranteed Resurrection. Lowell anticipates Marius Bewley in his Christological interpretation of Moby Dick.[8] The two-stanza epilogue attached to the forceful poem, with the title "Our Lady of Walsingham," clinches the point by transforming the anguished address into a serene prayer.

This is the "wisdom" that the dove of Jesus has given to the "exile" ("Where the Rainbow Ends"); but it is, Melville would say, a wisdom that is woe, and the disinherited heir of the Puritans inverts the route of the *Mayflower*. His "Exile's Return," counterpointing Malcolm Cowley's book by the same title, shows Europe as a shell-torn battlefield, where, despite the presence of "lily-stands" in the Rhineland and of a "rough cathedral," death lurks; a brief quotation from Dante's *Inferno* lines in Canto III ("lasciate ogni speranza o voi ch'entrate") warns us that these towns are a hell gate. "The Dead in Europe" tells us, through the imagined chorus of the European victims, what that hell was like:

After the planes unloaded, we fell down
Buried together, unmarried men and women;

Not crown of thorns, not iron, not Lombard crown,
Not grilled and spindle spires pointing to heaven
Could save us. Raise us, Mother, we fell down
Here hugger-mugger in the jellied fire:
Our sacred earth in our day was our curse.

A daring metamorphosis of the voice expands the significance of the poem in its concluding stanza, the third, by making the poet himself the speaker and thus implicating America in the spiritual fate of bombed Europe:

. . . Shall I bear,
(O Mary!) unmarried man and powder-puppet,
Witness to the Devil? . . .

The very last lines restore the initial chorus, but as an enlarged "we" that associates Lowell, indeed all of America, with the prayer of the dead:

. . . Mary, hear,
O Mary, marry earth, sea, air and fire;
Our sacred earth in our day is our curse.

A reshuffle of the elements seems in order to renew life, or perhaps to end history as such in a Final Judgment; Mary the Marrier will then be a death-giver, but also a life-giver in the spiritual sense. The transition of the verb tense from the past of stanzas 1 and 2 to the loaded present of stanza 3 ("*is* our curse") heightens the effect of the plural-singular-expanded-plural sequence as a direct way of prophetically relating past history (recent though this past may here be) to the day that is still being lived by mankind.

The prodigal son goes to Rome, hoping to find there a promise of salvation; and Rome, the cradle of his culture, is violently addressed by him in "Dea Roma"[9] as the locus of sixteen centuries wasted by Christendom "since Maxentius fell;" not only all the roads, but "many sewers" lead to it, yet St. Peter, providential fisherman,

> Walks on the waters of a draining Rome
> To bank his catch in the Celestial City.

Evidently a decisive event is approaching, a Second Coming, to seal history; the apocalyptic mood is in tune with the anguish of a Cold War overshadowed by the threat of an atomic cloud. Lowell's sense of history is eschatological and not, properly speaking, "historical," for he speaks like an angry prophet, not like a Hegelian historicist or hopeful humanist. Later poems concerned with Rome, such as "Beyond the Alps," "Falling Asleep over the Aeneid," "For George Santayana," develop in a more meditative tone, but still questioning history in the alternatives of power, reason, and faith; and the eschatological note is not wanting either.

Because his commitment to spiritual values is so thorough, whatever direction his religious allegiance may have taken since his conversion to Catholicism, Robert Lowell can sustain his poetry at a declamatory pitch that would prove dangerous to a less gifted imagination. There is despair in his faith, and cruelty in his love; but he agrees with his countryman Robert Frost that fire is better than ice. If rebellion is the best way an American has to establish a connection with his tradition, then Lowell's New England ancestry counts for something. The sociologist, the scientific historian has to do with facts and laws; who but the poet can afford to have "a lover's quarrel" with history? This is his way of being available to history-ridden mankind.

Notes

One / *Space, Experiment, and Prophecy*

1. Gabriele Baldini, *Edgar A. Poe* (Brescia, 1947).

2. See Introduction to *The Portable Edgar Allan Poe,* selected and edited by Philip Van Doren Stern (New York, 1945).

3. Elio Vittorini, "Nascita della letteratura americana," in *Prospetti* No. 8, Summer 1954; later included in *Diario in pubblico* (Milan, 1957). Vittorini's opinion seems particularly important in view of his internationally acknowledged achievement as a novelist and of the stimulation that American literature avowedly exerted on his creativity.

4. D. H. Lawrence, *Studies in Classic American Literature* (New York, 1923).

5. Charles Feidelson, *Symbolism and American Literature* (Chicago, 1953).

6. Allen Tate, *On the Limits of Poetry* (New York, 1948); *The Forlorn Demon* (Chicago, 1953).

7. At the moment of translating these pages into English (Winter, 1961) I should like to add that I look forward to the publication in book form of a very accurate doctor's dissertation on Melville's poetry, done by Mr. James Camp at the University of Michigan in a way that makes it an authoritative statement on the subject. When and if it appears in print, this book will bring toward completion the critical rediscovery of Melville's verse.

8. See Walter Bezanson's Introduction to his scholarly edition of *Clarel* (New York, 1960) for illuminating comment on the significance of this much overlooked poetical effort.

9. Henry James, "Mr. Walt Whitman," a review of *Drum-Taps* (1865) later reprinted in *Views and Reviews,* edited by Le Roy Phillips (1908) and included in *The Portable Henry James,* edited by Morton Dauwen Zabel (New York, 1941).

10. Henry D. Thoreau, letter of November 19, 1856 to Harrison Blake, and letter of December 7, 1856 to the same correspondent, published in *Henry D. Thoreau, Selected Writings on Nature and Liberty,* edited with an introduction by Oscar Cargill (New York, 1952).

11. F. O. Matthiessen, *American Renaissance* (New York, 1941).

12. For a challenging interpretation of Whitman as a poet of death see Leslie Fiedler, "Images of Walt Whitman," in *An End to Innocence* (Boston, 1955).

13. This applies particularly to Yvor Winters. See his *In Defense of Reason* (Denver, 1947).

14. Cesare Pavese, *La letteratura americana e altri saggi* (Turin, 1953). It may interest the American reader to know that Pavese, the Italian novelist and champion of leftist democracy, started on his literary career with a doctor's dissertation on Whitman, an excerpt of which is included in the above-mentioned book, posthumously published. Pavese's essay on Whitman is among the finest contributions to Whitman criticism, and parts of it have been translated by Roger Asselineau for Gay Wilson Allen's symposium on foreign Whitman literature: *Walt Whitman Abroad: Critical Essays from Germany, France, Scandinavia, Russia, Italy, Spain and Latin America, Israel, Japan, and India* (Syracuse, N.Y., 1955).

15. A new testimonial has come from sundry quarters in connection with the first centennial of the publication of *Leaves of Grass.* Besides the above-mentioned *Walt Whitman Abroad,* of which he was the general editor, Professor Gay Wilson Allen published in 1955 *The Solitary Singer, A Critical Biography of Walt Whitman* (New York). In the same year Richard Chase published *Walt Whitman Reconsidered* (New York); Milton Hindus published *Leaves of Grass One Hundred Years After, New Essays by W. C. Williams, Richard Chase, Leslie Fiedler, Kenneth Burke, David Daiches and John Middleton Murry* (Stanford, California); Fredson Bowers published *Whitman's Manuscripts, Leaves of Grass (1860)—A Parallel Text Edited with Notes and Introduction* (Chicago).

A few years before, there had appeared Randall Jarrell's essay of revaluation ("Whitman—He Had His Nerve," in *Kenyon Review,* Winter, 1952, afterward reprinted in *Poetry and the Age* (New York, 1954). And in France, the year 1954 saw the publication of Roger Asselineau's monumental study, *Walt Whitman: L'évolution du poète* (Paris, Didier). In 1950 Enzo Giachino had published his translation of *Leaves of Grass* with the

Einaudi firm of Turin, a fine piece of interpretive and stylistic work that came to supersede Luigi Gamberale's old translation, first published in 1887 to the prolonged inspiration of many Italian men of letters. Giovanni Papini's 1908 essay, included by Allen in his 1955 symposium, may serve as a typical illustration of Italian authoritative reactions to Whitman's poetry. But even before the repeated editions of Gamberale's translation made *Leaves of Grass* available to a wide circle of Italian readers, the poet Carducci had expressed his enthusiastic appreciation of Whitman's free epic song in two letters to his friend, the Anglist Enrico Nencioni, who in 1879 and 1881 had given sample translations and comment in two Italian literary journals. And Carducci's two greatest disciples, Gabriele d'Annunzio and Giovanni Pascoli—who share with him the rank of unofficial "laureates" in late nineteenth-century Italian poetry—were both deeply interested in Whitman. This interest of the three most important poets Italy produced in the latter half of the nineteenth century is documented also by significant parts of their creative work. As for the later Futurists, like Marinetti, Ardengo Soffici, and Paolo Buzzi, their iconoclastic posture, their cult of sensation, their anarchistic reshuffle of syntax, their ego-cult, and their allegiance to free verse were bound to make them recognize in Whitman a direct source and a kindred spirit. The same holds true of German Expressionists like Ernst Stadler, Franz Werfel, and Iwan Goll.

16. These lines, and those below, are taken from the poem numbered 285 in the definitive critical edition, *The Poems of Emily Dickinson, including variant readings critically compared with all known manuscripts,* edited by Thomas H. Johnson (Cambridge, Mass., 1955). From now on, each Dickinson poem quoted will be identified with the chronological numbering of this edition, which has put us heavily in its debt by restoring the original texts, sometimes unrecognizably maimed or bowdlerized by the early editors.

17. D. H. Lawrence, *Studies in Classic American Literature,* cited.

18. Allen Tate, *On the Limits of Poetry,* cited.

19. Henry W. Wells, *The American Way of Poetry* (New York, 1943); *Introduction to Emily Dickinson* (Chicago, 1947).

20. Constance Rourke, *American Humor* (New York, 1931).

21. George F. Whicher, *This Was a Poet* (New York, 1938). This fine study retains its value even after the careful, but perhaps too limiting, evaluation attempted by Richard Chase (*Emily Dickinson,* New York, 1951),

and after the well-focused explication of Charles Anderson (*Stairway of Surprise,* New York, 1961). Mr. Anderson's book is the first sustained study to appear after the epoch-making textual restoration of Thomas H. Johnson, if we exclude Johnson's own *Emily Dickinson, An Interpretive Biography* (Cambridge, Mass., 1955).

22. The profound affinities between Emily Dickinson's poetry and that of Rilke have been explored in a revelatory essay by Kurt Oppens in the January, 1960, issue of *Merkur,* while in its Summer issue of the same year *Sewanee Review* published my own article (written in 1958, and partly drawing on previous work of mine) on "Violence and Abstraction in Emily Dickinson." In this study, which develops cues from the Italian edition of the present book and from my 1956 Italian review of Johnson's critical edition in the magazine *Aut-Aut,* I tried to show certain parallels between Dickinson's heightening concentration of language and European *poésie pure* as practiced by Mallarmé, Valéry, Ungaretti, and Rilke.

23. After completing the present study, I was able to compare notes with Henry Wells and Theodora Ward, whose approach to Dickinson's poetry on the basis of the new or renewed texts set at everybody's disposal by Thomas Johnson's edition, though more psychologically oriented, shows important similarities to mine. Professor Wells was kind enough to send me from America the typescript of an unpublished article of his ("The Unfolding of Emily Dickinson's Poetry") and the reprint of Miss Ward's article as published by *Harvard Library Bulletin,* Winter 1956 issue ("Ourself Behind Ourself—An Interpretation of the Crisis in the Life of Emily Dickinson").

24. "Circumference," as George Whicher and several other interpreters have noticed, is one of the key words in Emily's verbal universe, and she seems to inherit it from Emerson (notably in the essay "Circles") and Thomas Browne. This favorite word of hers, however, does not have a fixed connotation, since from poem to poem she readjusts its meaning to a different context. Here, for instance, it implies a finite amplitude, the horizon of time, which despite its vastness may become a prison for the soul aspiring to God's own immensity. In other poems it denotes an inaccessible, self-contained perfection ("Circumference, Thou Bride of Awe"), or again the total range of human experience, or the scope of ultimate reality. To revert to the present poem (No. 802), a second look will reveal that two "circumferences" are in question here, one limited and limiting ("this Cir-

cumference"), the other limitless and liberating ("the stupendous vision/ Of his Diameters—"). The limitless "circumference" or sphere of God includes the limited one of human time, while the latter excludes the former. But the two aspects of experience are not statically and externally juxtaposed, since the limitless one supervenes as a process, whose transcending function is emphasized by the choice of a word like "Diameters"—suggesting the infinite thrust of transcendence, perpendicular to the finite "circumference." Beyond Browne and Emerson, Emily's debt in this regard goes back to Nicholas of Cues (Nicholas Cusanus), the fifteenth-century thinker who symbolized God as a "circle whose center is everywhere and whose circumference nowhere." But the highly personal use of the symbol on her part leads us to think she was really drawing on an archetypal pattern. Though very abstract, the pattern arises from concrete experience in the cosmos (the horizon, the heavenly vault, the sun) and, charged with the cultural enrichment that goes from Parmenides and Empedocles in Greece to the American Transcendentalists in Emily's own time, becomes available for manifold symbolic use. It will be recalled that Parmenides thought of Being as a perfect Sphere, while Empedocles believed that, when integrated by the harmonious sway of Love, the cosmos took a spherical form, subject to further disruption by Hate. In the contemporary scene, it is amazing to notice how close to Emily's own use of the archetype is Karl Jaspers' existentialist positing of an ultimately encompassing reality (*das Umgreifende*) to which man can have access only in "shipwreck," i.e., when finite reason founders. Though I doubt that the twentieth-century German thinker has Emily Dickinson's poetry in mind, I find that his terminological usage would be the ideal German translation of Dickinson's "circumference." Finally, since we are dealing with a poet here rather than with a philosopher, it will be advisable to direct our attention as readers to Emily's specific treatment of this symbol, among others, in the context of a style that seems to purify itself into a supreme abstraction without losing its expressive power. The answer is that, in burning out all sensory attributes of language, Emily Dickinson retains and intensifies its dynamic component; this enables her to make poetry beyond the atmosphere of concrete imagery, in the stratosphere of language, where utter rarefaction poses a challenge that only the finer type of imagination can meet. It is this that justifies my attempt to draw a comparison between Emily and Mallarmé. And, to clinch the point, one may observe how the "abstract," rarefied use of language in the poem on hand (and in the several others of the same type) perfectly fits the transcendent theme.

25. This is one of the poems where Johnson's restoration work has proved invaluable. The early editors had lopped off the whole fifth stanza, choosing to stop the poem short at the last line of the quatrain here quoted. The fifth stanza develops the idea of "wreck" in a very pre-Jaspersian way, to conclude on a note that might imply both a dizzying fall from reason and a breakthrough to mystical knowledge.

26. Rhythm and onomatopoeia become themselves serpentine here.

27. If she can have peace only at the price of "subjugating consciousness," it is easy to see how the fall into unconsciousness that concludes poem No. 280 conveys release and not only fear.

28. Mark Van Doren, "Nerves Like Tombs," a review of *Further Poems of Emily Dickinson,* in *The Nation,* Vol. 128, No. 3324, March 20, 1929; Conrad Aiken, "Emily Dickinson," in *The Dial,* April 1924; Preface to the Modern Library edition of Emily Dickinson's selected poems (New York, 1938); Allen Tate, cited; John Crowe Ransom, "Emily Dickinson," in *Perspectives,* Spring 1956. I should like to refer the reader also to Austin Warren's article, "Emily Dickinson," in *Sewanee Review,* Autumn 1957 issue, as well as to the same writer's chapter on E. D. in his book, *Rage for Order* (Ann Arbor, Mich., 1948).

29. For this momentous topic see René Taupin, *L'influence du symbolisme francais sur la poésie américaine* (Paris, 1929). Considering the pioneering value of this work and the amount of original research that went into its making, it is a pity that it should remain as yet untranslated into English, the more so as the original French edition is marred by numerous misprints and poor typography. One caution to be advanced against this otherwise excellent study is that it follows a positivist view of literary influences and overemphasizes the American poets' debt to French *symbolistes* as if the former were to be considered purely derivative. But a literary "influence" has a meaning when it arouses creative response! As a lively corrective to Mr. Taupin's dogmatic approach, no better book could be advised than Harold Rosenberg's *The Tradition of the New* (New York, 1960), which imaginatively compares the typical American experience of space with the French cultural experience from which *symbolisme* arose, and thus justifies the elective affinity that led so many modern American poets to use French models for technical inspiration.

Two / *Edwin Arlington Robinson*

1. While translating the present book from the original Italian, I was able to examine several Robinson manuscripts at the Houghton Library. These included poems with variant readings consisting of added or omitted stanzas, and a sustained correspondence with Amy Lowell, who kept urging him to acknowledge himself an Imagist because she saw through his traditional prosody and syntax to the modern and sometimes elliptical imagery. Robinson's replies are as courteous and unassuming as his handwriting is elegant and painstakingly minute, but he stands firm on his principle of distrusting manifestoes and programs for poetry. He will judge poetry only by its intrinsic accomplishment, whatever the proclaimed aesthetics of the poet; and he declines the flattering invitation of his fellow New Englander, whose enterprising spirit made her an impresario of poetry and a perfect opposite of the withdrawn Robinson. One could not imagine a more picturesquely hopeless meeting, with her vociferously missionary spirit vainly trying to convert him. About three-quarters of a century before, the enterprising Peabody sisters had had more luck in their efforts to draw another withdrawn New Englander out of his bachelor refuge, though Hawthorne's morbidly brooding inwardness survived Brook Farm and marriage itself.

2. For instance, Horace Gregory and Marya Zaturenska, in *A History of American Poetry 1900-1940* (New York, 1946), put Robinson in an "interregnum" period antedating World War I even though they recognize at least his intermittent accomplishment, and Babette Deutsch, in *Poetry in Our Time* (New York, 1952), p. 55 on, sees him as a belated nineteenth-century romantic without any stimulating power for the new generations. James Southworth, in *Some Modern American Poets* (Oxford, 1950), curtly dismisses Robinson as a long-winded epigone of Browning, and Louise Bogan, in *The Achievement of American Poetry* (Chicago, 1951), cannot accept the long Arthurian poems—she is obviously embarrassed by them and confines her praise to the New England sonnets and short pieces. On the other hand, a revaluation in terms of the modern sensibility has been advanced by Yvor Winters with *Edwin Arlington Robinson* (Norfolk, Conn., 1946), and by Edwin Fussell with *Edwin Arlington Robinson: The Literary Background of a Traditional Poet* (Berkeley, Calif., 1954). Fussell shows how Robinson really anticipates certain themes and attitudes

of T. S. Eliot, among others. Other positive appraisals are to be found in Henry Wells, *The American Way of Poetry* (New York, 1943), and in F. O. Matthiessen, *The Responsibilities of the Critic* (New York, 1952). Hyatt Howe Waggoner, in *The Heel of Elohim* (Oklahoma City, 1950), brings to light an important factor of authenticity in Robinson's deeply felt conflict between natural science and religious values, but unfortunately he limits his exegesis to one of Robinson's less successful poems, "The Man against the Sky"—a poem whose brillancies are overshadowed by frequent rhetoric. An impressive bibliography of American and European studies of Robinson's verse has been gathered by Fred Millett, *Contemporary American Authors* (New York, 1943), and more items will be found in *The Literary History of the United States,* edited by Spiller, Thorp, Johnson, and Canby (New York, 1948, 1953).

For the text of the Robinson poems here discussed, the standard source is *Collected Poems of Edwin Arlington Robinson* (New York, 1948).

3. Van Wyck Brooks, *New England: Indian Summer* (New York, 1940).

4. Van Wyck Brooks, *The Flowering of New England* (New York, 1936). Another useful source for background study of this moment in American culture is *Transitions in American Literary History,* edited by Harry Hayden Clark (Durham, N.C., 1953).

5. Rolando Anzilotti, *Poesie di Robert Lowell,* with English text, Italian translation, introduction, and notes (Florence, 1955). This painstaking work has been later emulated by Alfredo Rizzardi in dealing with Melville's poetry (*Poesie di Melville,* a cure di A. Rizzardi, Bologna, 1960). The intensive work of translation and commentary that has been going on in Italy during the recent decades is unrivaled in Europe, and represents a tribute to the vitality of American poetry even beyond its native boundaries.

6. Melville's dominant tone, of course, is more loudly tragic and, at times, melodramatic, while Robinson's stays closer to meditative elegy. Melville's predilection for hyperbole is the reverse of Robinson's constant understatement. As a result, even the comical vein present in both writers tends to take on a different coloring, for Robinson's is really dry New England humor, while Melville's has the exuberance and theatricality of his tragic phases.

Three / *Wallace Stevens: "Notes toward a Supreme Fiction"*

1. This chapter originally appeared as an independent essay in *Studi*

Americani No. 1, Rome, 1955, and was subsequently incorporated in the Italian edition of the present book.

2. Malcolm Brinnin, "Modern American Poetry,' in *New World Writing* No. 5 (New York, 1954).

3. Richard P. Blackmur, *Language as Gesture* (New York, 1952).

4. Malcolm Cowley, "The Time of the Rhetoricians," in *New World Writing* No. 5, cited, later included in *The Literary Situation* (New York, 1954).

5. Harold Watts, "Stevens' Rock of Summer," *Kenyon Review,* Winter 1952.

6. Lloyd Frankenberg, *Pleasure Dome* (Boston and Cambridge, Mass., 1949).

7. William Van O'Connor, *The Shaping Spirit* (Chicago, 1950).

8. Eugenio Montale's sophisticate verse has seemed to Robert Lowell to be comparable in some respects to Stevens' rather different poetry. I hope my American readers will not find it inappropriate that I should occasionally relate poetry and thought across whatever political or academic boundaries. I like to think of civilization as a conversation or concerto.

9. Whether Stevens was acquainted with the philosophy of Edmund Husserl or not, the parallelism between his poetry as a process of dialectical discovery and Husserl's phenomenology as an exercise in objective awareness of the quality of reality is too striking to be overlooked. Both Husserl and Stevens aim at a focused apprehension of the *essences* of things (*Wesenheiten*) by a process of "stripping" or "unhusking" (reality is not this, nor that, nor that . . .), which Stevens calls "abstraction" and which appears in so many of his poems as a kind of preliminary negation of the given object, or of our construed interpretations. Husserl and the whole phenomenological school with him speak of a preliminary "suspension" (Greek *epoché*) of judgment vis-à-vis the object; they mean by this a reductive operation that brackets whatever is a cultural assumption or superstructure, in order to enable consciousness to place itself before the object of knowledge with the maximum purity and the least prejudice. Thus consciousness "discovers" the object as if for the first time and corrects the incrustations of history. All of *Notes toward a Supreme Fiction* is conformable to this principle. On the other hand, Stevens' use of the term "first idea" here shows an indebtedness to Plato, only Plato believed in ideas as utterly transcendent to our world, insulated in ethereal space. Thus I have to speak of a "Husserlian Platonism" in Stevens, without thereby implying

that the American poet necessarily drew on Husserl's philosophy. The elective affinity or *Wahlverwandschaft* is what interests me here.

10. Stevens has here in mind Descartes' "cogito ergo sum," the act by which the French philosopher proceeded to derive certainty from the thinking self by a "geometric" method of logical deduction. Later idealists were to derive reality itself, and not only certainty, from the conscious self, and this arrogance Stevens will not have. Man should *see through* the enveloping air, not just mirror himself in it (like Eve here) in intellectual narcissism. Reality antedates and directs our knowledge ("myth"), the "clouds" are "pedagogues." We should not wall ourselves in our own self and commit the *hybris* of regarding our own thought as the only reality there is. Solipsism is a sin to Stevens, and realism (of his sophisticated brand) a salvation. Compare this poem with poem Number 8 of "It Must Be Abstract."

11. This seraph among violets echoes Stéphane Mallarmé's "Apparition": "Des séraphins en pleurs/ Rêvant, l'archet au doigt, dans le calme des fleurs/ Vaporeuses, tiraient de mourantes violes/ De blancs sanglots glissant sur l'azur des corolles." Often Stevens uses a literary datum for a start, which confirms our interpretation of his "estranged" attitude as given at the end of the present essay.

12. Also the last poem, of "It Must Change" contains an explicit reference to the Shelley ode, since it names the west wind as a joyful force of renewal.

13. Yvor Winters, "The Anatomy of Nonsense," in the volume *In Defense of Reason,* cited. On Stevens' abstract mannerisms, see also Jarrell, *Poetry and the Age* (New York, 1953).

14. Again, our purpose in comparing the American poet's work with the ideas of the well-known German existentialist in his recent phase is not to suggest an improbable indebtedness. Heidegger's philosophy has taken a turn for the positive, and in his essay on Hölderlin's poetry he speaks of the poet as a "shepherd of Being" who is "housed in language." Heidegger's metaphors are highly suggestive of the posture of symbiotic acceptance of reality that underlies so much of Stevens' writing, and the very fact that the philosopher deliberately employs imaginative, rather than drily logical, language makes the comparison more viable. That Heidegger is a disciple of Husserl helps to establish the relevance of such an attempt. Heidegger's "house of language" is not the pompous mansion Stevens describes in *Notes*

toward a Supreme Fiction; it affords shelter, separation from and communion with circumambient reality, and it has windows and doors. Permanence and perspicuity are certainly important attributes of language according to Wallace Stevens, who seems always to go out to reality from the house of words, without really abandoning the latter.

Four / *Hart Crane's "The Bridge"*

1. This chapter originally appeared as an independent essay in the Florence magazine, *Paragone,* No. 70, (October 1955).

2. Malcolm Cowley, *Exile's Return* (New York, 1951).

3. Allen Tate, *On the Limits of Poetry* (New York, 1948) and *The Forlorn Demon* (Chicago, 1953). I have been privileged to discuss the subject with him in a personal meeting after he had read my essay in its original Italian form.

4. *The Collected Poems of Hart Crane,* edited by Waldo Frank (New York, 1933).

5. Henry Willis Wells, *The American Way of Poetry* (New York, 1943).

6. Yvor Winters, "Primitivism and Decadence," in the essay collection *In Defense of Reason* (Denver, 1947).

7. Brom Weber, *Hart Crane* (New York, 1948). A useful monograph, to be complemented by the earlier biography published by Philip Horton in 1937; it has a rich Appendix with previously uncollected writings, rough drafts, and work sheets. Brom Weber has also edited the *Letters of Hart Crane* (New York, 1952), a fascinating literary and spiritual document.

8. Babette Deutsch, *Poetry in Our Time* (New York, 1952).

9. Horace Gregory and Marya Zaturenska, *A History of American Poetry, 1900-1940* (New York, 1946).

10. F. O. Matthiessen, *The Responsibilities of the Critic* (New York, 1953).

11. Karl Shapiro, *Essay on Rime* (New York, 1945).

12. Cowley, cited, p. 115.

13. *The Autobiography of William Carlos Williams* (New York, 1951).

14. Waldo Frank, *Our America* (New York, 1919), and *The Rediscovery of America* (New York, 1929).

15. Gorham Munson, *Destinations: A Canvass of American Literature since 1900* (New York, 1928). This book, which collects various essays pre-

viously published in periodicals, includes also a study of Crane's poetry, one of the earliest defenses.

16. For this information I am indebted to A. M. Ripellino's anthology of modern Russian poetry in Italian translation: *Poesia russa del Novecento* (Parma, 1954).

17. René Taupin, *L'Influence du symbolisme francais sur la poésie américaine (de 1910 à 1920)* (Paris, 1929).

18. R. P. Blackmur, *Language as Gesture* (New York, 1952).

19. Wells, cited, pp. 203-204.

20. James Southworth, *Some Modern American Poets* (Oxford, 1950).

21. Hyatt Howe Waggoner, *The Heel of Elohim* (Oklahoma City, 1950).

22. Joshua Whatmough, "One Use of Language: Literature," in *New World Writing* No. 6 (New York, October, 1954).

23. These are "The Bridge at Estador" and "Porphyro in Akron," published in 1921, then repudiated by the author and finally reprinted by Weber in the Appendix to his critical biography.

24. *The Letters of Hart Crane,* cited.

25. Sonia Raiziss, *The Metaphysical Passion* (Philadelphia, 1952), p. 19.

26. This symbology is to be found also in Shelley, particularly in *The Revolt of Islam.*

27. *Cutty Sark,* a clipper ship built in 1869, was famous for breaking all the speed records, and has been used for a long time as a training ship.

28. Obviously, the East River here becomes the Lethe of a Purgatory where the poet, delivered from the burden of memory and the past, symmetrically concludes the central part of his song, which the hurdy-gurdy of "Rip Van Winkle" had begun with an entrance into memory. From here, passage will be sought toward the paradise of an ideal Cathay in "Atlantis," clearly anticipated by the pun on the name of the East River itself.

This is a significant nexus with the shorter poems, enabling us to look at *The Bridge* as a drama of memory and release from memory. Attention should be given to the concentrated symbolism of "coil of ticking towers," where we have the time-measuring clocks with their springs, installed in Manhattan's skyscrapers, and at the same time the "coil" of the Time Serpent.

29. A summary critique is to be found in William York Tindall's *The Literary Symbol* (New York, 1955), pp. 154-55, and a detailed exegesis in "Crane's Voyages" by H. C. Morris (*Accent,* Autumn 1954). Tindall

sketches in this connection a comparison of "Voyages" with Rimbaud's "Bateur Ivre," at some cost to Crane's poem, and does not seem far from Van Wyck Brooks' position. The latter critic maintains, in *The Writer in America,* that the perturbing influence of Rimbaud was to blame for Crane's personal and literary troubles because it prevented his being integrally American. As a corrective to this nativist approach we would indicate Wallace Fowlie's article, "Rimbaud et Hart Crane," in *Arts et Lettres* (Paris, No. 17, 1950).

30. Charles Olson, *Call Me Ishmael* (New York, 1947), p. 114.

31. Hart Crane's letter to Gorham Munson, October 6, 1921, *Letters,* cited.

32. "New Thresholds, New Anatomies" is the title of Blackmur's essay on Crane in *Language as Gesture,* cited, where he devotes particular attention to this poem.

Five / *William Carlos Williams*

1. This chapter originally appeared as an independent essay in the Florentine magazine *Paragone,* No. 62 (February 1955). Quotations from *Paterson* have been taken from the 1951 New Directions edition.

2. Afterward completed as "Of Asphodel—Coda," in *Poetry,* August, 1954.

3. Samuel Beckett, ed., *Our Examination Round His Factification for Incamination of Work in Progress* (Paris, transition, 1929).

4. It is also the central theme of most significant American literature.

5. William Carlos Williams, *The Collected Later Poems* (Norfolk, Conn., 1951), p. 4, from the author's foreword.

6. William Carlos Williams, *The Collected Earlier Poems* (Norfolk, Conn,. 1950), p. 9.

7. Originally published in 1936 and then included in *The Collected Earlier Poems.* It may interest the American reader to know that this Williams poem was translated in the early fifties by Vittorio Sereni, one of the important contemporary Italian poets, and that as the translation of the present book was nearing the end (Winter 1961-62), a beautiful bilingual edition of Williams' selected poems appeared in Italy thanks to Vittorio Sereni's and Cristina Campo's inspired work (William Carlos Williams, *Poesie,* Tradotte e commentate da Cristina Campo e Vittorio Serini, Turin; Einaudi, 1961). And I have it from Mr. Sereni himself that translating the

American poet was to him a refreshing experience that stimulated his own creative vein to a new upsurge. The translation volume contains parts of *Paterson.*

8. It was also to Dante, in part.

9. Lewis Mumford, *The Culture of Cities* (New York, 1938). The Italian edition and translation dates from 1954.

10. James Southworth, *Some More Modern American Poets* (Oxford, 1954).

11. Randall Jarrell, *Poetry and the Age* (New York 1953).

12. A poet whose work has left a strong mark in modern Italian verse, Ungaretti has been presented to the American public in a bilingual edition by Mr. Allen Mandelbaum (New Directions, 1958).

13. In his *In Defense of Reason* (Denver, 1947), Yvor Winters defines Williams as a "primitive" poet to be contrasted with "decadents" like Stevens or Crane. For further evaluations of Williams see Vivienne Koch, *William Carlos Williams* (Norfolk, Conn., 1950), and Marianne Moore, *Predilections* (New York, 1955). One of the first Italian contributions was that of Paola Bompard, in *Studi Americani* No. 1, Rome, 1955.

Six / *Robert Lowell*

1. The present chapter was not part of the original Italian edition; it was published as a separate essay by the *Papers of the Michigan Academy of Science, Arts, and Letters,* Vol. XLVII, 1962.

2. Here I have in mind only the part of Croce's philosophy that regards time past as the domain of absolute necessity. Once things have happened, they are unchangeable. Since, on the other hand, Croce also maintains that true history is the awareness we gain of past events in the logical act of the conscious mind, and that in this awareness all history is contemporary, a case could be made for his partial relevance to Bergson's (and Lowell's) approach. Croce sees history as "the history of freedom," as the movement of mankind toward freedom. But there is nothing apocalyptic, nothing eschatological about his conception; in this respect his dialectical humanism is poles apart from the spirit of a poet like Lowell. Even if the problem of history, philosophy, and poetry as mutually relevant is open to endless debate, I take my stand for their positive and complex relevancy. Their distinction does not escape me, but I refuse to see it as an insulation.

3. The appropriate reference here implied is to Henri Bergson's early

work, *Matière et Mémoire* (Memory and Matter), but an even closer one could be found in his later *Les Deux Sources de la Morale et de la Religion* (The Two Sources of Morality and Religion), where he describes mystics and social innovators as promoters of an open society as against the conservative religious or political administrators who inevitably cling to inherited forms and to a closed society. The prophetic spirit that Lowell expresses in his poetry is clearly on the side of the former; and Randall Jarrell has shown how it would be impossible to dissociate that incandescent spirit from the poetry as poetry (see John Ciardi, *Mid-century American Poets* [New York, 1950], section devoted to Robert Lowell).

4. The "toward" here could be read as "against," thus implying the gesture of the rebelling child who calls his parents to account *because* they matter to him. Lowell's poetry is addressed to and aimed at America.

5. This is of course not peculiar to Robert Lowell's verse, for he clearly inherits the use of multiple or oblique reference from Eliot, Pound, Crane, and Joyce, and, through them, from one common source to be identified with Elizabethan and Metaphysical poetry. Yet it is fair to say that his own poetical punning often tends to lift the actual discourse into a transcendent sphere by twisting its historical basis, as if he were wrenching his statements from their logical-horizontal plane into an antinomic, "vertical," "metahistorical" dimension. In this respect, Lowell is very close to the baroque preachers and specifically to his own New England ancestors, Edward Taylor, Cotton Mather, and Jonathan Edwards; his affinity for them, or for John Donne's sermons, is much more direct than that of Eliot, whose irony in the use of literary references is (like Joyce's) far more detached and sophisticated. Lowell's splenetic sarcasm has a directness that makes it very un-Eliotic, I am almost tempted to say "barbarous;" and this directness of tone is perhaps the main factor behind his initial choice of tight iambic rhythms and closed meters, which he reinstated forcefully after Pound's, Williams', and Eliot's divergent experiments with a non-iambic prosody. With this goes the declamatory aggressiveness that seems best suited to a prophetic poet, and that, combined with Lowell's alternately flaming or abstract imagery, makes for a unique style. That style fuses the Whitman-Williams type of open utterance with the Taylor-Dickinson tradition of strict form (intensity being a quality both share).

6. This book shows Lowell's style at a turning point, with few poems conformable to the compact iambic pattern and tight statement of his first phase. What now prevails is an "open" prosody and a formally more re-

laxed statement, really music in the ears of Dr. William Carlos Williams, who, visiting the Indiana School of Letters at Bloomington during the summer of 1960, told me how earnestly he wished a gifted poet like Lowell would stop writing iambs. . . . One consequence is that a new subtlety informs the writing, and Lowell begins to lower his loud tone without losing poignancy. The quality of awareness has a weird piercing power, as in "Skunk Hour," "Memories of West Street and Lepke," or "Waking in the Blue," a poem more sharply focused on personal experience, yet not so that the public world should remain "outside" the poem's field of force. It describes Lowell's life in the Boston mental hospital during one period of treatment, and in so doing balances the ferocious directness of observed detail and straightforward confession with a network of literary references that reinforce, instead of attenuating, the directness. The main references are to Mallarmé's "Fenêtres" and "L'Azur" (even in the title), and to *Moby Dick*. Mallarmé's condition of "absence," his obsession with the haunting "blue" of the sky, his description of hospital confinement, are deeply relevant to Lowell's own experience, and he brings the literary source into a personal poem to stress the shock of recognition. The word "absence," a keynote of Mallarmé's poetry, appears in line 8 of Lowell's poem, charged with the specific implication of mental alienation, a real "absence from the public world," the more strongly felt as Lowell the thinking man rejects that world anyway and thus finds his "insanity" an appropriate response to it and the "asylum" a real "refuge." Lowell's "absence" is not merely intellectual, as Mallarmé's stance was, but a polemical gesture that Lowell relates to Ahab's brandishing of the harpoon against Moby Dick. Its import is finally recapitulated in the sinister ending, which mentions the "locked razor" each inmate keeps. The humor Lowell injects in his self-portrait, and into the description of the asylum, strengthens the ferocity and the sinister overtones. The fact that one nurse should be reading *The Meaning of Meaning* is not casual; it is both humorous and disquieting, for since the existence of the asylum implies that the "public" world has drawn the line between meaning and meaninglessness, it is fitting that the very "private" world of the asylum should shelter those who question "the meaning of meaning." Which world is really meaningless—the public one, which begot and surrounds the hospital, or the hospital's private one, whose diseased minds show, in their derangement, a greater awareness of contemporary reality than the "tranquilized" outside world generally does? Thus the public world is polemically drawn into the picture of what arose as a private poem. A similar combination of humor, relaxed phrasing (initially at least), and literary reference accounts for the remarkable success of the epitaph "For George Santayana," a poem that tightens and glows as it gathers momentum from the calculated looseness of its beginning. Santayana, "lying outside the consecrated ground," is likened to Dante's erstwhile mentor Brunetto Latini, whom the medieval poet meets among the damned in *Inferno* XV; and the complex relation of esteem and affection for the dead thinker whose sin (in Santayana's case, unbelief) places him forever beyond the reach of Christian grace is expressed by Lowell by inserting in his poem a translation from the last tercet of Dante's Canto which glorifies Latini even in the act of condemning him theologically. Lowell speaks, like Dante, from a situation of faith, but since this faith is not serene, and actually puts him at loggerheads with most of his surrounding world, he sees a relation between his dissent and Santayana's "outsideness;" thus the poem can have an intimate tone and structure as an address to the deceased teacher, as Dante's Canto does. The final lines are as taut as anything Lowell ever wrote, and they stand out because of the over-all flexibility.

7. This conversion was only temporary, but it left a mark. And it was in itself very "personal" indeed.

8. See Marius Bewley, *The Eccentric Design* (London, 1959).

9. In a later poem, included in the *Life Studies* volume with the title "Beyond the Alps," Lowell symbolically leaves the Eternal City and doubts the possibility that mankind will adequately respond to the Pope's anti-positivist, anti-bourgeois, anti-materialist and therefore anachronistic gesture in proclaiming the bodily ascension of the Virgin Mary to Heaven. Intimations of disaster are voiced here, in a suppler form, with science and faith battling for predominance; if in "Dea Roma" the poet seemed to be addressing a statue, more or less officially, here he is questioning his own experience in the very act of considering man's different thrusts beyond Nature, whether of the body, of the intellect, or of faith-powered imagination. In an article published by *Accent* in its Summer 1960 issue I had interpreted this poem as written still from a Catholic point of view, but Robert Lowell wrote me that it wasn't, even though it was far from indifferent or hostile to the Catholic faith he had earlier embraced. The difference is thin, but it reflects on the symbolic action of the poem (leaving Rome behind).

Index

Aiken, Conrad, 192; on Emily Dickinson, 47, 49
Anzilotti, Rolando, on Robert Lowell, 59

Baldini, Gabriele, 4
Barlow, Joel, 144
Bergson, Henri, 219
Bishop, John Peale, and Emily Dickinson, 49
Blackmur, Richard, on Wallace Stevens, 79-80; and Hart Crane, 126, 127 f, 173
Blake, William, 224
Bogan, Louise, on E. A. Robinson, 58
Breton, André, 192
Brinnin, Malcolm, on Wallace Stevens and Marianne Moore, 79

Conrad, Joseph, and Emily Dickinson, 43; and E. A. Robinson, 77
Cowley, Malcolm, 80; on Hart Crane, 120 f
Crane, Hart, 79, 195; and Emily Dickinson, 49, 50, 161; and Walt Whitman, 50; and E. A. Robinson, 78; and Dante, 100, 161, 172; and W. C. Williams, 100, 205, 212-213; *The Bridge,* 120-182; and Malcolm Cowley, 120 f; and Harold Stearns, 122; and T. S. Eliot, 122; and E. A. Poe, 124, 161 f; imagism, 124-126; Richard Blackmur on, 126 ff; and Walt Whitman, 126, 153 ff; and Yvor Winters, 127 ff, 146; and H. H. Waggoner, 128, 135; and Allen Tate, 129, 146; and Otto Kahn, 129 f, 131; craftsmanship, 130 ff, 180 ff; and Waldo Frank, 131; and Joseph Stella, 133; and Sonia Raiziss, 134 ff; and Henry Wells, 135; and Einstein, 141; and Emily Dickinson, 143; and Brom Weber, 146; river theme, 146 ff; and Herman Melville, 150-152 *passim,* 156; and Gerald Hopkins, 157; "Three Songs," 158 ff; "Atlantis," 164 ff; "Lachrymae Christi,"
Crane, Hart—*Cont.*
170 f; "Passage," 171 f; "The Wine Menagerie," 173 ff

Dante Alighieri, 211, 212, 226; and James Joyce, 100; and Hart Crane, 161, 172 f; and W. C. Williams, 189, 212
Deutsch, Babette, on E. A. Robinson, 74; on Hart Crane, 121
Dickinson, Emily, "self" and "otherness," 27-52; and Walt Whitman, 27 ff; death, 29; nature, 29 f; "domestic comedy," 30; religion, 31; imagism and symbolism, 33 ff; critique of success myth, 36 f; privacy symbolism, 41 ff; "circumference," 47-48, 49; and Wallace Stevens, 48-49; and Hart Crane, 143, 161, 178; and W. C. Williams, 206-208 *passim,* 216 f
Dos Passos, John, 191
Dostoevski, Feodor, and Emily Dickinson, 44

Eddington, Sir Arthur Stanley, 128 f
Einstein, Albert, 141
Eliot, T. S., 79, 125, 194, 200 f, 205, 208, 213; and E. A. Poe, 6-7; and E. A. Robinson, 60, 78; and Wallace Stevens, 115; and Hart Crane, 160, 163 f; and W. C. Williams, 183-198 *passim,* 205
Emerson, Ralph Waldo, 49, 167, 222

Faulkner, William, 27, 223; and W. C. Williams, 188
Feidelson, Charles, 181; and E. A. Poe, 7 f
Flaubert, Gustave, 204
Fletcher, John Gould, *Irradiations,* 35
Frank, Waldo, on Hart Crane, 121 ff, 131
Frankenberg, Lloyd, on Wallace Stevens, 82
Freneau, Philip, 49
Frost, Robert, 56, 228

Handlin, Oscar, on Robert Lowell, 223
Hardy, Thomas, and E. A. Robinson, 64
Heidegger, Martin, on Wallace Stevens, 119
Hemingway, Ernest, 208
Hopkins, Gerard Manley, 224; and Hart Crane, 157
Huxley, Aldous, 4

James, Henry, 16; and E. A. Robinson, 77
Jarrell, Randall, and Wallace Stevens, 118; on W. C. Williams, 214
Johnson, Thomas H., edition of Emily Dickinson's works, 47
Joyce, James, 191, 208; and Dante, 100; and Hart Crane, 160; and W. C. Williams, 186 ff

Kahn, Otto, and Hart Crane, 129 f, 131
Keats, John, and Walt Whitman, 24
Kierkegaard, Soren, and E. A. Robinson, 65; and Wallace Stevens, 115-116

Laforgue, Jules, 79, 125; on Walt Whitman, 29
Lawrence, D. H., 5; on Walt Whitman, 29
Leopardi, Giacomo, and E. A. Robinson, 64
Lowell, Amy, and E. A. Robinson, 60
Lowell, Robert, history as eschatology, 219-228; Handlin on, 223; and Herman Melville, 225 f

Mallarmé, Stéphane, and Emily Dickinson, 33 ff, 41
Mather, Cotton, 220
Matthiessen, F. O., 181; on Walt Whitman, 26; on Hart Crane, 121
Mayakovsky, Vladimir, 123
Melville, Herman, poetry, 9 ff; "self" and "otherness," 9-15; craftsmanship, 11 ff; and E. A. Poe, 12 ff; American myth, 14-15; and Walt Whitman, 16 ff, 25-26; sea image in *Moby Dick,* 21, 225 f; and Hart Crane, 150-152, 156, 176, 179 ff
Monroe, Harriet, and *Poetry,* 50
Montale, Eugenio, 85
Moore, Marianne, 79, 203; and Emily Dickinson, 35, 47; and W. C. Williams, 203
Morris, H. C., and Hart Crane, 176
Mumford, Lewis, "megalopolis," 193
Munson, Gorham, and Hart Crane, 122, 169

Nietzsche, Friedrich, and Wallace Stevens, 88

O'Connor, William Van, on Wallace Stevens, 82-84 *passim,* 110, 118
Olson, Charles, on Herman Melville, 167
d'Ors, Eugenio, 137
Ouspensky, Theodor, 167

Pascal, Blaise, and Emily Dickinson, 41
Pavese, Cesare, on Walt Whitman, 26
Perse, St.-John, 126, 190
Poe, Edgar Allen, 79; "absolute otherness," 4-9; romanticism, 5; craftsmanship, 5-6; hallucinations and logic, 5-6; "The Philosophy of Composition," 5-6; adventure, 5-6; symbolism, 6-8; evaluation, 8-9; and Herman Melville, 12 ff; and Emily Dickinson, 44; and Hart Crane, 161 f
Pound, Ezra, 79, 80, 125, 129, 144, 167, 208; and W. C. Williams, 183, 191, 204

Raiziss, Sonia, on Hart Crane, 134 f
Ransom, John Crowe, on Emily Dickinson, 47
Rilke, Rainier Maria, 36, 126; and Emily Dickinson, 33
Rimbaud, A., and Hart Crane, 181
Robinson, Edwin Arlington, 224; "Knight of the Grail," 53-78; New England compositions, 53 ff; Arthurian romance, 54 ff, 65 ff, 70 ff; Tilbury Town, 54 ff; craftsmanship, 57 ff, 63; "Isaac and Archibald," 58-59; and Rolando Anzilotti, 59; and Robert Frost, 59; "Tristram," 59, 65-68; evaluation, 59 ff, 78; "Miniver Cheevy," 60; and Amy Lowell, 60; and T. S. Eliot, 60; "Captain Craig," 60-61 ff; "Hillcrest," 63 ff; and Giacomo Leopardi, 64; and Thomas Huxley, 64;

Robinson, Edwin Arlington—*Cont.* and Kierkegaard, 65; Merlin, 70 ff; Lancelot, 70 ff; the Grail, 71 ff; and Henry James, 77; and Joseph Conrad, 77; and William Butler Yeats, 77 f
Rourke, Constance, 30

Santayana, George, 193, 221, 228
Schiller, Friedrich, 219
Shakespeare, William, 211
Shapiro, Karl, on Hart Crane, 121
Southworth, James, on Hart Crane, 128; on W. C. Williams, 214
Stearns, Harold, 122
Stein, Gertrude, 6, 208
Stella, Joseph, and Hart Crane, 133
Stern, Philip Van Doren, 5; on E. A. Poe, 8
Stevens, Wallace, 203; *Harmonium,* 35; and Emily Dickinson, 48-49; *Notes toward a Supreme Fiction,* 79-119; place in history, 79-80; and William O'Connor, 82 f, 110, 118; "abstraction," 82 ff; Plato in *Notes,* 85 ff, 88-89; Nietzsche in *Notes,* 88; theme of Paradise lost, 89-91; poetry and reality, 91; anthropomorphic constructions, 92; transcendence, 92 ff, 116; Truth, 93; Bergsonian Nature, 95; human values, 97-98; triadic structure, 98-100; cycles, 100 ff, 109; and Dante, 102; and Shelley, 103 ff; problem of language, 108 ff; "first idea," 110 ff, 116; and W. B. Yeats, 115; and T. S. Eliot, 115; and Kierkegaard, 115-116; and Randall Jarrell, 118; evaluation, 118-119; and Hart Crane, 181; and W. C. Williams, 203 f

Tate, Allen, on E. A. Poe, 8; on Emily Dickinson, 29, 31, 47; on Hart Crane, 120 f, 129, 146; on W. C. Williams, 206
Taupin, René, on Hart Crane, 125
Thoreau, Henry David, 16, 49, 167, 222
Toynbee, A. J., on Thoreau, 16

Ungaretti, Giuseppe, and W. C. Williams, 218

Valéry, Paul, 177; and Emily Dickinson, 34 f
Van Doren, Mark, and Emily Dickinson, 47
Vittorini, Elio, 5

Waggoner, Hyatt Howe, on Hart Crane, 128 ff, 135
Watts, Harold, on Wallace Stevens, 81
Weber, Brom, on Hart Crane, 121, 123, 146
Wells, Henry, 134 f; on Emily Dickinson, 30; on Hart Crane, 121, 127, 135
Whatmough, Joshua, on Hart Crane, 128
Whicher, George, 30
Whitman, Walt, 49, 202; "total identity," 15-27; individualism, 16; and Herman Melville, 16 ff, 21; romanticism, 23; and Keats, 24; craftsmanship, 26-27; and Emily Dickinson, 27 ff; and Hart Crane, 126, 153 ff, 160; and W. C. Williams, 206 f
Williams, William Carlos, and Hart Crane, 100, 121; and Herman Melville, 181; *Paterson,* 183-218; and James Joyce, 186 ff; and American history, 186 ff; and William James, 187; and Nathaniel Hawthorne, 189; and Dante, 189, 212; and John Dos Passos, 191; and Ezra Pound, 191; "megalopolis," 193 ff; 212; sea symbol, 195 ff; fire symbol, 197 ff; wind symbol, 198 ff; language, 200 ff; and Marianne Moore, 203; and Wallace Stevens, 203 f; and Walt Whitman, 206 f; and Emily Dickinson, 206 ff, 216; craftsmanship, 208 ff
Winters, Yvor, 4; and Hart Crane, 121, 127, 128, 132, 146
Wolfe, Thomas, 27

Yeats, William Butler, and E. A. Robinson, 77 f; and Wallace Stevens, 115

Zaturenska, Marya, on E. A. Robinson, 68